STRAY DOG
OF ANIME

D0933339

STRAY DOG OF ANIME

The Films of Mamoru Oshii

BRIAN RUH

First published 2004 by
PALGRAVE MACMILLAN™
175 Fifth Avenue, New York, N.Y. 10010 and
Houndmills, Basingstoke, Hampshire, England RG21 6XS.
Companies and representatives throughout the world.

PALGRAVE MACMILLAN is the global academic imprint of
the Palgrave Macmillan division of St. Martin's Press, LLC and of
Palgrave Macmillan Ltd. Macmillan® is a registered trademark in
the United States, United Kingdom and other countries. Palgrave
is a registered trademark in the European Union and other
countries.

ISBN 1-4039-6329-0 hardback
ISBN 1-4039-6334-7 paperback

Library of Congress Cataloging-in-Publication Data
Ruh, Brian.
    Stray dog of anime : the films of Mamoru Oshii / Brian Ruh.
       p.   cm.
    Includes bibliographical references and index.
    ISBN 1-4039-6329-0 — ISBN 1-4039-6334-7 (pbk.)
       1. Oshii, Mamoru—Criticism and interpretation.   1. Title.
PN1998.3.O83R84   2004
791.43'34023'092—dc22
                                                          2003068903

A catalogue record for this book is available from the British
Library.

Design by Letra Libre.

First edition: June 2004
10 9 8 7 6 5 4 3 2 1
Printed in the United States of America.

CONTENTS

ACKNOWLEDGMENTS

FIRST AND FOREMOST, I MUST THANK MY WIFE, Sarah Ruh, for helping with everything related to this book. She was extremely patient with me as my attitudes vacillated throughout the course of the project. She also offered crucial insights into the work and read (and reread) many of the drafts. Without her support, I do not think I would have been able to complete this project.

I am indebted to Professor Susan J. Napier at the University of Texas at Austin, who served as my mentor and guide while I was working on my master's degree. It was through her classes that I began to appreciate the artistry of Oshii's films. She also introduced me to Toby Wahl, my editor at Palgrave, paving the way for the publication of this book. I hope that through this volume I am able to do justice to what she has taught me. I would also like to thank the other professors from whom I took classes while at the University of Texas or who have given me assistance: Hiroshi Aoyagi, Robert Khan, Patricia Maclachlan, Charles Ramirez Berg, and John Traphagan.

Additionally, I need to thank: Frenchy Lunning at the Minneapolis College of Art and Design, for inviting me to present a draft of a couple of chapters at the Schoolgirls and Mobilesuits conference; Scott Frazier, for being my first interview victim early in the project; Carl Gustav Horn, for the fascinating info and the Anchor Steam; Mark Schilling, for his insightful e-mails about Japanese film and his timely review of *Killers* (from which I gleaned much of my knowledge of the film); Jerry Chu at Bandai Entertainment; Ivette Perez at Central Park Media; Yoshiki Sakurai at Production I.G., for helping to arrange my visit to the studio;

Kukhee Choo, Todd Tilma, and Kara Williams, my graduate school compatriots at Texas; Brent Allison, Lawrence Eng, Mikhail Koulikov, and everyone else in the Anime and Manga Research Circle; Marc Hairston; Karen Zarker at PopMatters.com; everyone from the fifty-third Japan-America Student Conference in 2001; and all of the fine folks who post on the Production I.G. message board.

I must also thank my friends and family, who have kept me sane (or just ever so slightly insane) while I've worked on the book: my parents, Richard and Christine Ruh; my parents-in-law, Daniel and Barbara Skinner; my grandfather, Charles Brenner; the Brenner and McGlothlin clans; my grandmother-in-law, Hilda Eibert; my sister-in-law, Mandy Skinner; Bryan Bick; Kerensa Durr and Brandon Hatcher; Chris Miller; Casey Mumaw; and Sara Weiser.

The basis for what I have written was my master's thesis in Asian Cultures and Languages at the University of Texas at Austin. Titled "A Cyborg Mephisto: Mythology in the Science Fiction Films of Oshii Mamoru," the thesis examined how Oshii uses religion and myth in his two *Patlabor* films, *Ghost in the Shell,* and *Avalon*. It was the culmination of my work at U.T., and I am glad that I am getting the chance to expand on and share my analysis of Oshii's films with a wider audience.

Note: In the text, all names are given in Western order, with given name first and surname second. Japanese words are romanized according to the modified Hepburn system, except in cases in which there are already accepted English spellings of the Japanese words. (For example, I use "Oshii" rather than "Oshī" and "Shirow" rather than "Shirō.")

PREFACE

TO BE HONEST, MY FIRST EXPERIENCE of one of Mamoru Oshii's films left me unimpressed. After hearing the film hyped in the small presses for some time, my girlfriend (now wife) and I rented a tape of *Ghost in the Shell*. Unfortunately, the only version of the film the small video store in Indiana carried had been dubbed into English. Although the visuals were outstanding, the story seemed muddled. By the end I felt as if I had completely missed the point of the story. As I rewound the tape, I wondered why there had been so much acclaim for such an incoherent film. It was not until a few years later when I decided to give the film another chance and watched the subtitled version that I grasped the subtle complexities of Oshii's filmmaking. I gained a renewed appreciation for the anime medium, as well as renewed scorn for films that have been overdubbed in a different language. The horrendous dub of *Ghost in the Shell* had almost turned me away from one of the greatest directors in animated Japanese cinema. (I recommend that readers watch Oshii's films in the original Japanese dialogue with English subtitles whenever possible.) My academic interest in anime continued to deepen, but it was not until graduate school at the University of Texas that I began to take a serious interest in Oshii's films. I took a cue from my mentor, Susan J. Napier, who encouraged me in my analysis of anime and Oshii's films in particular. Her work caused me to reexamine my initial assessment of *Ghost in the Shell* and led me to a further study of Oshii's works.

As of this writing, I have yet to meet Mamoru Oshii in person, although it is not for lack of effort. I set up an interview with him in March 2003, arranged for an interpreter, and flew to Tokyo to interview the director at the studios of Production I.G. Unfortunately, he was sick at home for the duration of my stay. Needless to say, I was disappointed. I had thought that by being able to apprehend the man in the flesh, I would be in a better position to understand the films that have sprung from his imagination. In a sense, though, failing to meet with Oshii led me to a better understanding of some themes in his works. Just as his later films demonstrate the mediation of daily life through technology, so were my interactions with the director mediated, through both computer technology and the barrier of language. Oshii did answer my questions about his films, translated and passed on to me from my ever-helpful contact at Production I.G., Yoshiki Sakurai.

In some respects, I think it is good that I was not able to meet with Oshii in person. His answers to direct queries about the meanings of his films invariably generate more questions than they resolve. Although I have used quotes from him to support specific assertions I make in the book, Oshii has always been a proponent of letting the viewer make up his or her own mind about the meanings of his films.

Thus this book is not the final authority on Oshii's works. I have provided my own interpretations to serve as a guide while viewing the films, but in the end it is up to viewers to determine their nature. This is what Oshii's films ultimately are about—the subjectivity inherent in concepts of reality.

CHAPTER ONE

AN INTRODUCTION TO OSHII

MAMORU OSHII IS A FILMMAKER WHO EXEMPLIFIES the breadth and complexities of modern Japanese cinema like none other. As a director, Oshii has made the majority of his complex and intelligent films in anime (Japanese animation). The term "anime" does not denote any particular style or content; it simply means animation from Japan. While anime has been gaining a broader audience in recent years, some critics still dismiss the medium as frivolous or lacking in depth based on a limited understanding of anime's breadth. For example, Donald Richie, noted critic of Japanese film, has said that "the reason anime are so fast, and so violent, [is that] they have to make themselves apprehendable through splash alone."[1] Although Richie's statement may be true of some popular anime programs (keeping in mind Theodore Sturgeon's maxim that "ninety percent of everything is crud"), Oshii's deeply complex films directly contradict such a generalization. Despite conceding that many animated Japanese films serve merely as lightweight entertainment, in his book *Dogs and Demons: Tales from the Dark Side of Japan,* Alex Kerr writes that anime is the "one bright spot in [the] otherwise gloomy picture" of modern Japanese cinema.[2] Animation as a medium possesses much more artistic and creative potential than many critics and casual viewers appreciate; Oshii tries to make his films fulfill this grand potential of anime cinema, with a certain amount of success. Along with Academy Award–winning director Hayao Miyazaki (*Spirited Away, Princess Mononoke*), Mamoru Oshii is at the forefront of this cinematic movement. As a director, Oshii refuses to be pigeonholed in medium or genre. He has worked in both live action and anime, directing everything from absurdist comedy to technological thrillers to meditations on the nature of dreams and reality.

As of this writing, Oshii has directed fifteen films in addition to his production and screenplay work on various other films and television series. His most recent full-length directorial work, *Avalon,* has received high praise from Academy Award–winning director James Cameron, who called it "the most artistic, beautiful and stylish [film] in Science Fiction history."[3] Directorial duo Andy and Larry Wachowski have cited Oshii's *Ghost in the Shell* as an influence on their groundbreaking science fiction hit *The Matrix.*[4] Two of Oshii's films have been screened at the prestigious Cannes Film Festival, and a retrospective of his work was shown at the 2000 International Film Festival Rotterdam. As a director, Oshii is both a popular and critical favorite; upon the 1996 release of *Ghost in the Shell* on video in the United States, the film went straight to number one on Billboard's sales charts. Of course, Oshii is also well regarded in his own country; he is one of the best-known anime directors and has been praised by Japanese critics for his "efforts to make Japanese animation the best in the world, not only in terms of techniques and execution but also in terms of popularity."[5] In addition to working in film, Oshii has written for *manga* (Japanese comics), video games, and even two novels. He is one of the true renaissance auteurs of modern Japanese film. However, unlike his contemporaries, such as Hayao Miyazaki, Oshii is a loner, an outsider who has been known to refer to himself as a "stray dog."

In spite of the accolades he has received, Oshii remains remarkably contrarian, eschewing the limelight in favor of his own personal cinematic vision. Although his films have been well received in America, Oshii does not generally care for Hollywood fare. He has been said to prefer European and Russian films, especially the filmmaking of Russian director Andrei Tarkovsky, to which Oshii's moody and atmospheric cinematic style is often compared. Said Scott Frazier, an American animator who has worked with Oshii, in viewing Tarkovsky's films, "you can see where Oshii's sense of timing and his atmosphere come from. . . . [Oshii] loves independent films, he doesn't like blockbusters."[6] The influence of live-action cinema is noticeable in Oshii's works, allowing him to create a believable universe filled at times with violence, contemplation, and absurdity. While a significant portion of anime in Japan is directed toward young children, Oshii takes the medium one step further by creating film and animation well suited for a thoughtful, sophisticated audience; James Cameron has called *Ghost in the Shell* "the first truly adult animation film to reach a level of literary and visual excellence."[7] Oshii's films are simply a joy to watch, each one a visual feast not soon forgotten.

Additionally, Oshii's works are an example of how a person can successfully balance both commercial and artistic concerns in the anime industry. Oshii has been able to remain loyal to his personal filmic vision while still garnering a remarkable fan base. Part of his success lies in the emphasis placed on the role of the director in the Japanese anime industry. Said Scott Frazier, "The Japanese anime director is similar to the American film director in that [he has] power over everything."[8] However, in practice, many Japanese and American directors are forced to waive their rights to the producers or sponsors of a television series or film; Japanese animation, like many other film industries worldwide, is both a commercial medium and a collaborative effort among many individuals. In spite of such restrictions, Oshii has demonstrated himself to be a talented and skilled director, capable of turning any story into one of his own. Each of his films bears his unmistakable imprint.

This book is intended to serve as a primer for the films of Mamoru Oshii. It does not cover every film he has directed, but focuses instead on the major films in which he has been creatively involved. Most of the films discussed in this book are commercially available in English, either on videotape or DVD. Of the films that are not commercially available outside of Japan, many are forthcoming, can be obtained within the anime fan community, or can be ordered from overseas without much difficulty.

BIOGRAPHY

Mamoru Oshii was born in Tokyo on August 8, 1951, the youngest of three children. Oshii was exposed to film from a young age—he has said that he remembers watching films like *This Island Earth* (1955) even before he was old enough to go to kindergarten.[9] When Oshii was young, his family went to the movie theater every weekend, and his father, an often-unemployed private detective, sometimes sneaked the boy out to the movies during the week as well. This began Oshii's conceptualization of the movies as something dangerous, although almost gleefully so. "I used to feel thrilled stealing change from my mom's purse in order to go to the movies," said Oshii. "In other words, movies are something evil: You wouldn't become somebody if you loved movies; you'd skip school, steal your parents' money, you wouldn't get a decent job, get married, or ever save money—your life would be a disaster. In my case, if I weren't a movie director, I'd be homeless or a professional eater at one of those stand-and-eat noodle places."[10]

Through junior high and high school, Oshii's interest in science fiction began to deepen, and he even contemplated becoming a science fiction writer. He began to correspond with the well-known Japanese science fiction writer Ryū Mitsuse, one of the founders of the Science Fiction & Fantasy Writers of Japan in the early 1960s. However, many of the books Oshii read were from English-language writers in translation—he has cited Robert Heinlein, J. G. Ballard, and Theodore Sturgeon as some of his formative influences.

In high school, inspired by the student protest movement (see chapter 5 for more details), Oshii began to become more politically active, participating in antiestablishment rallies and demonstrations. This interest in politics, and its intersection with Oshii's devotion to science fiction, is reflected in many of his later films, most notably *Patlabor 2* (1993) and *Jin-Roh* (2000). After graduating from high school, Oshii attended Tokyo Gakugei University, where he studied arts education and graduated in 1976. In 1977 Oshii, out of work, saw a sign advertising a job at Tatsunoko Productions, an animation company. He got the job and soon began drawing storyboards and doing production work for the company. Prior to this job Oshii had little experience in the entertainment industry, although he had been the director of a radio music show for about a year. An episode of the animated series *One-Hit Kanta* (*Ippatsu Kanta-kun*), for which Oshii wrote the storyboards, aired in December 1977. It was the first of his many credits in the field of anime. Some future anime directors began their careers by writing scripts for television episodes. Oshii, however, had little interest in the scriptwriting process, preferring to draw the storyboards. Said Oshii, "In the animation industry the writer's power is much weaker than the director's. . . . I always felt that scripts were written primarily to give the financier something to read."[11] Oshii did not begin writing scripts until he began to become established as a director and his ideas would be taken more seriously.

At Tatsunoko, Oshii continued to work on a number of different anime series through the late 1970s, mostly drawing storyboards and doing direction work. He left in 1980 to work for Studio Pierrot, where he continued his study of directing under Hisayuki Toriumi. Both men worked on the animated series *Nils's Mysterious Journey* (*Nirusu no Fushigi-na Tabi*), Studio Pierrot's first production, for which Oshii again did some directing and drew storyboards. They would collaborate again on the *Dallos* (1983–84) series of OVAs. The term "OVA" stands for "Original Video Animation," meaning anime films released straight to video, and *Dallos* was the first title to take advantage of the new format.

While at Studio Pierrot, Oshii began to work on the first major project of his career, becoming chief director of the *Urusei Yatsura* television series, which was based on the popular manga by Rumiko Takahashi. Oshii's lengthy involvement in the series was a testing ground for his own artistic vision of what can be done in the medium of animation and also led him to direct his first feature-length film, *Urusei Yatsura: Only You* (1983), and its sequel,

Urusei Yatsura: Beautiful Dreamer (1984). Later in 1984, Oshii left the staff of *Urusei Yatsura* and the employ of Studio Pierrot; from then on, he would not be tied to any one studio.

Oshii's first work as an independent director was the fantastic OVA *Angel's Egg* (1985), a collaboration with former Tatsunoko animator Yoshitaka Amano. In this film, Oshii would take advantage of his newfound freedom to the fullest, creating a lush and contemplative, if somewhat confusing, anime art film. He would direct two more films, the live-action *The Red Spectacles* (1987) and the animated OVA *Twilight Q 2: Labyrinth Objects File 538* (1987), before joining the creative team of Headgear to work on what would become the *Patlabor* series of OVAs, films, and television episodes (1988–93). Because of Oshii's reputation for producing "artistic" anime, initially some members of Headgear were skeptical that he would be the right person for the director's chair on the *Patlabor* project.[12] However, those doubts soon faded. With the success of the second *Patlabor* film, which he also directed, Oshii received an offer to direct the film adaptation of Masamune Shirow's cyberpunk manga *Ghost in the Shell* (1995). This internationally backed film, partially financed by Manga Entertainment, became one of the high points of the anime medium and one of the best-known anime films in the West. Oshii utilized only certain elements of Shirow's expansive manga for the film, creating a work that, although based on a preexisting storyline, bears all the traits one has come to expect from an Oshii film.

Oshii's next directorial project was *Avalon* (2000), a live-action film that explores many of the same issues of technology, the spirit, and alienation as *Ghost in the Shell. Avalon,* elements of which are based loosely on the events and characters of the legend of King Arthur, was filmed in Poland with Polish actors and a joint Japanese/Polish crew. Always a director who enjoys challenging an audience, when Oshii released *Avalon* in Japan, it was shown in Polish with Japanese subtitles. Other projects on which he worked during this time were an original story and screenplay for the film *Jin-Roh* (2000) as well as planning on *Blood the Last Vampire* (2000). Oshii's most recent projects have been a screenplay for *MiniPato* (2001), a series of comedic shorts set in the world of *Patlabor,* and the screenplay and direction of a segment of a live-action film called *Killers* (2003). As of this writing, Oshii is directing *Innocence,* the sequel to *Ghost in the Shell,* currently slated for a spring 2004 release in both Japan and the United States.

THEMES AND IMAGES IN OSHII'S FILMS

Oshii is well deserving of his status as an anime auteur. He does not simply direct films; he uses the media of film and animation to express his unique view of the world. Although his films span a diverse range of genres, they manage to maintain similar visual elements and discuss common themes.

One reason why Oshii's films exhibit such unity is the consistency of his collaborators, particularly music composer Kenji Kawai and screenwriter Kazunori Itō. Kawai first met Oshii on the set of *The Red Spectacles,* and Oshii has used him to score all of his films ever since. The pair has worked together so much, Kawai says, that they do not have to communicate very much when they are working on a project together; each knows what the other is thinking.[13] Similarly, Itō has written the scripts for many of Oshii's later directorial works, including the two *Patlabor* films, *Ghost in the Shell,* and *Avalon.* The two began their serious partnership while working together on the *Patlabor* OVA project as members of Headgear. (Although after the completion of *Avalon,* Oshii said that he does not think he will be working with Itō again.) This continuity in music and writing staffs has enabled Oshii to maintain a similar continuity in meaning and style. Each chapter discusses in more depth the themes present in each film, but in general six themes recur.

Ruins

Images of decaying cityscapes are a common element in Oshii's films. A few scenes in the first *Urusei Yatsura* film presage this, but Oshii's use of ruins does not become prevalent until the second *Urusei Yatsura* film. Decrepit cities and landscapes are featured in nearly every subsequent one of his films, from the abandoned city of *Angel's Egg* to the run down grit of *Avalon*. Oshii shows himself thoroughly to be a man of the city, expressing great concern about the survival of urban humanity.

Birds, Fish, and Dogs

Oshii is a great lover of animals, and they are a recurring motif in many of his films. Fish are featured as looming shadows on the sides of buildings and as airplane-size carp swimming through the sky in *Angel's Egg* and *Twilight Q 2: Labyrinth Objects File 538*, respectively. Birds, and especially their feathers, are highlighted in *Angel's Egg,* the two *Patlabor* films, and *Ghost in the Shell*. The fish and birds, especially because both seem to have the propensity for flight in Oshii's films, are perhaps symbolic of a sense of freedom from the mundane. Dogs, especially Oshii's beloved basset hounds, appear in a number of his later films and represent the director himself. Oshii does not call himself a "stray dog" as a mere metaphor. His love of, and identification with, animals is legendary; he has even drawn caricatures of himself as a dog. As the character Haruko states in an episode of the self-referential anime series *FLCL,* "Anime directors like cats because they don't have to take care of them. You know, they can't even take care of themselves. Oshii is probably the only director that loves dogs. He thinks he's a dog himself."[14]

Dreams

The confusion of dreams with reality is one of the main themes in Oshii's films. His first exploration of this topic, in the film *Urusei Yatsura: Beautiful Dreamer,* presents a world in which the dreamers do not realize they are dreaming. The confusion of dreams with reality appears again in *Angel's Egg* and *Twilight Q 2*. Oshii later expands this theme of confusion to examine the role technology plays in altering the reality of our daily lives. In *Ghost in the Shell,* a man's brain is hacked and he is given memories of a life he never had; here technology serves to blur the line between what is real and what is not. Similarly, at the end of *Avalon,* the protagonist must choose between the computer-generated "reality" in which she has found herself and the reality she had known until then. Although dreams are a trope he employs frequently, Oshii has stated that he is more interested in showing how dreams help to shape reality than in trying to distinguish between the two. Said Oshii, "I've never really differentiated between [dreams and reality]. I mean, it may be my imagination or interpretation, but I think that's the way dogs live. A dog doesn't really care about who it is, as long as it knows who it needs to live, and who is in its surroundings. Other than that, it doesn't need to know anything else."[15]

Military Hardware and Cyborg Technology

Although Oshii's films may have a philosophical bent to them, often they are visually grounded in a technological reality. For example, in preparation for work on *Ghost in the Shell,* the staff traveled to Guam where they fired actual guns in order to more realistically animate the performance of such weapons. (Because of Japan's strict gun control laws, such weapons testing would not have been possible in that country.) Oshii's fascination with military hardware and paraphernalia can be seen in the second *Urusei Yatsura* film, where the main characters set up a World War II–themed coffee shop for the school festival, complete with military regalia and a real tank. A column of tanks makes an appearance in *Angel's Egg,* and military technology is one of the main elements of the *Patlabor* films and *Ghost in the Shell.* One of the reasons Oshii filmed *Avalon* in Poland was the low cost and ease of access to many weapons, tanks, and helicopters.

Religion and Myth

Nearly all of Oshii's films have allusions to or make use of elements of religion and mythology. Even from a young age, Oshii had an interest in different religions. Although not raised Christian, he considered attending seminary not in order to become a priest, but simply to study religion further. Many allusions to Japanese myths can be found in the *Urusei Yatsura* films, and *Avalon* is structured around elements of Arthurian legend. However, Christianity is the religion Oshii most often uses and alludes to in his films; such references form a critical component of *Angel's Egg,* the two *Patlabor* films, and *Ghost in the Shell.*

Control and Surveillance

Issues of privacy and surveillance are closely tied into the progress of technology in Oshii's films. As technological sophistication increases, concerns that privacy will be eroded arise. For example, in *Ghost in the Shell,* the main character is a cyborg that works for a special section of the government. Although she is theoretically free to do as she pleases, the government owns her body and the memories contained within. Through this character, Oshii shows that as technology becomes a larger part of our everyday lives, it can inscribe us within new circles of control. Similar technological issues appear in the *Patlabor* films as well as *Avalon.* Oshii problematizes the progression of technology in a very technological fashion, through his use of sophisticated computer animation. He examines the downfalls of technology without succumbing to paranoia or seeming a Luddite. His response to invasive technology is quite playful; technology can be resisted through its proper subversion.

In the end, Oshii's films share the qualities of all good cinema. They are fascinating meditations on the nature of reality, spirituality, and the nature of humanity. Mamoru Oshii, a director with a vast artistic vision, uses the film and anime media not only to express his personal thoughts, but also to open doors to worlds heretofore unseen.

CHAPTER 2

URUSEI YATSURA (1981–84)

THROUGHOUT THE LATE 1970s, Mamoru Oshii worked in the anime industry, mainly drawing storyboards for various television series. After starting his career at Tatsunoko Productions, Oshii followed his mentor, Hisayuki Toriumi, to Studio Pierrot where he began to hone his skills at directing animation. While there, Oshii worked on a number of shows, most notably *Nils's Mysterious Journey*. An adaptation of a Swedish fairy tale, *Nils* is a tale of a young boy's quest for identity that features geese as the boy's traveling companions. It is noteworthy that Oshii was involved in a retelling of this tale at the beginning of his career; the story of Nils also has been cited as an early influence by Nobel Prize–winning Japanese author Kenzaburo Ōe.[1] As Susan J. Napier states, "Just as the young Ōe would grow up to commingle the Western Other in both his art and his life, so Nils seems happier among the alien geese than with humans."[2] Perhaps, like Ōe, Oshii could see something of himself in Nils and his quest.

The relationship with an alien Other would be highlighted in a more comedic manner in the first major project of Oshii's budding career. Oshii began work on the *Urusei Yatsura* television series in the early 1980s, marking the first time he was able to exert creative control on the course of an entire series. The program ran from October 1981 to March 1986 for 218 episodes, of which Oshii was chief director of the first 106. Like many popular animated franchises, *Urusei Yatsura* began life as a manga series. First published in 1978 in the weekly manga magazine *Shonen Sunday,* the manga became the first hit by artist Rumiko Takahashi. With future titles like *Maison Ikkoku, Ranma 1/2,* and *Inu Yasha,* Takahashi would go on to become one of the most popular (and wealthy) manga authors in Japan, not to mention the best-known female manga author. "*Urusei Yatsura* is a title I had been dreaming about since I was very young," said Takahashi. "It really includes everything I ever wanted to do. I love science fiction because sci-fi has tremendous flexibility. I adopted the science fiction–style for the series because then I could write any way I wanted to."[3] Takahashi has cited her influences as ranging from American sources like *Spiderman* and *Archie* comics and the *Bewitched* television show, to the writings of Japanese novelist Yasutaka Tsutsui. Of Tsutsui's novels, which have been called "metafiction" for the way in which they play with and conflate notions of what is real, Takahashi has said, "I've wished I could draw manga that was as absurd as that."[4] Oshii's work on *Urusei Yatsura* continued this idea of playfully toying with reality. As chief director of the series, Oshii could influence the tone and mood of many episodes, although his unique artistic vision for the series eventually led to creative conflicts with Takahashi. "I had to struggle with the ideas and views of the original writer," Oshii has said. "I only met with [Takahashi] a couple of times—there is no friendship between us."[5]

Oshii was able to become a director so quickly in his career due to a combination of talent and luck—his rise to the position of chief director of the *Urusei Yatsura* series was primarily because there were not enough qualified staff at the studio. Studio Pierrot's president therefore ordered Oshii to direct the series. Oshii's involvement with *Urusei Yatsura* also allowed him to develop some of his cinematic ideas and direct his first two full-length films, *Urusei Yatsura: Only You* (1983) and *Urusei Yatsura: Beautiful Dreamer* (1984). Although a light romantic comedy on the surface, the *Urusei Yatsura* television series and films that followed served as a proving ground for Oshii's skills and conceptual forms. It is through his involvement with *Urusei Yatsura* that he gained the early knowledge and experience to mature as a director.

The story of *Urusei Yatsura* chronicles a decidedly goofy tale of love, loss, and alien invasion, described by Takahashi as "a school comedy/romance with some science fiction and what-not, based on a foundation of slapstick."[6] In the series, the lecherous yet still somehow likable high school boy Ataru Moroboshi is chosen by random lottery to be the savior of the earth after aliens begin to invade. The format for such a decisive battle for the future of the planet is a game of tag on the streets of the fictional Japanese city of Tomobiki, where much of the series' action takes place. Ataru must touch the horns on the head of alien princess Lum within a given time period, or the earth will become the property of the aliens. (Of course, when he accepts this challenge Ataru doesn't know that Lum can fly.) Ataru's drive to win the game is for more personal reasons than the salvation of the world—his girlfriend, Shinobu, promises him they will marry if he wins. Additionally, Ataru is driven by libidinous desire to get close to the sexy Lum, who always wears a tiger-print bikini. Ataru's nature turns out to be to his advantage, however, as he wins the game of tag by yanking Lum's bikini top from her chest, making her pause to cover her immodesty and giving him the opportunity to touch her horns and win the game. In his excitement, Ataru yells that now he's going to be getting married. Lum, however, interprets Ataru's cheer as a proposal to her, and she accepts, forcefully wedging herself and her friends into Ataru's life. Although Ataru appreciates Lum for her curvaceous figure, he is wary of her temper and her tendency to subject him to electric shocks when she is upset. Although the premise of the series may sound bewildering, *Urusei Yatsura* is part of a tradition of much Japanese science fantasy, using folklore and myth to inform commentaries about contemporary life. Writes science fiction scholar Mark Siegel: "In the most common pattern of Japanese science fantasy, stupendous, god-like creatures come out of the skies, the mountains, the swamps, and the oceans to mingle in (and mangle) contemporary Japanese society. Perhaps because science fantasy, while a fairly recent development, fits into this well established tradition, it has been readily accepted by the adult as well as the juvenile population as a kind of modern legend."[7]

From this beginning, the series and films explore Ataru's relationships with Lum, Shinobu, and an ever-growing cast of supporting characters, showing how such interactions can cause chaos in daily life. In the course of the series, viewers are introduced to the large ensemble cast of Ataru's friends, family, and other attractive women (often supernatural or alien) after whom the lecherous lead lusts. The series frequently showcases exaggerated scenes and situations, and is filled with jokes and Japanese-language puns, many of which are lost on a younger and/or foreign audience. Many of the earlier episodes of the TV show were strongly based on Takahashi's original manga, but as the series progressed, Oshii began to take the show in his own artistic direction.

Urusei Yatsura participates in (and may have been one of the progenitors of) two subgenres of Japanese anime: that of the magical girlfriend and that of the loser boy. In the first category, the story's emphasis is on the relationship between the male lead and the female lead(s). The female characters often are imbued with both an unrealistically blind and undying love for the male protagonist, as well as special, seemingly magic powers. Examples of such anime can be found in series like *Oh My Goddess!* (1993) and *Tenchi Muyo!* (1992). The loser boy category features often painfully earnest male leads who just want to be loved, but cannot seem to make their relationships work. This anime genre often overlaps with the magical girlfriend category, as most males in such magical stories are loser boys. However, the loser boy category has more range, and the female love interests in such stories do not necessarily have any special powers. Examples of anime series featuring such loser boys are *Love Hina* (2000) and Takahashi's own *Maison Ikkoku* (1986). However, *Urusei Yatsura* has a decidedly different tone from all of its thematic descendants. Perhaps this is due to creator Takahashi's perspective as a woman in Japanese society and in an industry that was (and is) dominated by men. The male creators of magical girlfriend and loser boy manga and anime are demonstrating a form of wish fulfillment— they see themselves as the male protagonist, desperately wanting to be fawned over by an accepting woman (or women). Takahashi, perhaps in anticipation of such manga and anime, demonstrates what may happen when one receives too much of that for which one wishes. Ataru's consistently lecherous soul gets him into trouble by having him pursued by, and pursuing, a score of women. *Urusei Yatsura* was one of the first shows to employ such popular categories. Subsequent series often treat such themes in a much less creative fashion.

The character archetypes in the series also serve as a commentary on Japanese society. Through the character of Lum, the series throws light on the Japanese relationship with foreigners and foreign cultures. Lum is located at a unique point as both insider and outsider as she is both an *oni* (a figure from Japanese mythology) and an alien from outer space. Because she is outside of Japanese society, Lum provides a comedic counterpoint to the imagined stability of that society, yet her location as an insider allows her to participate fully in Japanese culture and ritual. In his analysis of character archetypes in Japanese animation, Jonathan Clements points out six basic female categories: the Girl Next Door, the Tomboy, the Maiden, the Older Woman, the Alien, and the Child.[8] Because much of the story of the *Urusei Yatsura* TV show centers on Ataru's romantic attractions to various female characters, these archetypes are particularly useful, and each does appear in the course of the series. The main conflict is between the Alien (Lum) and the Girl Next Door (Shinobu), although, as Clements states, "The dramatic tension in many episodes of *Urusei Yatsura* springs from the dangerous moments when Shinobu's prissiness threatens to relegate her to the Maiden scrapheap, or Lum veers towards promotion to Girl Next Door."[9] Rather than being mere romantic archetypes, these character classes are indicative of a larger social tension that has been occurring within Japanese society since Japan was forced to Westernize in the mid-nineteenth century (and probably even before). Lum and Shinobu represent the conflict between the appealing sexiness of the foreign and the stability and security of the native. However, in his two *Urusei Yatsura* feature films, Oshii chose not to focus on this cultural clash between Lum and Shinobu, examining instead the relationship between Ataru and another alien in *Urusei Yatsura:*

Only You and Lum's own desire for stability in *Urusei Yatsura: Beautiful Dreamer.*

In addition to its critique of roles in Japanese society, *Urusei Yatsura* was timely in its skewering of current events. For example, in one of the early episodes of the manga and the TV series, the earth is drained of all its oil due to Ataru accidentally taking a cosmic taxi from his school to home. Such a scenario pokes fun at the oil shocks Japan underwent in the 1970s by recasting the energy crisis on such a far-fetched premise. Further timely in-jokes and wordplay are scattered throughout the series.

Urusei Yatsura was Mamoru Oshii's first long-term job in the animation industry, lasting nearly three years. The first episode of the series aired on October 14, 1981, and the last episode of the series in which Oshii was involved aired March 28, 1984, nearly a month and a half after the second *Urusei Yatsura* film was released in theaters. In addition to serving as a proving ground for Oshii's creative and directorial skills, the contacts Oshii made with his fellow staff members proved beneficial. Through his work on the series and films, Oshii met Kazunori Itō and Akemi Takada. The three would go on to form part of the creative team called Headgear for the *Patlabor* series of OVAs, TV episodes, and films. Additionally, during his time at Studio Pierrot, Oshii had the opportunity to become involved in the *Dallos* animation project. *Dallos* would make anime history not because of its story or animation, but because of the way it was marketed and sold—it was the first anime to be released directly to video, becoming the flagship release of the OVA format.[10] Oshii directed all four episodes of *Dallos,* and worked on the storyboards and screenplay for three episodes.

Although it is often difficult to separate art from commerce in Japanese animation, *Dallos* began as a commercial enterprise for the Japanese company Bandai. According to Shigeru Watanabe, executive producer for Bandai Visual, in 1982 he was given the task of helping to develop a television show that would increase the sales of toys for boys. A number of different animation studios pitched ideas for this show, including a team from Studio Pierrot that included Hisayuki Toriumi, Itō, and Oshii. Although Oshii would go on to direct the series, many of the story ideas were not originally his; Watanabe says that Shintaro Shinchiya of Bandai came up with the idea of a *Rambo*-like main character, and others at Bandai contributed ideas for elements such as robots and guns that could be easily merchandisable.[11] However, because of commercial concerns, the projected *Dallos* television series was turned into a direct-to-video project. Released in December of 1983, the first of the *Dallos* OVAs was thirty minutes in length and used cover artwork by Yoshitaka Amano, an illustrator and graphic designer who would go on to work with Oshii on *Angel's Egg.* Three more thirty-minute installments would follow, as well as an edited compilation of the four OVAs. Only this compilation version, further edited and recut, has been released (dubbed) in English, as *Battle for Moon Station Dallos.*[12]

The story of *Dallos* replicates standard space opera–style science fiction. While the story is not terribly original, involving a band of colonists on the moon who are fighting for their freedom from the earth, the *Dallos* OVAs are an example of solid space drama. (The story is not based on the most original of concepts. It is similar to another landmark of Japanese animation, the TV series *Mobile Suit Gundam;* anime critics Helen McCarthy and Jonathan Clements have deemed *Dallos* an "unremarkable rip-off of Robert Heinlein's *The Moon Is a Harsh Mistress.*"[13]) Although Oshii directed the OVAs, they bear few of his stylistic visual touches. However, the police and dogs in the film are a precursor to some of his later works in the *Kerberos* world (the films *The Red Spectacles, Stray Dog: Kerberos Panzer Cops,* and *Jin-Roh*) and *Mobile Police Patlabor.* The cybernetic attack dogs in *Dallos* are the canine forerunners of the police in the *Kerberos* world, down to their glowing red eyes. Also of interest is Oshii's professed sympathy for the rebels as well as the motif of combat in underground tunnels, which appear again in *Patlabor 2* and *Jin-Roh. Dallos* is not Oshii's strongest directorial work, possibly because of the overt commercial considerations. As it was the guinea pig for the OVA format, there would not have been the willingness by the producers to indulge the experimentation Oshii was fostering in some episodes of *Urusei Yatsura.* This space drama would have been lost in anime history had its release format not been so novel. Another reason why *Dallos* is not as stylistically interesting as

Oshii's other films is that at the same time as work on *Dallos* was progressing, Oshii was pouring his efforts into the visually arresting film *Urusei Yatsura: Beautiful Dreamer.*

THE CHARACTERS OF *URUSEI YATSURA*

ATARU MOROBOSHI—The main male protagonist of the series, Ataru exhibits some of the worst traits of men. He is a lecherous, covetous loser who through sheer luck (not all of it good) is at the heart of most of the love triangles of the series.

LUM—An alien oni (a Japanese demon of legend), Lum sets herself up as Ataru's fiancée when she misinterprets his cry of joy upon winning the game of tag with earth in the balance. Although she can be sweet and kind, she is also very jealous; in the original Japanese dialogue she calls Ataru by the possessive term "darling" (in heavily accented English). As an alien, Lum's powers enable her to fly and shoot rays of lightning, with, more often than not, Ataru as the target. The design of the character is thought to be named after and based on late 1970s bikini model Agnes Lum, who, hailing from Honolulu and sporting a mixed racial background, was a curvaceous alien in Japan like the fictional Lum. It has also been theorized that Lum is creator Takahashi's alter ego, as "Lum" could be a nickname for "Rumiko" (owing to the indistinctness of "l" and "r" in the Japanese language).

SHINOBU—Ataru's girlfriend at the beginning of the series, Shinobu agrees to marry him if he wins the tag competition against the alien invaders. Although this promise has the desired effect of spurring Ataru on to win the game, it also results in the unintended consequence of Ataru becoming engaged to Lum. As the series progresses, Shinobu becomes less romantically attached to Ataru.

MR. AND MRS. MOROBOSHI—Ataru's mother and father often feel that their son's brazen antics are a disgrace to the family. Mrs. Moroboshi constantly laments that she ever gave birth to such a son, and Mr. Moroboshi is a caricature of the Japanese father figure, always sitting at the table, hidden behind the newspaper as events unfold around him.

SHUTARO MENDOU—The son of the richest family in Japan, Mendou is a source of constant surprises, due to his access to unrestricted capital and his family's private army. Like most of the male characters in the series, he is infatuated with Lum and often is angry with Ataru, who does not seem to appreciate his newfound alien girlfriend.

LUM'S STORMTROOPERS—The gang of Chibi, Perm, Kakugari, and Megane are collectively known as Lum's Stormtroopers for their constant protective supervision of Lum. Each member of the Stormtroopers is obsessed with the alien girl in his own way, but since Lum is in love with Ataru, none of them tries to woo her. Rather, they set themselves up as her guardians, trying to protect her and her happiness. (The threat to Lum's happiness often comes in the form of some thoughtless thing Ataru has done.) The individual characters are named for their respective physical characteristics. Chibi (literally: "runt") is the smallest of the four, Kakugari (literally: "crew cut") is the largest and sports a short military hairstyle, Megane (literally: "glasses") wears his eponymous spectacles, while Perm is so named for his styled hair.

TEN—Ten is Lum's baby cousin who, like his older relative, wears tiger-skin clothing and can fly. Unlike Lum, who can shoot bolts of electricity, Ten can breathe fire. He is a constant source of irritation to Ataru.

CHERRY—A crazy Buddhist monk, Cherry is the source of much consternation for Ataru, as he often causes more problems than he solves. Cherry often says he sees foreboding in Ataru's countenance, signifying Ataru's rash of bad luck.

SAKURA—A Shinto priestess and a nurse at Tomobiki High School, Sakura is a stunning woman. Her connection with the ancient religion of Japan seems to give her supernatural insights into the ways in which the world works, as evidenced in the second *Urusei Yatsura* film. She is also Cherry's niece.

ONSEN MARK—A teacher at Tomobiki High School, Onsen Mark is the first person to notice there is something amiss in the world in *Urusei Yatsura: Beautiful Dreamer.*

BENTEN—One of the seven lucky gods of Chinese mythology, Benten, the only female in the group, is also the goddess of love. In the *Urusei Yatsura* universe she plays a more rough-and-ready character than her mythological origins suggest, appearing as a scantily clad biker. She appears in *Urusei Yatsura: Only You* to help Lum figure out a way to get Ataru back from Elle, a rival alien love interest.

KURAMA, OYUKI, RAN, REI—Kurama the *karasu-tengu* (crow-goblin) princess, Oyuki the snow woman, and Lum's childhood friend Ran all play relatively minor roles in the first film and appear in the second film only in brief cameos in the harem scene. Equally minor is the role of Rei, a male oni and Lum's former fiancé, who appears briefly in the first *Urusei Yatsura* film.

SYNOPSIS OF *URUSEI YATSURA: ONLY YOU*

Two silhouetted children are playing tag against an abstract backdrop of trees, playground equipment, and city streets. They run across the landscape until the girl stops and the boy is able to catch her, leaping joyfully onto her shadow. The girl explains that on the planet from which she comes, the act of stepping on someone else's shadow is a marriage proposal. As her spaceship comes to pick her up, she tells the boy that she will be back to pick him up in eleven years so they can get married.

A large pink birdlike creature pedals his mail-delivery bicycle through the bright sky, touching down to deliver to Mendou's residence the invitation he carries. The compound guards leap into action, speeding the mail to the main house via a military motorcycle through the forest of tanks and jets that populate the Mendou compound. As the sun is setting, the messenger finally arrives at Mendou's residence to find the young master practicing his swordsmanship in a courtyard. Mendou is dismissive of the letter, a wedding invitation, until he is told that the prospective happy couple is Ataru Moroboshi and someone named Elle. At the news, Mendou becomes enraged and half crazed. He manages to calm himself quickly, doubting the letter's veracity, but vengefully vows to cut Ataru in half if the news is true.

At Tomobiki High School, everyone is talking about Ataru's upcoming nuptials, wondering who this mysterious Elle person is. The only two who are unaware of the commotion are Ataru and Lum, who walk to school together as if nothing out of the ordinary is occurring. Megane manages to lure Ataru to the school's clock tower with the promise of meeting a beautiful girl. There he and the other Stormtroopers accost Ataru, accusing him of bigamy. They intend to punish Ataru and to interrogate him about Elle and why he will be breaking Lum's heart. Ataru cannot confess because he does not know anything about the pending marriage. Even Sadoyama, a member of the school's farcical torture club, cannot make him talk (admittedly the torture consists mostly of tickling). Shinobu's arrival puts an end to the torture, and although Ataru thinks she has come to save him, he discovers that she is just as upset as are the Stormtroopers; in fact, her growing anger frightens even them. Lum arrives shortly thereafter, freeing Ataru from his chains with a blast of lightning. Ataru runs to her, crying that Megane and Shinobu have been picking on him. However, Lum has just received an invitation to his purported wedding and has arrived only to interrogate him further, and her repeated electric shocks to Ataru blow out the clock on the tower.

After Mendou arrives at the school to challenge Ataru with a division of armored tanks from his family's personal army, the skies above the school darken and a mysterious light begins to emanate from the clouds. As a shower of rose petals falls from the sky, a gigantic alien ship descends, filling the sky with its pointed cold metal and flashing, blinking lights. Everyone on the ground stares dumbfounded, including Lum, who says she has never before seen such a ship. A bridge of energy extends from the ship to the hole in the clock tower where the clock face used to be. A young woman crosses it to come within speaking distance of the group. The woman tells Ataru that she is from Planet Elle and has come to take him away with her. When Lum protests that she and Ataru are as good as married, the woman says that Ataru got engaged eleven years ago. Ataru is more than willing to go along with such an attractive woman. When Lum tries to shoot a lightning bolt at

Ataru to stop him, a protective barrier covering Ataru stops the blast. Ataru and the rest of the group are informed that he is actually engaged to Lady Elle, queen of Planet Elle, and that they will be back to pick him up tomorrow; they are giving him time to take care of any unfinished business he may still have. When Lum gets upset and tries to zap Ataru again, she sees he is still protected by a powerful shield. As Ataru returns to the ground, he tells Lum that he is excited if Elle is as beautiful as promised. Lum, upset beyond words, flies crying into the distance.

Later that evening, Lum sits with Ten at a coffee shop. Lum is absorbed in her thoughts as Ten struggles to remain awake. As Lum gets up and walks into the cold night air, a strange woman at the table next to hers stands and leaves too. Lum feels lonely and displaced, as if she has nowhere else to turn. Walking along, Lum encounters her friend Benten, who flushes out the agent from Elle who had been tailing Lum, making the agent quickly retreat. Lum and Benten discuss the details of Ataru's upcoming wedding over beef bowls at a Japanese fast food restaurant. They decide that Lum needs to launch a preemptive strike this evening. Lum leaves to make plans while Benten calls a taxi service for the use of an armed "interplanetary microbus" and driver.

As Ataru makes plans to marry Elle, Lum launches her counterattack, kidnapping Ataru, his parents, and Cherry using a gigantic vacuum attached to her spaceship. Lum plans to stage a preemptive wedding so Elle cannot possibly marry Ataru. Benten, in the space taxi, proceeds to kidnap the other necessary members of the wedding party via a tractor beam aimed directly into their homes. Along the way the beam also picks up incidental debris like a giant statue of a *tanuki,* a raccoon dog of Japanese legend. Once everyone is onboard, Lum and Benten take their ships into deep space to rendezvous with the spaceship of Lum's father, where they meet Kurama, Oyuki, Ran, and Rei as well.

A further series of shocks onboard the oni space cruiser eventually removes the protective barrier surrounding Ataru, leaving him worse for the wear. After a group discussion with Lum's parents and his own, Ataru seems to resign himself to marrying Lum. However, later, when Lum tries to give him a wedding ring, Ataru blurts out that he'd rather be with Elle, causing Lum to erupt in fury. Before further wedding preparations can be made, a fleet from Planet Elle materializes in front of the ship, blocking their way. Determined not to lose the fight, Lum's father calls for alert status, and space fighters from both sides begin to battle.

In the confusion, an infiltrator from Planet Elle on the oni ship (who had been hiding in the tanuki statue and had been tailing Lum earlier) manages to kidnap Ataru away from Lum again. They take off on an oni shuttle, but it is the one on which Shinobu, Mendou, Ten, and the Stormtroopers happen to be. Lum chases after them in a high-speed space fighter, but the one she chooses had been undergoing repairs, and when she engages the afterburner the plane explodes, leaving her floating in space by herself. The stolen shuttle makes its way back to the main ship, which warps back to Planet Elle.

Planet Elle is an alternately lush and urban world, looking like a parallel world to Earth, even down to the beef bowl restaurants being advertised. As Ataru's friends (especially Megane) worry about the lives they will lead on this new world, Ataru reveals his plan: By marrying Elle, he will become king, take over the planet, and create a great harem. When Elle first meets Ataru and the rest of the group, she mistakes the dashing Mendou for her promised love. Later, as Ataru and Elle walk around, flirting and getting to know each other, she reveals why she is so obsessed with his love: As queen of Planet Elle, she has always had everything she desires, yet Ataru is special because he freely chose her so many years ago.

Later that evening the scheming Mendou meets Elle in a secluded location for what he thinks will be a secret tryst. However, Elle takes him down into her inner sanctum, revealing rows of handsome young men in suspended animation; it is where Elle keeps her lovers, to be called on as she needs them. She reveals to Mendou that he is to be number one hundred thousand in this "refrigerator of love." Ataru, Ten, and the Stormtroopers, having followed Mendou and Elle, are shocked by what they see and try to escape from the planet. Just as the freezing process is about to begin, Shinobu rushes in and saves Mendou, demonstrating her superhuman strength by lifting the freezing contraption off him. Before anyone can escape, they are all taken prisoner by Elle's soldiers. When Ataru tells Elle that he wants to call off the wedding, she has him imprisoned until the ceremony the next day and has everyone else thrown in prison. In their cell together, Ten berates Ataru for mistreating Lum for all these years, and Ataru comes to realize the folly of his ways, realizing that all along Lum has cared only for him.

Creatures from across the universe have come to Planet Elle to witness the marriage of Elle and Ataru, and the capital is swarming with security forces to prevent any interference with the ceremony. At the altar, Ataru stands motionless in a state of shock with sunken cheeks and dark rings around his eyes. Having made her way to the planet, Lum manages to steal one of the patrolling aircraft while Benten creates a diversion, leading most of the other aircraft away from the cathedral. At the same time, Oyuki creates a snowstorm and Rei (in his monster form) rampages through the restaurant district. The group also manages to defrost all of the young men in suspended animation, who begin to riot because of Elle's impending nuptials. Lum reaches the cathedral before Ataru and Elle can kiss and flies him away, with Elle hanging onto his legs. All three are vacuumed into Benten's space taxi, which is shot at by Planet Elle's ground forces, causing the taxi driver to accidentally hit the warp switch, propelling the group into an alternate universe in which they are able to view the past.

At the playground from eleven years ago, the group watches young Ataru and Elle play. They learn that Ataru wanted so badly to catch Elle that he lied about stepping on her shadow, thus nullifying their engagement. When the taxi warps back to the present, Elle tells them to leave and never come back. She will make do with her male harem, most of whom have been recaptured.

The taxi lands back on Earth in another cathedral for another wedding—this time, that of Ataru and Lum. During the exchange of vows, Ataru cannot bring himself to commit to Lum and runs off. Lum flies after him, with the rest of the congregation following closely behind.

COMMENTARY AND ANALYSIS

As Mamoru Oshii's feature debut as a director, *Urusei Yatsura: Only You* merely hints at the director he would become. The storyline is overly melodramatic and the large ensemble cast of characters feels forced and underused, as if Oshii felt compelled to include nearly every character from the series for fear of upsetting fans. The story's flow is interrupted in places by interludes of pedestrian pop music, padding the film's running time, but adding to neither plot development nor depth of character. Years after making this film, Oshii seemed to acknowledge the follies of his youth, saying "Fairly often a first-time director puts too much into his first film and strikes out. That has happened to me too."[14] In spite of its faults, however, *Urusei Yatsura: Only You* showcases a number of issues and visual themes that presage the direction in which Oshii would take his filmmaking. Although the story relies too heavily on character and plot archetypes, the skill of Oshii and others on the film crew make it worth watching.

The first scene stylistically sets the tone for what is to come, both paralleling and inverting the story of how Ataru and Lum met. The opening shows the silhouetted children running across an image of a white reflected sun against a red background. More than just a stylistic abstraction, this sun is the reverse of the Japanese flag. Such an image indicates that this first scene is occurring in a world that is different from the "usual" one inhabited by the characters. It also serves to show that the events in the film will be similar to what the audience expects, yet in some ways crucially different, serving as an inverted parallel to the standard world of TV's *Urusei Yatsura.*

This opening scene reinforces the game-of-tag metaphor that had been used in the series since the first episode. Tag is an appropriate game to play because the name of the game in Japanese is *onigokko,* with the one who is "it" being the oni. (Of course, Lum herself is supposed to be an oni.) It is an interesting reversal that in the first game of tag in the series, Ataru has to play the role of the oni by having to tag Lum. Ataru's role is similar in *Only You*—he is the one who is doing the chasing at first, and it results in the similar consequence of unwanted attention. Elle is a parallel of Lum, both in how she and Ataru became engaged (accidentally, through a game of tag) and in her overprotective attitude toward him. Yet Elle is also a reflection of Ataru, in her attitude toward love and her maintenance of a harem.

The scene of the wedding invitation being delivered to Mendou demonstrates many of the styles and themes of Oshii's films. It is remarkable that in his very first film, Oshii is able to show both where he is in his career and where he is going; he deftly juxtaposes the silly comedy that is inherent in the *Urusei Yatsura* series and some of his earlier works with the emphasis on technology and the military that are integral parts of his later films. The pink delivery bird begins the scene pedaling his bicycle across the sky, gliding through a fantastical world without limits. When the bicycle touches down on Earth, the viewer is soon brought around to a world of the concrete everyday, a world of men and machines rather than pink mail-delivering birds. Oshii is signaling a transition from the unreal to the real. His subsequent films, and particularly the second *Urusei Yatsura* film, will continue this clash and combination of fantasy and reality.

Yet another skillful juxtaposition is when Elle's ship descends in a flurry of rose petals. The technological hardness of the dark ship and Mendou's tanks contrasts with the organic softness of the falling flowers. This hard/soft dichotomy can refer to both the tactile nature of the objects as well as their colors. Oshii loves to play with visual and conceptual dichotomies in his films, using them to amplify the differences and similarities inherent in personhood, religion, and technology.

In his early films, such as *Urusei Yatsura: Only You*, Oshii was just as likely to use such odd juxtapositions for comedic effect as he was to use the technique as a tool to further introspection. In a discussion of filmmaking with fellow anime creator Yūji Moriyama, Oshii reportedly mentioned the American film *Used Cars* by Robert Zemeckis. Says Moriyama, "He raved about it [*Used Cars*]. 'In this film,' he said, 'one little thing leads to another, and the story keeps snowballing, till the whole thing becomes a big hurly-burly.' Oshii felt that that was the greatest kind of storytelling."[15] Oshii's affection for such an approach to telling a story can be seen in *Only You*. The entire *Urusei Yatsura* story is filled with examples of premises that spin wildly out of control, and this film is yet another example. A simple game of tag and a childhood lie escalate into interstellar war for the love of a young man nobody really likes. In the battle with the ships of Planet Elle,

Lum's father tells his soldiers to allow no harm to come to his son-in-law, even though Ataru is a lecher ready to dump Lum for Elle (or any other beautiful woman) at a moment's notice. The soldiers' exhortations of glory and honor are contrasted with the inglorious and dishonorable actions of Ataru, the man they are fighting to protect.

Although the fight over Ataru is played for its comedic value, it is also a critical parody of Japanese attitudes toward war and sacrifice. One of the most direct indications of this parody is the captain of the oni's lead ship, a lean man with a scar on his face and an eye patch. This character is a direct reference to Captain Harlock, created by manga artist Leiji Matsumoto. In the original manga *Space Pirate Captain Harlock* (1977), the eponymous character fights to defend Earth against both an alien invasion and an acquiescing planetary government. This Captain Harlock "lives by Matsumoto's ideal of how life should be lived—under debt to no man, to no cause, and with no code to guide him but his own."[16] Harlock is a stoic fighter, yet his appearance in such a fracas as that which swirls around Ataru lessens his stature. The space battle portion of *Only You* is Oshii's response to the anime in the late 1970s and early 1980s that allegorically revisited World War II, such as *Space Battleship Yamato* (1974, also written by Leiji Matsumoto). By incorporating such references, Oshii shows that the ideals and people for which one fights are not always what one thinks they are. Oshii would revisit the ideals of war and peace in more serious terms in *Jin-Roh* and most notably the second *Patlabor* film.

In the climax of *Only You,* Oshii experiments with a stylistic device that he will continue to use and modify throughout his filmmaking. It is what can be called the *satori* moment of the film. Satori, a term from Japanese Zen Buddhism that has entered the English lexicon, commonly is understood to mean a sudden flash of insight. Said D. T. Suzuki, "[The] supreme moment in the life of an artist, when expressed in Zen terms, is the experience of *satori.* To experience *satori* is to become conscious of the Unconscious (mushi, no mind), psychologically speaking. . . . The *satori* experience, therefore, cannot be attained by ordinary means of teaching or learning . . . *Satori* thus refuses to be subsumed under any logical category."[17] Suzuki continues, "This self-realization is known as 'seeing into one's own being,' which is *satori. Satori* is an awakening from a dream. Awakening and self-realization and seeing into one's own being—these are synonymous."[18] Satori is an important concept to keep in mind when examining Oshii's films, as they often deal with differences between what is real and what is a dream. Satori by its very nature confounds communication; the awakening of satori must be experienced, not merely discussed. This idea of satori, and of meaning as experience, could be why Oshii often is reluctant to tell the meaning of any particular film. Oshii also has said that he thinks that people are not "waking up to reality," saying that if they did "I wouldn't have to make my films."[19] This statement implies that the idea of satori is central to his idea of how a film should be made. However, my use of "satori" to describe Oshii's films is not an attempt to subsume the films under a typically Orientalist idea of Japan. I am using "satori" less for its orthodox religious connotations than for its precise description of a type of awakening and its use in art.

The moments of realization in Oshii's films often occur within a special environment set aside for such a purpose. (In his later films the space in which the stories occur and this special space become more integrated.) In *Only You,* this moment of realization occurs on a different plane from the rest of the film. When it is time for the revelation, the characters are transported in space and time to the playground where Ataru and Elle played tag years ago, where it is revealed that Ataru lied when he told Elle he stepped on her shadow. This is the moment of enlightenment and revelation for Elle—all of her goals and plans for Ataru come crashing down. The result of one impetuous lie by a small boy triggered both a heated war of hearts and a giant war in space.

Although this revelatory scene was supposed to provide a sense of closure, its conclusion is drawn out far too long. As occurs earlier in the film, a musical number interrupts the flow of the story, allowing the moment to expand too much and losing the focus of the scene. Such musical interludes, consisting of songs detailing nostalgic loss, interrupt the action, allowing one to see Lum's rumination on her predicament, or the joy the characters felt when running and playing as children. Oshii has stated that the musical pauses in the narrative were not his idea and he disagreed with their inclusion in the film: "I was asked to do [the musical interludes] by the producer, and as a new director, I had no power to reject his intention. I truly think that they were meaningless sequences."[20] Thankfully, *Only You* is the last time Oshii would have to pad one of his films with such ill-conceived musical filler. (Oshii does use musical sequences in some of his later works; there they serve the overall effect and style he is trying to achieve, rather than working against them.)

This first feature film of Oshii's serves as a charming addition to the *Urusei Yatsura* television show. Although it did not break any new ground in terms of story or characterization, the film managed to showcase Oshii's developing style of storytelling. Incorporating many visual elements that would become his trademark, it established Oshii as a capable director of feature-length works. Oshii learned many lessons in the making of *Only You,* some of which meant that he had to relearn what his role as director should be. "When I made my first movie," says Oshii, "there was a certain understanding of what a director must be or do. And that would entail entertaining his audience, making an entertaining movie. Even if you do things in order to entertain the audience, I've come to understand that that doesn't necessarily make a movie."[21] After the light ensemble comedy of this first film, few people were expecting the turns Oshii would take in the second film in the franchise, *Urusei Yatsura: Beautiful Dreamer.* Although hailed in both Japan and abroad as a visual masterpiece, Oshii's treatment of the series' general plot and characters upset a number of Japanese fans. *Beautiful Dreamer* showed that Oshii would not be constrained by the commercial limitations of a popular franchise, even one he had helped to develop.

SYNOPSIS OF *URUSEI YATSURA: BEAUTIFUL DREAMER*

A brightly shining sun looms over a desolate landscape of a flooded, ruined city inhabited by the main cast of *Urusei Yatsura.* Some of them, such as Lum and Ten, are taking full advantage of the gorgeous day, riding Jet Skis and laughing. Others sit lounging in the detritus of modern consumer culture. Ataru, however, stands motionless in the water with a dazed look on his face, carrying a sign for *kakigōri* (a Japanese shaved ice dessert like a sno-cone). Tomobiki High School is partially submerged, the clock tower is cracked and crumbling, yet the tower bells continue to chime.

The scene switches to a prior time: the chaos at Tomobiki High as the students prepare for a school festival. In the midst of the confusion, Ataru and his friends are preparing a classroom to serve as the "Third Reich Decadent Coffee Shop," complete with German military paraphernalia and a working tank that strains the school's wooden floorboards. Lum's Stormtroopers complain that they probably will have to spend yet another night at the school working on the shop so it will be ready on time to open the next day.

After Onsen Mark enters the room to chastise the students for having a tank in school, Ataru, who has been in the tank the entire time, begins to cause trouble by fantasizing aloud in his sleep about all of the girls he would like to love. In the ensuing chaos (precipitated by Mendou jumping in and attacking Ataru because he heard Ataru say something about his sister) the tank turret swivels to the side, and Onsen Mark ends up hanging onto the main cannon as it points out the window a couple of stories above ground. Lum arrives and gives Ataru a good zap of her lightning, causing the tank to spin around and destroy much of the coffee shop the students had worked so hard to build.

After being subjected to a rambling lecture by the principal, Lum and Shinobu go off to get some hot water for tea. Shinobu complains about the time she has to spend at school on the festival, but Lum says she is enjoying it. As they discuss their relationships with Ataru and other boys, Lum says that her dream is simply to live with Ataru, his parents, and all of their friends together. Shinobu does not quite understand, saying that Lum's dream is no different from how things currently are, to which Lum replies that this is why she is so happy.

Ataru and Mendou take a break from the festival preparations and take a ride in Mendou's car to grab some food. As they drive down the dark deserted streets, they see their reflections in the many glass storefronts they pass, and Ataru wonders if the town is always so quiet at night. When stopped at a light, music begins to get louder until a group of traditional wandering musicians crosses the street in front of them and out of sight. (These musicians, known as *chindonya,* are often used in advertising to promote a sale or draw in customers. Ataru and Mendou react in horror because they are so out of place on a deserted street.) As the car drives farther into the night, Ataru and Mendou remain puzzled by what they have just seen.

The next morning the gang is groggily washing up at school after a long night of working on the festival coffee shop. They see Onsen Mark dragging himself across the schoolyard because he has worn himself out trying to supervise the festival. As they all begin a new day of work, the speech and actions of the students and teachers are remarkably similar to those of the previous day. Because Onsen Mark is so tired and overworked, school nurse Sakura sends him back home, giving him a large bottle of what she thinks are tranquilizers. When she is treating another patient, she realizes that what she gave Onsen Mark were high-potency laxatives. Sakura jumps on her motorcycle and speeds over to his apartment. When she bursts in, she finds everything in the apartment, from the walls to the floor, covered in a thick layer of dust and mold, with Onsen Mark sitting in the middle of the mess. Sakura flings him from his apartment through a window and follows close behind. (Owing to cartoon physics, Onsen Mark is unhurt when he falls back to earth.)

Sitting at a coffee shop, Sakura and Onsen Mark discuss what has been happening around the school. Onsen Mark explains that he had been absent from his apartment for a few days while overseeing the festival preparations at school, but had come home to find his room looking as if it had been abandoned for ages. Sakura draws the connection between what happened to Onsen Mark and the Japanese legend of Urashima Taro, comparing Tomobiki High School to the fabled Dragon Palace. In the legend, a young fisherman named Urashima Taro saves a beached turtle from some children who had been torturing it. In exchange for saving its life, the turtle takes Taro to the Dragon Palace below the sea, where Taro is welcomed by the beautiful queen. While there, Taro receives all the food, drink, and entertainment he desires. However, after a while Taro becomes homesick for his family and decides to leave. As a departing gift, the princess gives Taro a box with instructions not to open it. When Taro arrives back home, nothing is as he remembers it, as hundreds of years have passed as he has whiled away his time at the palace under the sea. Despondent that everything he loved is gone, Taro opens the princess's box, instantly ages a hundred years, and dies soon after. Sakura's comparison between the events taking place in Tomobiki and those of the legend indicate that she suspects something is amiss and that the city and the school have somehow been removed from the usual flow of time.

Onsen Mark explains that lately he has been having extended feelings of déjà vu, as if he has seen before the things that people around him say and do. Yet at the same time, everything is unfamiliar, and he keeps forgetting exactly what he has done even very recently. Onsen Mark wonders if everyone, maybe even in the entire world, keeps repeating the same day over and over again. Sakura tells him he is being delusional, yet when they return to the school to see Kakugari (who had been impersonating Onsen Mark earlier) being thrown out the window and hanging from the tank's turret, Onsen Mark decides to take action. Thinking the school may be the cause of the odd happenings, he kicks everyone out and locks the gate of the school. This is the last the group sees of Onsen Mark, as he disappears from Tomobiki after that evening.

The gang go their separate ways as it begins to rain. Lum flies off with Ataru; Perm and Megane get on the train to go home; Chibi and Kakugari ride the bus; and Mendou tries to take Shinobu home in his car. Sakura also departs in search of her uncle Cherry, thinking he may be able to explain the situation. However, only Lum and Ataru successfully reach their destination. The train's next stop puts Perm and Megane back at the exact same station from which they started, and Mendou's car constantly runs into dead ends. Unable to find Cherry, Sakura takes a ride from the Blue Turtle Taxi service; the cabdriver, who has comically exaggerated facial features, asks her if she has ever heard the legend of Urashima Taro. He wonders aloud what might have happened if everyone in the village had gone for a ride on the turtle rather than just Taro, theorizing that time and space are not objective things, but rather are created by the human mind.

Catching on that this is no mere human cabdriver, Sakura waves her Shinto *harai-gushi* wand,[22] causing the driver to lose control and swerve down the street. However, when Sakura looks again at him, the cabdriver's face is no longer the same; it has returned to a normal human countenance.

The Stormtroopers, Sakura, Mendou, and Shinobu all find themselves back at the gate to Tomobiki High School and, after deciding it is the only place to which they can go, make their way to Ataru's house. After calling around and finding no answer at anyone's home (not even the Mendou family compound, with its over two hundred telephones), they settle in for the evening while Shinobu compliments Ten on his new pet, a cute pig given to him by some strange man he met. The next day, after a communal breakfast, everyone walks back to the school through the puddled streets to continue preparations for the festival. However, when Lum turns around, Ataru sinks out of sight into one of the puddles. Looking down a side street, Shinobu sees a cart carrying *fūrin* (small bells with hanging strips of material to catch the wind), then a procession of fūrin floating through the air on their own. After being momentarily engulfed by their chiming, Shinobu finds herself alone in the middle of the street as a lone figure watches her from an upper-story room.

At Tomobiki High, Mendou's beloved tank has somehow appeared in the swimming pool. Recoiling at his prized possession's unexplained submersion, Mendou is even more surprised to see Ataru suddenly appear from the pool. Thinking Ataru is to blame for his tank's predicament, Mendou draws his sword and begins to chase Ataru, and stops only when Lum blasts the pool with one of her lightning bolts. At seeing this replay of events, akin to the previous tank fiasco, Sakura decides to take action. Over dinner that evening, Mendou, after consultation with Sakura, proposes that the group try to figure out what is going on. The Stormtroopers are not very interested in doing so, saying that they are glad that Cherry and Onsen Mark have disappeared. However, because the group forces Mendou to pay for the dinner, he makes them follow his lead to try to solve the mystery.

The group decides to explore Tomobiki High at night, as it seems to be a focal point of the weirdness that has been occurring.

Splitting up to take different floors, the group encounters a school unlike the one with which they are familiar, as if its labyrinthine structure had been designed by M. C. Escher. The characters run (and fly, in Lum's case) all around the school, their paths assuming impossible forms. In the end, the group ends up falling from a window into the car below, in which Shinobu and Sakura had been waiting the entire time.

As they speed away from the school, Mendou directs the car to a noodle shop that is really a secret base for his family; they have stashed a Harrier jet there for emergency purposes. When Mendou takes off to explore by air, the rest of the group hangs on to the plane so they do not get left behind. As they gain altitude, distancing themselves farther and farther from the city, they behold a shocking sight: the entire city is resting on the back of a giant stone turtle, floating through space. Flying around the perimeter of the city, they see giant stone images of Cherry and Onsen Mark serving as pillars, supporting the city on the turtle's back. When the jet begins to run out of fuel, the group is forced to return to the city, crash-landing just outside Ataru's house.

When the group returns from the Harrier escapade, the entire population of the town has disappeared. The town itself has crumbled, many of the buildings collapsing into rubble. Yet seemingly impossible things occur around the group of survivors: Ataru's house is still standing and has gas and electricity when all the surrounding homes are piles of debris; the nearby convenience store is always stocked with supplies, and somehow even the daily newspaper is delivered. Although content to live at Ataru's house for a while, some group members eventually drift off, with Sakura opening a beef bowl stand, Ryuunosuke and her father (peripheral characters who have somehow made it to the new world with the rest of the group) reopening their teahouse, and Mendou going off in his tank, seemingly firing shells at random. However, the group has lost track of time, unsure of exactly how long the world has been in such a state. Despite their feelings of displacement, most of the group members manage to have a good time, playing in the water, skating, sunbathing, and never having to worry about food. One scene even shows them in a theater watching an old print of *Godzilla*.

One day when speaking with Lum, Mendou asks her what she thinks of the world in which they now find themselves. Lum replies that this new world is very fun. After ingratiating herself with Mrs. Moroboshi, Shinobu unexpectedly disappears, as does Ryuunosuke. When searching the city yields no results, Mendou rappels down the edge of the city to discover that Shinobu, like Cherry and Onsen Mark before her, has become one of the giant stone pillars on which the city rests on the turtle's back. Sakura notices those who have disappeared were the troublemakers and the girls who turned Ataru's attention from Lum: Onsen Mark was the first to notice that things were off-kilter, Cherry would have been able to divine any spirits at work in this odd world, and Shinobu and Ryuunosuke frequently distracted Ataru. Because she is both a spiritual sleuth and a frequent object of Ataru's lust, Sakura believes that she will be the next to vanish.

Sakura arranges a private meeting with Ataru at night in the ruins of the clock tower of Tomobiki High. However, when Ataru arrives, Mendou is waiting there as well, and prevents Ataru from running away. They all sit down together, and Mendou reveals that while he has been driving the tank around, he has been trying to figure out how the world is built. He says he has discovered that Ataru's house is seated at the center of this world, and he goes on to describe everything strange about the world. As Mendou is about to tell Ataru his conclusion, that the world is just a dream, Ataru interrupts, saying that he and the others have already figured it out, but they do not know whose dream it is. Mendou informs Ataru that by process of elimination, it must be Lum's dream. Sakura postulates another person, who is bringing Lum's dream to fruition, pointing at Ataru. When he protests, Sakura brings out the *real* Ataru, who had been waiting in the darkness. The imposter Ataru, finding himself trapped in a box with *gohei* (paper folded in a zigzag pattern used in Shinto) around the sides, transforms into his true self, the demon Mujaki, the manipulator of dreams who has been responsible for much of the terror and sorrow of humankind's existence. (He has the face of the cabdriver who had been speaking with Sakura that rainy night.) Mujaki admits that he has caused the dreams of many different people, but only those dreams that they desired. Exhausted and trying to do some good in the world with his final job, Mujaki had given Lum the dream she wanted: to live happily with Ataru and his family and friends.

However, as Sakura and Mendou are listening to the story, Mujaki turns on them, imprisoning them behind the glass of the aquarium that had appeared as he recounted his meeting with Lum. As he walks away, it can be seen that each of the characters has disappeared in a separate pane of glass, showing the dream each is having. Ataru, however, manages not to get trapped, surprising Mujaki, who then gives him his true dream: a harem, composed of nearly every girl Ataru has ever met. However, the one girl who is not there is Lum, and Ataru yells at Mujaki to get Lum into his harem. Mujaki, in frustration, drops the horn he had been carrying that calls Baku, the eater of nightmares, who has been disguised as Ten's pet pig. Since Mujaki will not produce Lum in his dream, Ataru blows the horn, and the pig takes to the sky, sucking up the landscape of the dream into his mouth. As the dream crumbles away, Mujaki cries that he will not let Ataru go.

Ataru is back in Mendou's car as they are going out to get some take-out food. He begins to say that it was only a dream, but the driver speaks, and Ataru sees that it is in fact Mujaki. Not paying attention, Mujaki crashes the car, and Ataru is sent into another dream world. This time he is at the beginning of the *Urusei Yatsura* series, in the very first game of tag with Lum, before any of his misadventures had begun. However, now Ataru decides to not grab Lum's horns, time runs out, and an angry crowd (with Mujaki as one of the throng) closes in and beats him up. Ataru fades out of consciousness, only to reawaken as Frankenstein's monster. He and Mujaki hit each other again, and Ataru awakens in a future world in which he and Lum have been frozen, waiting for the time when science has advanced enough to awaken them. However, when he looks over at Lum's capsule, he sees that there was an accident four hundred years ago and realizes that she will never be waking up in this world. Ataru runs screaming, bursting through one of the walls, which is only a set piece. Mujaki, irritated that the next dream is not ready yet, hits Ataru with his large mallet. Ataru then finds himself in a world of DNA, of life itself, with Mujaki talking to him. Mujaki relates the story of the man who dreamed he was a butterfly and who, upon waking up, does not know if he is a man dreaming he is a butterfly or if he is a butterfly dreaming he is a man. Mujaki offers to make Ataru many good dreams that are, in his words, "the same as reality." A small girl, who appears throughout the film, tells Ataru that in order to return to reality, he must jump from where he is and that if he calls out the name of the person he most wishes to see, he will wake up. Ataru begins his screaming plummet, calling out all the girls' names he knows before finally saying "Lum" a fraction of a second before he hits the ground.

Ataru lands back at Tomobiki High, where everyone is sleeping in the room where the coffee shop has been created, exhausted from days of preparation. Seeing his sleeping form, Ataru kicks it, waking himself up. Sleepy and somewhat puzzled, Ataru kneels by Lum's bedside. When the clock in the tower chimes, Lum awakes, telling Ataru about the wonderful dream she just had. Ataru softly tells her it was only a dream and, as they are about to kiss, notices that everyone else has awakened as well. Lum tells Ataru he should be able to kiss her in front of others if he loves her, to which Ataru asks when he ever said he loved her. Lum delivers a fresh batch of electric shocks to her darling, and another day begins.

COMMENTARY AND ANALYSIS

While the first *Urusei Yatsura* film served as an introduction to the visual elements Mamoru Oshii would employ in his films, it is in this second film that a distinct artistic vision begins to develop. One of the lessons Oshii says he learned in making his first film is that "The audience does not have to understand [the film]. It might make the audience angry, but if you do your own thing, if you express yourself enough, even if the audience does not understand what you do, they can get some kind of enjoyment from it. . . . You don't have to *understand* a movie, as long as it makes you feel *something*."[23] This way of thinking inspired Oshii to take a gamble with *Urusei Yatsura: Beautiful Dreamer,* placing the emphasis more on deeper philosophical issues than the wacky hijinks that composed a critical part of the original series (although *Beautiful Dreamer* is certainly not without its moments of humor). This shift in filmmaking priorities angered a number of viewers when the film was released, and some fans were reportedly so upset by Oshii's treatment of the *Urusei Yatsura* characters that they sent him letters containing razor blades.[24] However, to this day *Beautiful Dreamer* garners accolades in Japan and abroad for its unique vision and stylistic presentation.

Urusei Yatsura: Beautiful Dreamer is a much more mature film than Oshii's first effort, the characters are much more developed. One of the problems with viewing films based on a long-running series is that they necessarily assume knowledge of what has come before, or at least a general familiarity with the characters. For the uninitiated, *Urusei Yatsura: Only You* can be a complicated mess of a tale. *Beautiful Dreamer,* on the other hand, presupposes less prior knowledge about the characters and allows them to stand more fully on their own. For example, Ataru had always been a one-dimensional character, ever the lustful male but demonstrating few other traits. Although his basic character is unchanged in *Beautiful Dreamer,* he grows more as a person and begins to truly understand the depths of Lum's love for him. It is telling that at the end of *Beautiful Dreamer,* Ataru finally gets the harem for which he has been constantly yearning. In fact, it was Ataru's quest for a harem that got him into so much trouble in the first film. The *Beautiful Dreamer* harem is filled with all of the girls Ataru has lusted after, yet he declines Mujaki's offer to stay in a dream world. In the end, through all of the confusion and false endings, Ataru comes to truly appreciate Lum and the world she represents, a far cry from his flight from the wedding chapel at the end of the first *Urusei Yatsura* film.

Another critical decision in this film was to remove nonessential characters. Although still composed of a large ensemble cast, *Beautiful Dreamer* pares away a number of the characters at the periphery of many of the *Urusei Yatsura* stories and concentrates on the relationships among the inner circle of main characters. Through their inclusion, the film shows that these are not only the main characters in the *Urusei Yatsura* universe, but these are the people to whom Lum feels closest. Gone are many of the competitors for Ataru's attention, such as Benten, Oyuki, and Kurama, which allows the plot to proceed in a direction that does not concentrate on Ataru's eternal quest for the opposite sex (but of course that quest is referred to, as it is one of Ataru's essential character traits). Such characters do not appear because Lum wishes it to be so—viewers are in the realm of Lum's dream from the very first scene, and it is not until the very end that "reality" is depicted. Thus the excising of peripheral characters serves not only to help along the flow of the story, but forms an essential part of the story itself.

What really sets *Beautiful Dreamer* apart from the rest of the *Urusei Yatsura* universe is Oshii's unmistakable visual style, using quiet, contemplative shots, often coupled with long monologues or dialogues. With this film, the main action and conflict in Oshii's works begin to be driven more by what the characters say than by the images onscreen. This is not to imply that the images are unimportant; they are obviously carefully crafted, but they provide supplementary meaning to what is being spoken. This approach can be contrasted with many other anime, in which it is the animation itself that takes precedence over story. At the same time, Oshii often employs a large amount of visual symbolism (often religious) that on initial viewing may not seem to relate to the plot of the story. Viewers often must puzzle out the true meanings of many of Oshii's films (if any film can be said to have a "true" meaning), using the dialogue and visual elements as guideposts.

Although all of the *Urusei Yatsura* series is heavily imbued with Japanese culture (especially the multilayered puns that are not easily translatable), Oshii makes elements of traditional Japanese mythology a central part of this film. This marks the beginning of another stylistic approach of Oshii's—the use of direct references to religion and mythology in his films. Of course, this use of mythology does not set a precedent in the *Urusei Yatsura* universe—myth and legend had been a part of the series from the very beginning, as all of the nonhuman characters have some historical basis in Japanese myth. (Consider Lum's status as an oni and Benten's position as one of the seven lucky gods of Chinese legend.) The series has referred to other Japanese myths, such as that of Momotaro, or Peach Boy, when Ten first appears. Because most of these myths would be culturally familiar to Japanese viewers, Takahashi (and Oshii in turn) could reformulate the legends in a modern setting. Thus, the previous use of myth and legend in the TV series allowed Oshii to transition seamlessly to using the Urashima Taro myth in *Beautiful Dreamer.*

Some of the mythological elements of *Beautiful Dreamer* had been used previously in the television series, most notably in the episodes "Wake Up to a Nightmare" ("Mokuzamereba Akumu") and "The Big Year-End Party That Lum Organized!" ("Lum-chan Shusai Dai-bounenkai!"). The film can be seen as a combination and reworking of these two episodes. The first episode introduces the characters of Mujaki and Baku; the character of Mujaki is a fictionalized creation, but Baku is taken from Japanese folklore. Similar to *Beautiful Dreamer,* the second episode references the Urashima Taro legend and places the characters in a maddeningly cyclical narrative structure. This reworking of previous material is a technique Oshii would go on to employ in the second *Patlabor* film, which uses elements from two of the original *Patlabor* OVA episodes.

At the heart of *Beautiful Dreamer* is the distinction between dreams and reality, a theme to which Oshii returns in many of his films. He is fascinated by the power of dreams to mimic reality. By taking up the subject of dreams, Oshii is necessarily questioning the dividing line between dreams and reality (if one can be said to exist at all). In *Beautiful Dreamer,* Oshii uses the Urashima Taro myth to play with ideas of time and memory. Almost the whole film takes place in a dream world, yet in the end Ataru is able to cross from the land of his dreams back to "reality" with remarkable fluidity. In the film, memory becomes compressed into a single instant that exists at no time. In the words of the cabdriver Mujaki, the only thing that is certain is the present.

Another idea central to Oshii's works is the concept of the labyrinth, in its physical, mental, and religious forms. The word "labyrinth" generally brings to mind physical entrapment, and the characters in *Beautiful Dreamer* are indeed physically trapped within a perplexing space. The group's expedition into Tomobiki High School at night is an excellent example of the labyrinth at work, as they keep wildly running (or flying, in Lum's case) around the same space but get nowhere. However, Ataru later discovers that their supposed physical confinement is not physical at all, but in fact mental. Additionally, a labyrinth is not the same as a maze, designed to ensnare; labyrinths have been used in religious worship and practice for hundreds of years as a metaphor of, and tool for, spiritual growth. However, the path of the labyrinth need not exist in physical space. *Beautiful Dreamer* employs a number of labyrinths, some physical and some mental. In the film, the entire city of Tomobiki becomes a labyrinth, shrinking smaller and smaller in order to contain the characters. When trying to get Shinobu home, Mendou even comments on this fact, saying that they have to be able to find some way out, as the city was not designed as a labyrinth. (Unknown to Mendou, Lum's dream version of the city was indeed constructed to be so.) Perhaps such a labyrinthine structure was designed to mirror the twisting forms of the modern Japanese environment; an article in *Japan Quarterly* has described the city of Tokyo itself as a labyrinth, an urban mass that seems to grow by itself.[25] In the film, the city is a mirror of the main labyrinth that is Lum's dream. However, this containment of the characters ironically leads to personal growth, as Ataru becomes more aware of Lum's true feelings. Although all the characters in *Beautiful Dreamer* are taken along the path of Lum's dream, the spiritual journey in fact belongs to Lum and Ataru. *Beautiful Dreamer* foreshadows the great concern for the future of urban humanity as well as the labyrinthine path of spiritual growth that Oshii would feature in subsequent films.

Also of note is the melancholic tone that pervades the entire film. This is evident from the very first note of the score, setting the mood for the film and serving as a contrast to the fun some of the characters are having in the first scene. Something is obviously amiss; viewers are left with the sense that something great has been lost. Equally sad is the glimpse of the lives of the characters among the detritus of popular culture. Although much else has been lost, these remnants of consumerism are what the characters cling to in order to find meaning in their newly confused lives. Oshii is commenting negatively on the capitalist culture of acquisition that spread throughout Japanese society, and especially among its youth, in the mid-1980s.

Beautiful Dreamer is such an effective film because it relies on the idea of what anthropologist Mary Douglas calls "matter out of place."[26] Although Douglas originally used the term to apply primarily to the concept of dirt and cleanliness, the idea can be expanded to give it a more general scope. When objects are removed from their proper contexts, they become a form of ideological pollution, confusing and upsetting the watchers. The chindonya (wandering musicians) in the early part of the film are just one such example. They appear where they do precisely because they should not be there. This is the first signal to the characters that there is something amiss. The audience, however, has already been forewarned in the film's opening scene: a giant tank, Jet Skis, a tape deck, fan, refrigerator, and kakigōri sign—all elements one would not expect to find among the flooded ruins of a city. Oshii tries to show that it is through the process of being perplexed and upset that one can gain insight into one's own biases of how the world does (and possibly should) work. It is this realization that enables Ataru to free himself from the confines of the dream and return to Tomobiki High with a greater understanding of Lum's innermost character.

One of the hallmarks of Oshii's works is showing characters through some sort of distortion. Often it is some sort of reflection, such as through water or glass. This is especially evident in the scene in which Sakura and Onsen Mark are discussing the latter's decrepit apartment. The perspective adds a touch of unreality to the scenes and emphasizes what the characters are saying. Oshii uses a different point of view particularly effectively in the scene in which Mendou's car is driving around, trying to get away from Tomobiki High. The scene represents what one can see from the front of a car and, as such, shows only an illuminated circle on the ground from the headlights. As they can see only a small portion of the path they travel, the characters' sense of urgent confusion grows. This scene is echoed a short time later by Sakura's cab ride. The scene out the window is a succession of streetlights, one after another, which contrast with the cabdriver's musings about time not being linear. Another such scene occurs when the group walks back to the school after the first night at Ataru's. As they walk along, their images are reflected in the puddles left over from the previous night's rain. Yet during this sequence, large fish quickly swim across the screen, indicating that the reflections are not mere puddles but are indicative of a deeper reflection and distortion of the "real" world.

Beautiful Dreamer gradually brings to the fore issues of time and space, first by playing with viewers' concepts of season. However, this play occurs through culturally specific representations of seasonality that non-Japanese viewers often would overlook. Although it is not explicitly mentioned, it is probably fall at the beginning of the film, as that is when most school festivals occur. Onsen Mark begins to question the seasons in his confessional to Sakura, wondering if he is so hot because it is hot outside or because he is nervous. As increasingly strange events begin to occur, Shinobu sees a procession of fūrin, a traditional sign of summer, down an alleyway, further adding to the confusion as to what time of the year it is. Subtle clues such as these deepen the spatiotemporal mystery at the heart of the film.

Even though it is about dreams and reality, *Beautiful Dreamer* is also a film about the end of the world. According to Susan Napier's analysis of Japanese animation, the apocalyptic is one of the "three major expressive modes" of anime (the other two being the festival and the elegiac).[27] Unlike most visions of the apocalypse, Oshii's vision does not end in a bang, but quietly, in a manner that is almost dignified. Yet Oshii does not take the end of the world too seriously. After the Harrier flight, the film is narrated briefly by Megane, in a parody of typical postapocalyptic survivors' tales. As one of the few remaining souls, he relates his tale of horror at what the world has become with a sense of self-importance because he will be one of the architects of the new human society he believes will rise from the ashes. However, his monologue is so clichéd and over the top that it is difficult to take him seriously. He even states that his monologue is an excerpt from a longer work of his called "The Prehistory of Tomobiki." The destruction of the city itself even becomes self-referential as the characters watch *Godzilla* in a dilapidated theater, viewing how the destruction of Japan was once envisioned. Perhaps envisioning the end of Tomobiki was a form of catharsis for Oshii as he neared the end of his tenure on the *Urusei Yatsura* staff. The director said of working on the television show, "I remember receiving threatening letters on a daily basis, as well as being involved in various troubles which made the company almost fire me." He added, "I could not bring myself to love [Rumiko Takahashi's original manga] characters."[28]

Many of the scenes in *Beautiful Dreamer* bear a striking visual similarity to elements Oshii would incorporate into later films. The visual links between this second *Urusei Yatsura* film and Oshii's next film, *Angel's Egg,* are clear. For example, in one of the first scenes in *Beautiful Dreamer,* Ataru stands just barely in the water as the waves lap his legs. Oshii later incorporated this shot into the end of *Angel's Egg.* Additional scenes referenced in *Beautiful Dreamer* include the presence of sirens during the first shot of Tomobiki High (like the sirens heralding the arrival of the giant sphere in *Angel's Egg*) and a shot of Mendou in his tank (a precursor to the column of tanks in *Angel's Egg*). The same year he finished *Beautiful Dreamer,* Oshii left Studio Pierrot to work independently on his own projects such as the fantastical *Angel's Egg* and the mysterious *Twilight Q 2.*

CHAPTER 3

ANGEL'S EGG (1985)

In 1984 Oshii left the staff of Urusei Yatsura and the employ of Studio Pierrot to begin working on his own projects. Oshii's departure not only marked the beginning of a new phase in his career, it also served as the impetus for his former colleagues to create the popular animated film *Project A-ko* (1986). Yūji Moriyama, director of animation and storyboard artist on *Project A-ko,* stated: "The crew [of *Project A-ko*] consisted mainly of people who had worked on *Urusei Yatsura.* Initially, that TV series was directed by Mamoru Oshii, but he stepped down along the way. His defection demoralized the crew and left us utterly unmotivated. We were ready to move on to something more interesting, something we could really sink our teeth into. Those of us who shared that sentiment got together and brainstormed. And this film is the culmination of all our ideas."[1]

Although both Oshii and the group that went on to make *Project A-ko* trace similar roots and influences to *Urusei Yatsura,* their end results could not be more different. The goal in *Project A-ko* was centered on the drive to make really interesting animation rather than to explore philosophical ideas. Said Moriyama, "The currents [at that time] were shifting favorably towards more serious works that were loaded with meaning and heavy themes. It was a frustrating time for animators who liked to animate. *A-ko* was a deliberate attempt to push all that aside, to provide some mindless fun, to make an action-packed film that would be fun to make and fun to watch. I guess you could say it was an animator's anime. Animators who wanted to animate big action but couldn't, came together on this project and let it all hang out."[2]

One reason why Oshii left *Urusei Yatsura* may have been that he recognized a viable market for the more introspective anime he wanted to direct. His next work was *Angel's Egg,* a drastic departure from the comedic lightness of Lum and Ataru. In this work Oshii would go on to explore many of the same themes of dreams and reality that he examined in *Beautiful Dreamer,* but in a much more serious and experimental fashion.

Angel's Egg is one of the most challenging anime films to be commercially released and served as inspiration for many anime that came after it. The film is rich in style and visual symbolism, but offers little in the way of dialogue or straightforward plot. Multiple viewings are required to absorb the full effect of the surreal visuals. Nearly twenty years after its production, it is still often thought to be one of the highlights of both "artistic" anime and Mamoru Oshii's career as a director.

Angel's Egg was the result of collaboration between Oshii and artist Yoshitaka Amano. Oshii wrote the screenplay and directed the film, Amano was in charge of the art direction, and both Oshii and Amano collaborated on the film's storyline. Like Oshii, Amano began his career at Tatsunoko Productions, working on such anime series as *Gatchaman* (1972) and *Time Bokan* (1975). In the early 1980s Amano began branching out into the field of illustration, creating his own style of fantasy art that combined elements of European and Japanese design. Thus, although Amano is a Japanese illustrator, his works do not have a stereotypical "manga" style to them; he eschews pen and ink in favor of a softer watercolor look. Since working with Oshii, Amano has done illustrations for the *Final Fantasy* line of video games and has collaborated with Neil Gaiman on the Hugo–nominated and Eisner Award–winning graphic novel *Sandman: The Dream Hunters.* Amano's illustrations and lithographs have been showcased in solo shows in Tokyo, New York, London, and Paris.

While Oshii controlled the content of *Angel's Egg,* Amano influenced the film's visual design. Amano's contribution created a moody atmosphere that is palpable in every scene. In a number of other projects, Amano's original artwork was altered significantly in the final product. A good example of this was the anime film *Vampire Hunter D* (1985), about which Clements and McCarthy wrote, "The character designs, based on Amano's illustrations for [Hideyuki Kikuchi's] novels [on which the anime was based], may entice lovers of his smoky, elegant watercolors and baroque game characters, but they were radically simplified to cut animation costs, with only traces of the artist's hand remaining, mostly in still frames."[3] However, *Angel's Egg* retains the look and feel of Amano's original designs, making it one of the most beautiful and lyric films in the animated medium. One Japanese animation guide has reportedly called it "animated art rather than story. It could be brought to a Soho gallery theater."[4]

In crafting the designs for *Angel's Egg,* Amano has said he "was deliberately trying to visualize Oshii's world,"[5] indicating that because of the concepts employed, the film was more Oshii's than Amano's. Many of the visual elements characteristic of Oshii's films are present in *Angel's Egg:* ruins and decaying cities, birds and feathers, heavy military machinery, and quotes and allusions to the Bible and Western mythology. Oshii began incorporating such elements into his films beginning with *Urusei Yatsura: Beautiful Dreamer,* and continued to use themes in *Angel's Egg* that are present in many of his later works.

Aside from being a collaboration between two very talented individuals, *Angel's Egg* is known for being remarkably difficult to understand. Oshii himself has said that he does not know what the film means. Similarly, Amano has said the film "was a rather private story, so I'm sure it's nearly impossible to understand it. So, it might be better for [the viewers] to watch it more for the visual images than for the story."[6]

THE CHARACTERS OF *ANGEL'S EGG*

THE GIRL—The girl is a mysterious traveler, carrying a large egg of unknown origin. Her purpose and destination are unclear, but she seems to attach great importance to the egg she bears.

THE SOLDIER—The soldier is a young, handsome man who carries a large weapon in the shape of a cross. Although the girl is initially suspicious of him, he later accompanies her on her journey. The soldier is on a journey of his own, though; he is questing for the answers to who he is and where he is from. He believes the girl and her egg may be able to help him.

THE FISHERMEN—The fishermen are constantly cloaked in darkness as they pursue their prey—giant shadow fish that appear on the walls of buildings in the city. Armed with a multitude of harpoons, the fishermen try valiantly to catch the fish, but to no avail.

SYNOPSIS

A young soldier stands on a surreal checkerboard landscape, watching as a giant orb filled with thousands of Greek-influenced stone statues descends from the sky. As it settles to the ground, sirens are triggered throughout the orb.

Whistling sirens in the distance awaken a young girl, sleeping in a room at the bottom of a tall staircase. After she rises from the bed, wrapping her blanket around her shoulders, she leaves behind a large egg the size of her head. As she walks up the stairs to the top of the staircase, the girl looks out wistfully on the city in the distance. Then she returns to the egg, places it underneath her skirt so she is carrying it next to her stomach, as if she were pregnant, and begins her journey across the land.

The girl makes her way through the darkened and desolate landscape, crossing a forest of tangled roots and misshapen trees. She stops at a small pond to fill a large glass flask that is the same size as the egg, holds it up to admire the way in which the world is reflected through its shimmering contents, and then slowly drinks from it. As a lone feather floats along the pond's surface, the girl sees a vision of herself slowly sinking into the water's flowing embrace then standing on the bottom of the pond as she holds her egg.

The girl reaches the city—a dark, seemingly deserted town of vaguely European design. Walking alone through the decaying streets, she looks up at the blackened windows reflecting the storm clouds overhead and gazes at the abandoned balconies and staircases. The small alleyways open on a large thoroughfare, and she pauses at the sound of approaching machinery. A division of large tanks rises over the hill in a seemingly endless progression, their priapic guns looming over the landscape. One of the tanks stops long enough for a young soldier to dismount, looking intently at the girl. The girl looks up at him and clutches the egg more tightly to her chest. The two stand staring at one another as the tanks drive off into the distance. Suddenly the girl turns and begins running, taking refuge in a small alley, and comes out only when she believes the soldier to be gone.

A short time later the girl searches a decrepit room in the city for further supplies, placing what she needs into her small shoulder bag. She picks up another large glass flask, pours out its red liquid contents, and carries it to a still-functioning fountain in the town plaza. She fills the flask and is about to drink when she notices dark, mysterious figures sitting on the other side of the fountain. As a clock in town begins to chime fourteen times, she drops the flask and runs away.

Taking a break in the sunken remains of a once-great building, she puts the egg down and moves off to gaze at the standing water that now fills the ruins. After a while, she turns to see the soldier a short distance away. He produces the egg from under his cloak and chides the girl, saying that she should keep precious things inside her to keep them safe. After he gives the egg back to her he asks her about it, saying that the only way to truly know what is inside is to break it open. The girl turns and runs away, and the soldier begins following her.

She continues to walk throughout the city, the soldier becoming her de facto traveling companion. A throng of fishermen with spears runs past them, and the girl comments that even though there are no longer any fish, the men still pursue them. As more fishermen begin to assemble, shadowy images of fish appear on the sides of the buildings. The men repeatedly throw their spears, but to no avail; the fish are, after all, only shadows, and they continue to swim across the buildings in spite of the harpoons being hurled their way.

The girl leads the soldier back the way she came and, after securing his promise that he would not do anything to her egg, takes him into a large building containing the fossilized remains of some large ancient creatures. Inside, the soldier sees a stylized painting of a tree on the wall, triggering a memory for him. He says he has seen a tree like this before and that the tree had contained a dreaming, sleeping bird within a giant egg. Noticing the rows of glass flasks lined up along a wall, the soldier asks the girl how long she has been living in this building, but she does not know. He confides that he does not really know who he is or where he is from either. He begins to tell her the biblical story of Noah and the ark, but changes the ending; instead of sending the dove out and finding land, the people on the ark begin to drift aimlessly, forgetting about their previous lives and even that the world had been flooded. The soldier theorizes that maybe they are all part of someone else's dream and that the giant dreaming bird he remembers never actually existed. The girl tells him that the bird does indeed exist and leads him to the fossilized skeleton of a giant bird in another part of the building. She tells the soldier that she found the skeleton like this, but that she is going to hatch a new bird from the egg she is carrying.

The soldier and the girl, cradling her egg next to her head, sit around a small fire on the floor of the girl's bedchamber. The soldier asks if she can hear anything in the egg, and she just looks at him and smiles, saying that she can hear the sound of breathing. The soldier retorts that she is just hearing her own breathing. She replies that she can hear the sound of wings, to which the soldier replies that it is just the wind outside.

It is raining hard outside when the soldier carries the now-sleeping girl and lays her on her bed. She awakens enough to ask the soldier again who he is, but he just returns the question and the girl falls back to sleep, clutching her egg. The soldier sits on the floor, watching the dying fire, his back against the bed. When the flame goes out, he stands up and takes the egg away from the girl. He places the egg on the ground and uses the pointed end of his cross-shaped weapon to smash it.

The rising waters have flooded much of the town, yet the fishermen continue to stand motionless, waiting for the shadow fish to arrive again. The girl awakens to find both the egg and the soldier are gone. As she walks around the room, she finds the hollow shell of the egg cracked open on the floor—there is no evidence that there was ever anything inside the shell—and begins to cry. She runs out of the building, across the barren landscape, and sees the soldier walking some distance away. Before she can reach him, she falls into a water-filled ravine, languidly sinking deeper into the murky depths.

The soldier stands alone on a desolate beach in a storm of bird feathers whipped around by the wind. The orb rises out of the ocean, its alarms going off yet again. This time, however, one of the statues on the orb's surface is of the girl holding the egg. The soldier stands in the surf and watches the orb rise in the distance.

COMMENTARY AND ANALYSIS

Oshii has reportedly said *Angel's Egg* was so unsuccessful in Japan "that it kept him from getting work for years."[7] While his filmography attests that this is something of an exaggeration, the film has indeed biased many viewers' perceptions of Oshii as a director. In *Angel's Egg*, Oshii is cultivating his budding reputation as a director of difficult-to-understand films, almost reveling in his use of abstruse symbolism.

After an initial viewing of *Angel's Egg*, it might be easy to call the film a nihilistic work—in the end, the soldier destroys the one thing so very precious to the young girl and is seemingly unrepentant in having done so. The girl becomes so distraught that she ends up dying by falling into a ravine while chasing after the soldier. To view the film as nihilistic, however, disregards much of its religious symbolism. The soldier is not an evil man and does not destroy the egg because he desires to hurt the girl. Rather, he destroys it to sate his burning quest for self-knowledge. He is not sure of his past and thinks his vague memories of a great bird may be related to the egg the girl plans to hatch. Although he violates his promise to the girl to do no harm to the egg, the soldier's breaking of it is consistent with what he says during their first meeting, when he tells her that to see what is inside the egg, she would have to break it open.

Angel's Egg, like many of Oshii's other works, deals with the question of identity. In this film, which has relatively little dialogue, it is important that the first lines spoken (in the girl's voice as the soldier's image fills the screen) are *"Dare? Anata wa dare?"* ("Who? Who are you?") It is a question that is asked repeatedly, and one the soldier even asks the girl. Neither ever responds to the question—in fact, the entire film can be seen as an attempt by the soldier and the girl to try to discover who they really are.

The element most closely related to the plot of the film is Oshii's use of Christian religious symbolism. While allusions to religion, both Japanese and Western, are not uncommon in anime,[8] serious explorations of religion are fairly rare. For instance, the TV series and films of *Neon Genesis Evangelion* (*Shin Seiki Evangelion,* 1995) made use of Christian symbolism, but this was more of a marketing gimmick than serious soul searching. Said Kazuya Tsurumaki, the program's assistant director: "There are a lot of giant robot shows in Japan, and we did want our story to have a religious theme to help distinguish us. . . . There is no actual Christian meaning to the show, we just thought the visual symbols of Christianity look cool. If we had known the show would get distributed in the US and Europe we might have rethought that choice."[9] Religious references in anime films are often superficial and used to impart an exotic and mysterious flavor. Oshii, on the other hand, utilizes his religious motifs in a much more meaningful way. Such serious explorations of religion are not out of character for a man who once considered attending seminary. Animator and Oshii collaborator Scott Frazier, recalling a conversation he had with Oshii on the topic of religion, says, "He knows Christianity better than most Christians do. He knows what the Christian symbolism means. He doesn't just know the outlines of the dogma, he knows it all the way down."[10] From this it can be deduced that the religious imagery in Oshii's films is not mere affectation, but is intended to convey meaning. Thus, unlike many other references to religion in anime and popular culture in general, Oshii alludes to religion to say something deeper about the human condition. Said Carl Gustav Horn, anime critic and a frequent writer on Oshii's films, "I think the use of Judeo-Christian ethics is a kind of intellectual tool for probing questions of meaning. [It is] fascinating for a lot of Japanese because it is a way to break out of the ordinary assumptions, to find the kind of absolutes that may not exist in their normal lives."[11]

The first religious allusion in *Angel's Egg* is, of course, in the title. While the imagery of the egg is readily apparent in the film, there is no direct reference to angels—neither traditional angel imagery nor the Japanese word *tenshi* (angel) appear in the film. There are two possible explanations of how the film relates to angels. The first is that the girl is supposed to be the angel. She sees as her duty the protection of the egg in order to bring back to life the great bird she believes to be inside. In this way, the girl is acting as the guardian angel of the egg. However, another explanation is that it is the egg that contains the angel and that the fantastic bird in question may not be a bird at all, but rather a messenger from the heavens. For example, the Japanese phrase "*interi no tamago*" can be translated into English as "budding intellectuals,"[12] suggesting that the term *tamago* (egg) may connote a degree of incipience. Each explanation has a different thematic ramification when the egg is revealed to be empty in the end. If we accept the interpretation that the girl is the angel, the film means that one cannot rely on angels for protection and, by extension, cannot depend on a god for salvation. If the angel is what will hatch from the egg, then the film indicates that angels do not in fact exist; all that the girl believed to be true was mere self-delusion. The destruction of the egg has a great metaphorical meaning involving religion and identity. If we take the view that the girl is an angel, then the soldier's actions demonstrate that in the quest for knowledge of the self, sometimes not even the heavens can be of use. The girl was powerless to stop him from destroying that which she held most dear. If it was the angel that was supposed to be in the egg, its emptiness is a telling sign—after all of the girl's care and faith, the egg ends up being hollow. Everything about the egg, as the soldier told the girl, had been a projection of her own belief, what she wanted to hear. In the end, there was nothing in which to have faith but the self. Although the film uses Christian imagery almost exclusively, such a message about faith has very Buddhist associations. (Many sects of Buddhism use the term "emptiness" in a positive manner, emphasizing self-reliance rather than reliance on a god.) Neither explanation of the egg's destruction is contradictory; both can be correct, yet point to similarly negative conclusions regarding traditional spirituality.

In spite of this negative portrayal of established religion, or perhaps because of it, Oshii does make extensive references to the Bible in many of his films. *Angel's Egg* is the first film he directed in which passages from the Bible are quoted, a technique he continued in the two *Patlabor* films and *Ghost in the Shell*. However, canonical spirituality often has negative connotations in his films; for example, in the two *Patlabor* films and *Ghost in the Shell,* the biblical quotations are all delivered by the films' antagonists. This does not necessarily mean that the soldier in *Angel's Egg* is to be perceived as an antagonist. The important aspect is that the biblical passage is changed in the soldier's telling of it, allowing the words themselves to have a negative impact. The biblical reference is from the book of Genesis and speaks of floodwaters coming to destroy the works of man. After the soldier speaks of the flood, the rain that had been drizzling begins to fall in earnest, flooding the city. A parallel is made between the biblical story and the events taking place in the film—it is almost as if the scenes in the film are playing out the great flood. As the floodwaters rise, the fishermen, who have tried so valiantly in vain to catch the shadow fish, stand immobile, unwilling or unable to move to higher ground. In the fishermen, Oshii captures not only the blind faith of religion (their belief that they will catch the fish, in spite of their constant and consistent failures), but religion's fatalism as well.

In terms of the film's symbolism, the egg should bear the brunt of the analysis. Its importance cannot be overstated; without an understanding of its meaning, we cannot comprehend the overall film. As the egg is an important symbol in many mythologies around the world, the meaning of *Angel's Egg* depends on the attitudes and cultural perceptions viewers bring to the film. Many cultures have creation myths based on the concept of the egg—one myth of the Letts (one of the groups of people occupying what is now Latvia) even involves angels and devils hatching from the egg that became the world.[13] I do not know if Oshii was aware of this myth, but given the vaguely European setting of *Angel's Egg* and the allusions to Hungarian history in his later *Avalon,* I would not be surprised if he consciously incorporated that myth into his film.

The egg plays a key role in the Japanese creation myth in the *Nihongi,* one of two official records detailing the ancient history of Japan. In the beginning of the world, "Of old, Heaven and Earth were not yet separated . . . they formed a chaotic mass like an egg which was of obscurely defined limits and contained germs."[14] The legend thus likens the swirling mass from which the universe formed to that of an egg; by saying it "contained germs," this egg-like proto-universe is set apart as something unclean and undesirable. In this context, the egg marks a transitional period to be overcome and traversed as quickly as possible. This mythological background could explain why the soldier in *Angel's Egg* is so willing to smash the egg to see what is inside: The egg is not important for what it is, but for what it will become.

Although Oshii comes from Japan and undoubtedly knows the legends in the *Nihongi,* his use of biblical quotes and other Christian references makes an examination of the allusions to eggs in Christian belief critical to understanding the film. The egg does not play a significant role in the Christian creation story, but it takes on special meaning during Easter, the celebration of the resurrection of Jesus Christ. It is thought that eggs came to be associated with Easter because of the fact that with eggs, life arises from what previously seemed to be a lifeless source. Eggs have been used as a symbol of rebirth and resurrection in Christian religious ceremonies since at least the Middle Ages, when "it was quite usual to place a coloured egg in the representation of Our Lord's tomb during the Easter liturgy."[15] According to some beliefs, it is important that the eggs be broken. A folklore study says that there is "a German belief, [that] to fulfill this ritual function [of the Easter ceremony] the shell must first be shattered—by breaking it the blessing of Easter will enter in."[16] Thus, in one reading of the film, the egg is representative of a form of rebirth. The girl imagines herself as the caretaker of the bird she thinks is contained within the egg. Her ideas are shattered when the soldier breaks the egg, a religiously symbolic and important action performed not out of hatred or spite, but as a part of his quest for knowledge. The egg turns out to be the girl's own rebirth—she lives on as a marker on the giant orb, leaving the soldier alone, still searching for his own truth.

Another important motif in *Angel's Egg* is that of fish. Not only is fish a traditional staple of the Japanese diet, but it has strong biblical connotations as well. For example, many of Jesus' apostles used to be fishermen; Jesus had said to them, "Come ye after Me, and I will make you to become fishers of men" (Mark 1: 17). Additionally, the Gospels tell the story of Jesus' feeding of thousands of people with just a few loaves and fishes. The image of the fish also has come to be a symbol of Christianity itself. The Greek word *ichthus* (meaning "fish") was appropriated as an acronym for "Iesous Christos Theou Uios Soter," meaning "Jesus Christ, the Son of God, the Savior." With such strong connections between fish and Christianity, Oshii is making a strong statement when the fish in the film turn out to be mere shadows, ephemeral and intangible. There is nothing real about the fish. The fish exist only because there are fishermen, not the other way around. If the fish indeed represent Christianity, it is telling that they have no substance in the world of *Angel's Egg*.

The cross carried by the soldier is another important symbol, as he bears it upon his back throughout the film. Such an image alludes to the suffering of Jesus Christ, who was made to carry his own cross before his crucifixion. Other than the presence of the cross, however, the soldier does not seem like a very Christ-like figure. He is directionless and unsure of himself and his place in the world. In fact, in the end he smashes the egg with the base of the cross. This may in fact be the action of a Christ-like or Buddha-like figure, and by destroying the egg, he destroys the false idol and false hope to which the girl has become attached.

Carl Gustav Horn has written that *Angel's Egg* "suggests the death of director Mamoru Oshii's youthful faith in Christianity."[17]

When asked if he thought *Angel's Egg* was optimistic or pessimistic in its view of religion, Oshii responded with the cryptic statement: "All religions start in pessimism and end in optimism. I admit I am a religious type, but I do not believe in any specific religion."[18] In spite of his use of Christian imagery, I believe that he is presenting a more general critique of religion—the film seems to suggest the death of his faith in the power of faith itself. Faith can be a useful and wonderful thing, but the events in *Angel's Egg* suggest that it must be accompanied by action. We see this in the instant the girl holds aloft the remains of the smashed egg, showing that it had been hollow all along. Faith alone was not enough to bring her dream of the bird to fruition. In fact, the girl's faith was deluding her into believing that something existed in the egg in the first place. The viewer is never shown the origin of the egg; the fact that giant birds have not roamed the skies in recent memory would seem to indicate that the egg did not come from such a bird. It is almost as if the mysterious egg was born from the girl; such a genesis is suggested by the fact that the girl often carries the egg under her dress, resembling a pregnant stomach. Thus, the egg is a product of the girl, and she is placing all of her faith into an object of her own creation. Oshii may be likening this to the construction of religion—it is said in the Bible that man was created in God's image, but Oshii suggests that it may be the other way around.

Another strong symbol Oshii employs in this film is that of the young girl, or *shōjo*. In contemporary Japanese society and popular culture, the shōjo occupies a unique position as being neither child nor adult; as Susan J. Napier has suggested, the shōjo in anime is a symbol of liminality, of being neither here nor there.[19] Correspondingly, the shōjo occupies a liminal space in the narrative of many anime stories, such as *Revolutionary Girl Utena* (*Shōjo Kakumei Utena*), *Magic Knights Rayearth* (*Mahō Kishi Rayearth*), *Escaflowne* (*Tenkū no Escaflowne*), *Fushigi Yūgi,* and *Serial Experiments Lain,* in which the heroine enters and must confront an unfamiliar world. It is in this liminal space that the extraordinary becomes everyday and previously held assumptions of how the world functions melt away. It is therefore appropriate that Oshii uses the symbol of the young girl in his meditation on dreams and spirituality in *Angel's Egg*. As in many of the aforementioned anime, the young girl serves as symbol of determined innocence. In this way the character of the young girl allows Oshii to draw parallels between spirituality and sexuality. *Angel's Egg* is the girl's coming-of-age story; it is the encounter between a girl, represented by the egg she carries, and a young man, first introduced astride a masculine tank. Although the girl asks the soldier to do no harm to that which is most precious to her (the egg), he takes it from her while she is sleeping. When he smashes the egg with a weapon that is simultaneously phallic and like the Christian cross, the girl's innocence is destroyed along with her faith in the egg. Water is an often employed symbol of femininity in Japanese culture, and it is into water that the girl falls after her egg has been destroyed. As she sinks deeper into the flooded ravine, the girl becomes older and begins to look more mature, symbolizing her loss of both spiritual and sexual innocence.

With such multilayered symbolism at work in *Angel's Egg,* viewers may wonder what the film is ultimately about. Oshii's reticence to comment on the meaning of the film is indicative of his approach to filmmaking in general. He has said, "When it comes down to it, I think the director doesn't know everything about the movie. Everyone always thinks if you want to know something, you talk to the director. I don't think that's true. I think the answers lie inside every single viewer."[20] Interpreting this statement literally, the meaning of the film can be whatever viewers glean from it. While this point is true to a certain extent, I do not think this is what Oshii had in mind. *Angel's Egg* is filled with his commentary on the role religion and faith play in the lives of humankind. Faith is that which gives the young girl the courage to persevere in a desolate world nearly devoid of human contact, but this faith is misplaced—there is nothing at the core of the egg but a pervading emptiness. Oshii seems to be saying that we must not abandon faith, yet we must not fall prey to the tempting lure of blind faith.

Angel's Egg has influenced a number of films, both inside and outside the realm of Japanese animation. For example, Carl Colpaert's *In the Aftermath* (1987) intercut redubbed scenes from *Angel's Egg* with scenes featuring live actors to create a film very different from the original. Subtitled *Angels Never Sleep,* the film grafts the story of the girl and the soldier in *Angel's Egg* to a tale of survival on postapocalyptic Earth. The girl and the soldier, rather than being strangers who meet in the near-deserted city, are cast as brother and sister angels. It is the girl's job to use the egg she carries to find and save people on Earth if she determines they are worthy. In the end, the girl gives the egg to a soldier named Frank, and he uses it to clear the toxins from the polluted atmosphere. *In the Aftermath* takes nearly half its footage from *Angel's Egg,* and although much of the subtle beauty of the original shines through, its impact is lessened due to the resequencing of events and expository voiceovers (which feature such priceless lines as "He should have spanked me with asteroids"). For example, after the scene in which the brother destroys the egg (presumably because the girl has fallen asleep, neglecting her duty as a guardian), he gives her a second chance with another egg. Thus, the destruction of the angel's egg, the pivotal event upon which the original film hinged, is of little concern in *In the Aftermath.*

Angel's Egg can also be seen as a strong visual influence on Kazuyoshi Okuyama's *The Mystery of Rampo* (1994). Although a live-action film, setting the tone and mood for the entire piece is a five-minute introduction animated by Studio 4°C and directed by Yasuhiro Nakura (who would go on to do designs and lead animation for Rintaro's *Metropolis* [2001], an adaptation of the classic manga by Osamu Tezuka). This introduction to *Rampo* uses a very similar drawing style and color palette to *Angel's Egg* and uses similar visual elements, such as water, eggs, and fish. *Angel's Egg* also serves as a spiritual predecessor of the breakthrough anime franchise *Neon Genesis Evangelion.* Although there may not be a direct correlation between the two works, it is interesting to note that one of the animators on *Angel's Egg,* Yoshiyuki Sadamoto, would go on to write the *Evangelion* manga and be the character designer for the TV series.

Shortly after completing *Angel's Egg,* Oshii began work on another collaborative effort, this time with Hayao Miyazaki and Isao Takahata. Called *Anchor,* this Studio Ghibli film would have featured Oshii as director and Miyazaki and Takahata as producers. As Oshii's films differ significantly in theme, pacing, and attitude from the films of Miyazaki and Takahata, this would have proved an interesting mix. However, the three of them got into an argument during the planning stages and Oshii quit the project.

Oshii was involved in another abortive project around the time of *Angel's Egg,* again related to Miyazaki (albeit somewhat distantly). Originally Oshii had been chosen to direct the third film in the *Lupin III* series, which was based on the exploits of a jet-setting international thief originally created by manga artist Monkey Punch. Two *Lupin III* television series had aired in the late 1970s and had spawned a set of feature films, the second of which, *Castle of Cagliostro* (*Lupin III: Cagliostro no Shiro,* 1979), had been directed by Hayao Miyazaki. The plot of the third film originally involved Lupin's theft of an artifact called the "Angel's Fossil" and the smuggling of a nuclear weapon out of Israel. (Oshii later incorporated the idea of nuclear smuggling into his work on *Patlabor.*) However, the project's producer decided that story was too complicated and that the idea was not suitable for a *Lupin III* film, so Oshii's work on the film was stopped.[21]

The film Oshii directed after *Angel's Egg* shows him taking further advantage of his newfound directorial freedom. *The Red Spectacles* was both Oshii's first foray into live-action directing and his first exploration of the world of the Kerberos Panzer Cops. The film, though intriguing, is remarkably uneven, and at some points it seems as if Oshii is trying to replicate anime conventions in a live-action setting. (We will return to this film in chapter 7 in the discussion of *Jin-Roh.*) The next animated film Oshii directed was *Twilight Q 2: Labyrinth Objects File 538,* a short OVA exploring many of the same issues of self and identity as *Angel's Egg.*

CHAPTER 4

TWILIGHT Q 2: LABYRINTH OBJECTS FILE 538 (1987)

IN THE SECOND AND FINAL EPISODE IN THE *TWILIGHT Q* OVA series, *Twilight Q 2: Labyrinth Objects File 538* (*Twilight Q 2: Meikyū Bukken File 538*), Oshii gives viewers a glimpse of a world where fiction and reality flow seamlessly into each other. The *Twilight Q* OVA series originally was intended to highlight the stories and talents of up-and-coming anime directors through a series of unconnected, imaginative short stories, but the project lasted only two episodes. The title of the series can be read as an homage to two influential television shows: *The Twilight Zone* and *Ultra Q*, a mid-1960s' series that was a cross between a Japanese version of *The Outer Limits*–style science fiction and a Toho monster film. Although the anime series was in color, the allusion to these two black-and-white television programs is indicative of the sense of noir and mystery aimed for in *Twilight Q*.

The first episode was directed by Tomomi Mochizuki, who would go on to direct the first *Kimagure Orange Road* film (1988) and Studio Ghibli's *Ocean Waves* (*Umi ga Kikoeru*, 1993), and featured character designs by Akemi Takada (who later did the character designs for *Patlabor*). Released in February 1987, this episode involves a girl who finds a mysterious camera on a beach that contains pictures of her with a man she has never met. Eventually the girl finds herself traveling forward and backward in time, leading to a rather open-ended conclusion. Oshii's "sequel," released in August 1987, treats the idea of reality as similarly plastic, although the ending is far more satisfactory. The second episode of *Twilight Q* garnered more attention due to Oshii's involvement, but the series did not ultimately catch on with the anime-buying public.

In addition to directing *Twilight Q 2,* Oshii wrote the original story and screenplay. The film demonstrates the influence of classic science fiction on Oshii—the tale could just as easily have been a short story rather than a film. Oshii has said that when growing up, he was influenced more by foreign science fiction writers than by writers of contemporary Japanese fiction like Yukio Mishima.[1] *Twilight Q 2* shows traces of Oshii's earlier desire to become a science fiction writer. Although he may have moved on to the medium of film, his love of good sci-fi still shines through.

Twilight Q 2 is also one of Oshii's most autobiographical works. The experiences of the detective in the film are drawn from the life of Oshii's father, a frequently out-of-work private detective (although it is safe to assume that Oshii's father never took on a case like the one described in the episode). *Twilight Q 2* is not the only one of Oshii's works to feature a private detective—the detective Mitsui, a minor character in the *Patlabor* OVAs and television series, is given a much larger role in the two *Patlabor* films Oshii directed.

CHARACTERS

THE YOUNG GIRL—The young girl lives in a decrepit apartment in the outskirts of Tokyo with a man who appears to be her father. She always wears a long T-shirt that says "FISH" on it in English letters, as well as an army helmet with a red star painted on it. She is fascinated by fish and airplanes, often seeming to confuse the two.

THE LARGE MAN—The large man is the young girl's caretaker. He may be her father, but their true relationship is unknown. He does not seem to do much, other than sit around the apartment and share meals with the girl.

THE DETECTIVE—The detective was hired to find out more about the large man and his relationship with the young girl. However, every fact he uncovers deepens the mystery, and he soon finds himself drawn into a labyrinth from which there may be no escape.

SYNOPSIS

Japan Air Lines passenger flight 538 is cruising through a partly cloudy sky. Suddenly pieces of the plane begin to fall away as a giant tear in the fuselage bulges out near the cockpit, triggering a cascading wave of cracks down the plane. As pieces fall away, the cracks are revealed to be giant scales, some of which darken into a red-and-black pattern. As an eye forms, it is revealed that the aircraft has completely transformed into a giant *koi* (Japanese carp), still shedding scales as it flies through the air.

In a small cramped apartment, a large man sits listening to the news of the disappearance of flight 538 on the radio, sweat flowing down his vacant face. The radio reports that a similar disappearance had occurred with an Air Zimbabwe flight just a day earlier. There are three main figures in the apartment—the large man, a small girl wearing a helmet with a red star on it, and a large koi in a tank that can barely contain its bulk. The girl stands facing the tank, imitating the movements of the fish's mouth, until the man taps her, indicating that it is time to eat. As they noisily slurp their plain noodles, the girl looks at the man and inquires "O-sakana?" ("Fish?") When she hears an airplane flying overhead, she rushes to the open window yelling "Fish! Fish!" She is wearing a T-shirt with the word "FISH" in English on it. The man follows her to the window, looking up, and then turns around. As the noise from the airplane recedes, the man gazes at the fish in the tank and begins to imitate its mouth just as the girl had done. He then turns to watch the girl staring out the window again.

A mysterious man wearing a trench coat and sunglasses (although it is nearly dusk) stands listening to the radio news on a small headset as he gazes at the city from across the bay. The reporter announces that another JAL flight has disappeared, bringing the month's total of missing airplanes to seventeen. The man turns and begins to walk toward the apartment building of the large man and the girl, the only building in a desolate field. The man enters the apartment to find the girl sleeping on one futon, with the koi on the futon beside hers, its mouth still moving.

The man sits down at a desk in front of a word processor and pushes the button labeled "execute," causing the machine to begin typing what is stored in its memory. The message, which had been typed by the large man, begins by stating that it is for the author's "successor." As the man in the trench coat reads aloud what is being printed, it is revealed that this man is a detective who was so desperate for a case that he took the unusual assignment of looking into the personal lives of the large man and the girl. The case had one specific rule: to never contact the subjects or enter the apartment. Having broken this rule, the detective reads on, narrating the large man's story.

Years ago, during a summer of intense heat, there had been a similar rash of airplane disappearances. Time had seemed to come to a standstill, with summer everlasting. The large man also had been a detective, perhaps without the one skill essential for a detective to have: the ability to find a client. He waited for innumerable days, losing track of time, unable to remember his last assignment or even if he had had a last assignment. With his money dwindling, he finally received a case involving the investigation of an apartment and a man and girl residing within—the same case as that on which the narrating detective had been working.

In the course of the investigation, the large man had difficulty finding any information about the residents; they were not listed in the *koseki* (family register), the post office did not deliver to the apartment, and although water, gas, and electricity were being used, no bills were ever sent. Even NHK, the Japanese public television station, did not come around for its yearly collection of fees. The large man began watching the pair, whom he suspected were not blood relatives, through a hole in the wall of an adjacent room. He saw the pair do little other than eat and sleep, never venturing outside the confines of the room. One day he saw the girl leaning out of the window yelling "Fish! Fish!" as the sound from an airplane passed overhead. As she did so, the plane's engines suddenly grew silent. That same evening the pair left the apartment to go to a public bath, and the large man decided it would be an opportune time to search their room. When he entered, it looked nothing like the room he had been observing all this time— the furniture had fallen into disrepair, and debris was scattered throughout. There were no signs that the room had been inhabited recently.

The large man received information from a friend who worked in real estate that the land where the apartment is located, an area overrun by *seitaka* (goldenrod), had once been scheduled for reclamation but was still, according to a city map, part of the sea. This additional mystery intrigued the man, who began to have little interaction with the world of the people around him, focusing all his energies on the case. Strange things continued to happen: The large man discovered the airplane disappearances seemed to be concentrated in the sky above the mysterious apartment; giant fish scales were found near the city; a fighter pilot said he saw a school of carp in the sky while on patrol one day. As more time passed, the large man realized he had forgotten everything about himself. The man found the question of who he was intimately intertwined with the question of the identities of the mysterious pair. Which was real: the apartment or the city beyond? If the apartment was not real, how could that be reconciled with the fact that the large man had been watching it for so long? The large man decided to enter the apartment while the pair was inside.

The letter goes on to explain that the man under investigation was in fact the large man's client, just as the large man was the detective's client. The detective is now part of a cycle, and it is not known how many have come before and how many will follow after. It is not by chance that these men became one in a series of fathers the girl has had; the letter states that the men were in fact created to be such. The detective now will become the girl's latest father, and the large man's letter suggests that the detective himself now take the time to write out a letter to his own successor. The large man continues that the detective in time will come to discover the girl's true identity and that the large man's spirit—in the form of a fish—should be lying in the apartment somewhere. He asks that the detective prepare it in a stew rather than keeping it in the aquarium. The letter concludes by saying that the detective should wake the girl in the middle of the night to go to the bathroom, explaining that, as a dark puddle begins to spread out from the girl on the futon, God sometimes pees in her sleep. After he finishes reading the letter, the detective removes his sunglasses to reveal the visage of none other than the large man.

It is morning in the apartment. The large man is on the telephone to his editor, telling him about a story he has just written called "Meikyū Bukken" ("Labyrinth Objects"). In the conversation, the man summarizes the events that have just been portrayed, saying that God is in fact a dumb little kid who has created a series of men to take care of her. The editor says he doesn't understand the story and does not think it will sell. Frustrated, the man begins preparing a large carp for himself and his daughter. As he slits the carp, the image changes to a passenger airplane being ripped fore to aft by an unseen force, with the people and luggage previously in the plane cascading into the air.

COMMENTARY AND ANALYSIS

Oshii's *Twilight Q 2: Labyrinth Objects File 538* illustrates how an interesting story can make effective use of rudimentary animation. Although the opening sequence of the airplane changing into a giant koi is lovingly detailed and beautifully animated, the animation in the rest of the episode does not measure up. A large portion of the episode consists of a voice narrating the details of the story over still images, some of which are retouched photographs. However, this is not to say that such a technique is not effective at conveying meaning and detail. Regarding later works like *Ghost in the*

Shell and *Blood the Last Vampire,* Oshii has said that even though computer graphics are capable of conveying rapid movement, he still prefers a flowing movement to his films.[2] It is remarkable that he can achieve such flow with so few images. For example, the scene in which the detective enters the apartment building is nothing but a series of still shots: the *genkan* (entryway) littered with shoes, a stairwell viewed from above, the end of a poorly lit hallway surrounded by blackness, and finally a beam of light casting its glow on the apartment door. This method of animation serves to focus attention on the story being told rather than the images on the screen. In *Twilight Q 2* the visual aspect is lessened due to the story's structure—the plot is told almost entirely in flashbacks, with little or no action taking place. The fantastical images of the flying fish that bookend the film stand in contrast to the dearth of movement in the main part of the film.

The introductory scene of the JAL plane turning into a giant carp sets the tone of the film. Like the invitation delivery scene at the beginning of *Urusei Yatsura: Only You,* the beginning of *Twilight Q 2* deftly juxtaposes the concretely real with the utterly fantastic. This time the comparison is between the highly detailed aircraft and the large fish into which it transforms. Another similar comparison contrasts the cartoonishly exaggerated design of the main characters with the photorealistic backgrounds used in certain shots. By incorporating such juxtapositions, Oshii tries to accentuate the plausible intrusion of the fantastic into the everyday world.

The setting of *Twilight Q 2* plays a crucial role in the meaning of the film; the ruins of the apartment and surrounding land serve to mirror the directionless desolation inside the characters. Oshii, in a conversation with Hayao Miyazaki, said he uses the image of the seitaka (goldenrod) to express how humanity has stalled,[3] although he does not explicitly mention *Twilight Q 2.* Oshii's statement is intriguing because the seitaka surrounding the apartment in *Twilight Q* is one of the few "nature" scenes in any of his films. Oshii, born and raised in Tokyo, is very much a man of the city, and his films present a very urban view, as opposed to the very nature-oriented works of Miyazaki. When this glimpse of nature does occur, however, it is very brief and is of a plant that is not even native to Japan. The *seitaka-awadachisō* (the plant's full name in Japanese) arrived from North America shortly after World War II and is commonly viewed as an undesirable weed. It grows and thrives in unused fields throughout Japan, as it does in the field outside the apartment in *Twilight Q 2;* it is a plant of desolation. Like the seitaka, humankind is growing like a weed, spreading throughout the world. This is not a directional growth; in the two *Patlabor* films, Oshii bemoans the loss of the old Tokyo he once loved. Buildings are razed and new ones put in their place at an alarming rate. It seems that nothing stays the same in Japan anymore, least of all nature. Even the area around the apartment where the seitaka now grow is scheduled to be part of a reclamation project. The seitaka is a symbol of nature, but it is an unreal nature, one created by the aimless expansion of a cannibal city. This image of the seitaka is mirrored by the twisting plot of *Twilight Q 2* and the labyrinth at its center.

The main focus of *Twilight Q 2* is the subjective nature of reality. Oshii enjoys playing with different points of view in his films, subtly changing the way in which the viewer reads them. In his later films, Oshii uses unusual shot angles and lenses to show the alteration of the point of view. In this work, he accomplishes this by placing the viewer in a maze of meaning, the "labyrinth" of the film's subtitle. The labyrinth itself is constructed from various points of view: of the detective, of the man, and of the child, further complicated by the fact that they are just part of a larger story. Oshii has said, "We've been focusing too much on humans, and animation isn't the exception. Even when two persons are talking, probably a bird is flying over their heads, a fish is in a pond, and a dog is watching you when you look down. In my case, the eyes of animals are always on my mind."[4] The large man and the girl are identified with animals by the T-shirts they wear—his says "BIRD" in English, while hers reads "FISH." Oshii further complicates the idea of the point of view by illustrating different transformations of men into fish. The first transformation occurs in the first scene, in which the passenger-filled airplane is changed into a giant koi; the second is when the detective realizes that the fish on the futon used to be the man he had been investigating.

This fish is one visual trope Oshii employs throughout the film. Some of the historical symbolism of the fish has already been mentioned in the chapter on *Angel's Egg*. Unlike *Angel's Egg*, *Twilight Q 2* is more driven by plot than thematic symbolism. However, this is not to say that symbolism is not present in this film. Oshii draws a direct connection between the fish and spirituality by depicting God as a little girl who is obsessed with fish, driven to transform the airplanes above her into giant carp. Yet while the film maintains the connection between fish and God, it is intentionally vague concerning the causal connections. God (the girl) is turning the planes into fish on a whim, using her extraordinary power with no real purpose; she is seemingly oblivious to the world around her and the humans going about their daily activities. Although this view of God is presented in a lighthearted manner and comes across as somewhat less pessimistic than Oshii's view of religion in *Angel's Egg,* the basic themes remain. Even if there is a god, it is not a god on whom one can rely. In both films, god does not exist for the benefit of humankind. Rather, it is a god that requires constant maintenance and supervision by people—as we see at the end, God is not even potty trained. God in *Twilight Q 2* is still growing and may learn to control her great powers, but she still requires constant care from human beings.

The use of the fish in *Twilight Q 2* is also important as a symbolic foodstuff. Many of Oshii's works incorporate or reference food in some fashion. In *Urusei Yatsura 2: Beautiful Dreamer,* this reference came in the form of the continually stocked convenience store and the massive meals that were prepared for the Tomobiki crew. In *Twilight Q 2,* the viewer is introduced to the large man and the girl as they are beginning a meal of noodles. Food in Oshii's films serves as a grounding element for the characters, and it serves to humanize them in the eyes of viewers. The little girl is given a particularly empathetic portrayal, as she struggles with her noodles. The image of food recurs occasionally in Oshii's subsequent works, most notably in *Avalon* and episodes of *Patlabor.*

It is intriguing, then, that in *Twilight Q 2,* the fish is never actually consumed. In his letter, the large man requests that the detective eat his essence, which has manifested itself as a fish, rather than keeping it in an aquarium. However, the large man had kept a fish of his own in the aquarium—presumably the essence of his predecessor. It can be supposed that the detective will do the same thing and not eat the large man's essence when he assumes the role of the girl's father. At the beginning of the OVA, we see the girl ask the man for fish as they eat noodles together. The man, who seems accustomed to this entreatment, simply gives her more noodles while the fish floats in its tank unmolested. The man's essence transforming into a fish is a novel interpretation of transubstantiation and, as such, entails that the fish be shared and consumed. Perhaps it is the man's unwillingness to partake of his own essence (as we know the detective and the large man to be the same person) that prompts the girl to change airplanes into giant carp. Had the pair eaten the fish, the hunger of the curious and playful god might have been satiated.

As in some of his other films, Oshii employs a conscious reference to the seasons in *Twilight Q 2*. In *Urusei Yastura 2,* he made use of conflicting seasonal symbols and referents to instill a sense of confusion in viewers. In *Twilight Q 2,* Oshii uses the opposite approach, maintaining a sense through the film of one continually overbearing summer. Summer becomes almost like another character—the oppressive rays of the sun beat the world into a sweltering submission. The summer sky is shown as a sickly, overexposed yellow that oppresses the mind and the soul, leading one down a tortuously sun-addled path. For the detective, the haze and delirium of a sweltering, never-ending summer add to the concept of the labyrinth of logic at the heart of the story.

The end of the film threatens to disappoint when it is revealed that the story being told is just that—a science fiction story being pitched by an impoverished author. The pronouncement that previous events were all just a dream or somehow did not really occur seems like "cheating," because it allows a filmmaker to wriggle free from the constraints of what the story would entail if "real." However, although it initially appears that Oshii has fallen prey to such trickery, in the end he brings viewers back to the realm of fantasy by showing a passenger plane being mysteriously sliced open as the man prepares a large carp on his cutting board. This technique is somewhat similar to the one Oshii employed in *Urusei Yatsura 2: Beautiful Dreamer*—he acknowledges that the preceding events were in fact a dream or a story, but he does not allow them to be *merely* so. These otherworldly events, Oshii suggests, do have some bearing on the real world; there is some slippage between dreams and reality.

Thus, while Oshii is continually concerned with what is real and what is a dream, he is most concerned with how they overlap and influence each other. Such themes have been featured in *Urusei Yatsura 2* and *Angel's Egg* and continue to appear in his later films, most notably *Ghost in the Shell* and *Avalon.* "For me personally, whether it's a dream or reality is not all that important," said Oshii in a recent interview. "You can't rely on memory, so the way you see yourself at any given moment is 'you'—and how you see the world around you is what makes up your reality."[5] In the context of this statement, the ending of *Twilight Q 2* is easier to reconcile. When the airplane at the end is split down the middle as the man slices the fish, it is happening *right then* at that moment. It is a fusion of the previous fiction and the present "reality."

The ending is also rather humorous when we consider Oshii's reputation as a filmmaker. The man's editor, to whom he is talking on the telephone, tells him that he doesn't like the story about the detective and the little girl. The editor says that he does not understand the tale and would prefer a story that is more "normal." Oshii has made a career out of defying expectations and telling stories that are not normal, including *Twilight Q 2.* The ending of the film adds a touch of self-deprecating humor; Oshii knows that his films are perceived as difficult to understand, but he seems to take such criticism in stride. In the wake of the utterly humorless *Angel's Egg,* such levity is a welcome change of pace.

Twilight Q 2 was a turning point for Oshii's films. After the final gasp of fantasy that ended this film, Oshii moved toward realism in his filmmaking for a time. His subsequent films were primarily of the mecha and cyberpunk genres for which he is best known in the West. After completing *Twilight Q 2,* Oshii joined the creative team of Headgear to begin work on *Mobile Police Patlabor,* a project that had a formative impact on his career. The initial six-episode *Patlabor* OVA series led to a television series, a second OVA series, and a set of comedic shorts. Oshii then went on to direct the first two full-length *Patlabor* films, the second of which is one of the benchmarks of the anime medium.

CHAPTER 5

MOBILE POLICE PATLABOR (1988–93)

MAMORU OSHII'S INVOLVEMENT in the *Mobile Police Patlabor* series of OVAs, television episodes, and films may seem out of place when compared to his previous work. Prior to *Patlabor,* Oshii's films had been science fiction comedies and meditations on the nature of dreams and reality. *Patlabor* was his first foray into the mecha subgenre of Japanese animation. Mecha films and shows place an emphasis on mechanical elements, especially robots and giant mechanical suits. Much of the early classic Japanese animation had emphasized mecha, and its lineage can be traced from *Tetsuwan Atom* (*Astro Boy*) and *Tetsujin 28-go* (*Gigantor*) in the 1960s, *Mazinger Z* and *Mobile Suit Gundam* in the 1970s, *Superdimensional Fortress Macross* in the 1980s, and *Neon Genesis Evangelion* in the 1990s. Beginning in 1989, the *Patlabor* series can be situated within the giant robot theme in Japanese animation. However, like all good mecha anime, *Patlabor* overcomes the limitations of its genre. It is not merely a show about giant robots, but serves as a basis from which to explore history, politics, and culture. Oshii said of his work, "In retrospect, *Patlabor* for me was a major film in many ways, and I think it became my turning point. I know I am what I am today because of *Patlabor*."[1]

The strength of *Patlabor* is its foundation of true-to-life characters and situations—if we overlook the presence of hulking anthropomorphic police robots in the stories. This world of *Patlabor* displays more verisimilitude than we might think. As Alex Kerr says in his book *Dogs and Demons,* modern manga and anime do in fact "reflect reality: only manga could do justice to the more bizarre extremes of modern Japan. When every river and stream has been re-formed into a concrete chute, you are indeed entering the realm of sci-fi fable."[2] Oshii's move toward more technologically oriented science fiction is not as odd or sudden as it may seem; his love of the mechanical can be seen even in the *Urusei Yatsura* films. Tanks, Harrier jets, and fighting spaceships all are depicted with a keen eye to detail. Oshii's direction of the *Dallos* OVAs also demonstrated that he is capable of handling straightforward action scenes.

There are additional connections between Oshii's previous films and his new direction. For example, one common thread running from *Urusei Yatsura* to *Patlabor* is the choice of voice actors. Actor Toshio Furukawa, the voice of Ataru in *Urusei Yatsura,* became the voice of Asuma Shinohara in *Patlabor.* Other voice actors used in *Patlabor* who had worked on *Urusei Yatsura* (*UY*) include: Shigeru Chiba (Megane in *UY,* the voice on the radio in *Twilight Q 2,* and a featured actor in all of Oshii's live-action films save *Avalon*) as Shige in *Patlabor;* Issei Futumata (Chibi in *UY*) as Mikiyasu Shinshi; Michihiro Ikemizu (Onsen Mark in *UY*) as Isao Ohta; You Inoue (Ran in *UY*) as Kanuka Clancy; and Yoshiko Sakakibara (Elle in *Urusei Yatsura: Only You*) as Shinobu Nagumo.

Although he became a powerful force in the direction of the *Patlabor* universe, Oshii was the last member added to Headgear, the creative team that envisioned the series. *Patlabor*'s genesis began with manga artist Masami Yūki (*Assemble: Insert, Tetsuwan Birdy*) and mecha designer Yutaka Izubuchi (*Gundam: Char's Counterattack, Gasaraki*). In the early 1980s, Yūki had an idea for an animated police drama featuring robots and pitched the idea to friend and colleague Izubuchi. Later in the decade, with the success of the OVA format, the project began to look promising. Joining the team next was writer Kazunori Itō (*Maison Ikkoku,* the new *Gamera* films) and character designer Akemi Takada (*Creamy Mami, Kimagure Orange Road*) both of whom had worked with Oshii before on the *Urusei Yatsura* series. (Takada had also worked as character designer on Oshii's *Urusei Yatsura: Only You,* while Itō had cowritten the screenplay for *The Red Spectacles* with Oshii). The principals of Headgear got along well together, which facilitated the creation of *Patlabor.* Said Akemi Takada, "We were all friends even before we formed Headgear. We decided to go to an onsen [Japanese hot spring bath] one time, but not just to go, but to go with a production plan for an anime to discuss!"[3] The anime project needed a director, and although Oshii ended up joining the team, there were initially some misgivings about his suitability. Izubuchi reportedly said that he did not want to create a show that would "turn out to be nothing more than a bad dream at the end."[4]

Headgear was formed so that the creators of the series would be able to control the rights to their own works, rather than having the production company or the sponsor own the rights, as is common practice in the production of anime shows.[5] Thus all five members of Headgear collectively hold the rights to *Patlabor,* with all members sharing the profits for new endeavors in the *Patlabor* universe, even if an individual member was not directly involved in a particular project. (This means that, for example, Oshii would share in the profits of the latest *Patlabor* film, *Patlabor WXIII,* even though the only Headgear members involved in its production were Yūki and Izubuchi.) This method of copyright holding avoids legal squabbling of the kind seen over the rights to the television program *Macross,* in which the production company, Tatsunoko Productions, was awarded the rights over Studio Nue, which did the planning and direction.[6] Another reason Yūki gave for Headgear's formation is that the involvement of large companies would have bogged down the project. While it was decided to produce both a *Patlabor* manga and an anime, the anime would not be based on the manga, as is so often the case. This is because, as Yūki said, "if 'Patlabor' were to be credited as *based* on my manga, my publisher Shogakukan would have gotten into the picture, and that would have complicated things. . . . So we decided that the animation should be the primary work, and come out first."[7]

Also significant about the work on *Patlabor* is the relationship that Oshii would develop with the studio of Production I.G. The studio was founded by Mitsuhisa Ishikawa and Takayuki Goto (the initials of whose surnames form the "I.G." of the company name) in 1988 as an independent animation studio dedicated to producing compelling series and films. Although Ishikawa, like Oshii, had worked at Tatsunoko Pro, they did not meet until both men had left the company; Production I.G. ended up being one of the subcontractors for the animation on the first *Patlabor* OVAs, and Oshii was so impressed with their work he began a lasting affiliation with the company.[8] In the fifteen years since the company was founded, nearly all of Oshii's filmic output has been somehow associated with Production I.G.

The world of *Patlabor* may be confusing initially, as the franchise encompasses three subtly different chronologies. The first time line starts with the beginning of the six-episode OVA series directed by Oshii in 1988.[9] Strong sales prompted the production of a feature-length *Patlabor* film, produced in 1989 and helmed again by Oshii, followed by the second *Patlabor* film in 1993. Shortly after the first *Patlabor* film was released, a forty-eight-episode *Patlabor* series aired on television, reintroducing the main characters and beginning a somewhat different, yet complementary, time line. A second OVA series of sixteen episodes that followed the same chronology as the TV series was released in 1990. The third chronology of *Patlabor* is Headgear member Masami Yūki's manga version, produced from 1988 until 1994. In 2002 a third *Patlabor* film, *Patlabor WXIII*, was released in Japan. This new feature film was shown along with a series of animated shorts called *MiniPato*, which depict the *Patlabor* characters in humorous situations in a superdeformed (cutely disproportioned) style. Mamoru Oshii wrote the screenplay for the shorts.

Set in the late 1990s, the world of *Mobile Suit Patlabor* (common to all three chronologies) seemed familiar to audiences, with a few crucial exceptions. In the story, technology has advanced enough to develop the Labor, a heavy-duty robot used mostly for construction, each piloted by a single operator. The advent of the Labor allowed for the construction of Project Babylon, a giant retaining wall in Tokyo Bay designed to protect the city from the rising oceans caused by global warming. However, besides being used for construction, Labors are being used to commit crimes. The Special Vehicles police division was created to combat Labor crime using customized Patrol Labors, or Patlabors. The series follows the adventures (and misadventures) of Special Vehicles 2 (SV2), Second Unit, a team of castoffs and misfits who have, inexplicably, been the recipients of the latest in Patlabor technology.

The *Patlabor* OVAs and films were Oshii's first forays into the realm of hard science fiction, rather than the fantastical science fantasy that had been the domain of his previous works. With the *Patlabor* series, Oshii began to be associated with cyberpunk, the genre with which his films are most associated in the West. As cyberpunk writer Bruce Sterling wrote, for cyberpunks, "technology is visceral ... it is pervasive, utterly intimate. Not outside us, but next to us. Under our skin; often, inside our minds."[10] Interestingly, this quote can be used to trace an arc through Oshii's latter films of humankind's relation to technology. *Patlabor* demonstrates the technology outside of and next to us, while *Ghost in the Shell* demonstrates the technology inside the body and *Avalon* the technology within our very minds.

Oshii problematizes the hierarchies surrounding the characters in the *Patlabor* films through the portrayal of the Labors themselves. Rather than being controlled by their pilots, the Labors end up being in control of the humans, due to the constant confinement and monitoring of the pilots inside such technologically powerful suits. The Labors are equipped with many different types of monitoring systems, both inside and outside; they not only act as mobile units surveying the world around them, but they also watch the pilot inside. And yet technology is always seen as being separate from the human body. Although sometimes threatening to attack or overwhelm the body, technology never threatens to invade it in the *Patlabor* films, in contrast to what occurs in *Ghost in the Shell* and *Avalon*. Additionally, the police force to which the *Patlabor* protagonists belong serve to inscribe the characters within realms of technological control. The hierarchical police force, while able to secure the safety of Tokyo twice in the films, is part of a larger, problematic system. In both films, the heroes must fight people within their own organization in order to proceed with the best course of action to combat the terrorist threats. Such a hierarchical system is portrayed to be as detrimental as the misguided zealotry of the films' antagonists. Additionally, both films take place mainly within the urban environs of Tokyo, further serving to contain and constrain the events portrayed therein.

The Labors themselves are fascinating as symbols of technology, as the name "Labor" points to the eponymous telos of such machines. This name also invites a comparison between the machines and a Marxist critique of the nature of labor. Indeed, in the first of Marx's "Economic and Philosophic Manuscripts," written in 1844, the philosopher states: "The externalization [*Entäusserung*] of the worker in his product means not only that his labour becomes an object, an *external* existence, but that it exists *outside him,* independently of him and alien to him, and begins to confront him as an autonomous power; that the life which he has bestowed on the object confronts him as hostile and alien [brackets and emphasis in original]."[11] This quote accurately describes the Labors that appear in *Patlabor.* The Labor as machine is a perfect example of Marx's idea of the alienation of the worker from that which is produced. The films and episodes that constitute the *Patlabor* universe are a meditation on the nature of work and technology, lending credence to the assertion that "technology is nothing less than labor in concretized material form—labor embodied—and that every piece of machinery can only work if it exists, can only exist if it works."[12] The Labors are extensions of the desire for increased productivity, for the creation of great marvels of engineering such as the hubris-inviting Babylon Project. *Patlabor* takes as a given that the overreaching extension of such human labor will be misused; hence the deployment of the Patlabor team to protect the city.

The work on *Patlabor,* especially the two feature films, marks the beginning of Oshii's analysis of the cyborg. In their daily lives and actions, the members of the SV2 become almost like cyborgs in their intimate relationships with technology. Technology has become woven into the fabric of their daily lives. The intimacy with technology even threatens to become amorous, as illustrated in the opening theme song of the first OVA series. This theme, which prepares the viewer for the events about to unfold in the series, is sung from the viewpoint of the main female character. While the song begins like a generic pop tune, extolling the virtues of love, we soon learn that she is actually singing to her Patlabor. As the series develops, Oshii's sense of play and parody shine through, suggesting that the opening theme song is to be viewed similarly as parody. The upbeat music and exaggerated lyrics make it a delightful skewering of mecha conventions, perhaps poking fun at the prevalence of giant robots in manga and anime in general. However, Oshii is not afraid to deal with issues of technology in a more serious manner, as illustrated in the later OVA episodes and the *Patlabor* films; there is an element of truth to the OVA theme song, which serves as a playful reminder not to become too obsessed with our own technological creations. To the credit of the *Patlabor* characters, they do not invest themselves fully in the mechanical devices they pilot everyday. Technology, though a large part of their lives, is not all-encompassing. Each member of the SV2 displays his or her own unique foibles and eccentricities, culminating in a display of sympathetic humanity that contrasts with the mechanized surroundings. (In *Ghost in the Shell,* Oshii explores more fully the relationship among work, technology, and the individual body.)

Thus, *Patlabor* is as much about the interesting characters of the SV2 as it is about the Labors. It is a tale of how humans change and adapt against a background of technology that is rapidly altering our social interactions, contrasting the individual characters' humanity against the giant Labors and the hierarchy of the Tokyo police system. Headgear manages to create wonderful characters that play off archetypes but never succumb to them. *Patlabor* not only shows how people are changed and affected by technology, it explores the idiosyncrasies that make us all human.

In addition to critiquing the advancement of technology in a science fiction setting, in *Patlabor* Oshii examines Japan's tumultuous past and controversial present. A number of the Oshii-scripted *Patlabor* episodes, and especially the second *Patlabor* film, require an understanding of post–World War II Japanese politics, especially Japan's relationship with the United States. Following

World War II and the subsequent U. S. occupation of Japan, the Japanese government accepted a new constitution drafted by the occupation forces. One of the most contentious parts of the constitution is Article 9, or the "peace clause." This article states that the country of Japan officially renounces war and the use of force and that the country will not maintain land, sea, or air forces or any other potential for making war. In the years since the end of that war, Article 9 has been interpreted to allow for the use of military force for the purposes of "self-defense," often at the urging of the United States, which needed a strong ally against the spread of communism in East Asia. Although Japan is still technically a pacifist nation, the Japan Self Defense Forces, or Jieitai, have grown into one of the largest military forces in the world as the country's economy has grown. This situation puts Japan in the contradictory position of feeling that it should assume a greater leadership in world affairs while being constrained by its own constitution. Oshii illuminates Japan's modern political schizophrenia through the *Patlabor* series and films.

Also of concern to Oshii is the student protest movement of the postwar period. As mentioned in chapter 1, Oshii was a student activist himself, and participated in activities such as distributing flyers and putting up posters. One of the main points of contention for the student protesters was Japan's security treaty with the United States, which allowed America to base troops in Japan for its exploits in Korea and Vietnam. Many Japanese believed that since Article 9 of Japan's constitution prohibited the country from going to war, Japan should not help to facilitate a war in other countries. Protests against the security treaty became a part of Japanese popular consciousness, and "the experience of the 1960 treaty crisis was so salient as to create a generation of students who, to this day, are referred to as the 'Ampo [security treaty] generation' and whose leaders' names became household words in Japan."[13] However, this acclaim was rather short-lived, and student protest went from a "relatively unified movement with widespread popular support in the late 1950s to a much smaller, badly divided movement which had lost most public support for its increasingly violent tactics by the 1970s."[14] A participant in such student struggles, Oshii incorporates such ideas of conflict and protest in much of his work, especially those dealing directly with the police, such as *Patlabor, Ghost in the Shell,* and the films in the *Kerberos* universe (*The Red Spectacles, Stray Dog: Kerberos Panzer Cops,* and *Jin-Roh*). In these films, those in positions of power are forced to respond to a threat or an uprising from a disgruntled populace, and institutionalized forces often are cast in an unflattering light.

THE CHARACTERS OF *PATLABOR*

Noa Izumi—Noa is a young and eager Patlabor pilot, one of the least-experienced members of SV2. The daughter of a bartender in Hokkaido, Noa worked her way through police school so she could fulfill her lifelong dream to be a Labor pilot. She is overly protective of her own Patlabor, which she has named Alphonse after a dog and a cat she used to have. Because of her affection for such machines, Noa is too timid with her own Labor and those she must fight; often she is afraid to do anything that may cause even incidental damage to them.

Asuma Shinohara—Asuma is the command backup to Noa's forward position, guiding her in his command car. Asuma's father is the president of Shinohara Heavy Industries, the company that manufactures the SV2's Patlabors.

Isao Ohta—The second pilot in SV2, Ohta is often at odds Noa due to how she performs her duties. While Noa is overly cautious, Ohta rushes headlong into nearly any and every situation, guns blazing. A good pilot and an able marksman, Ohta often leaves a swath of destruction in his wake.

Mikiyasu Shinshi—Shinshi serves as Ohta's backup, his meek manner contrasting with Ohta's outward brashness. Shinshi is the only married member of SV2, and his job is a constant strain on his marriage.

Hiromi Yamazaki—A giant of a man, Yamazaki is too large to pilot a Labor and thus is relegated to driving the large vehicles that carry the Labors to emergency calls. Like many other large men in popular fiction, Yamazaki is gentle and shy, preferring to grow tomatoes than to go into combat.

KANUKA CLANCY—An officer in the New York Police Department, Kanuka comes to Japan to learn about the Labors and how they can be integrated into a metropolitan police force. Although a skilled Labor pilot, Kanuka serves in a support position, helping to direct the strategies of Noa and Ohta.

TAKEO KUMAGAMI—Introduced in the *Patlabor* television series, Kumagami joined SV2 after Kanuka returned to New York. Kumagami's character does not appear in any of the *Patlabor* OVA episodes or films Oshii directed, and she appears only peripherally in the television episodes he scripted.

CHIEF SAKAKI—In charge of all maintenance for both SV1 and SV2, Sakaki is a man of few words. Considered almost a god by the men in his crew, Sakaki also is well respected at police headquarters for the many years he has served as a mechanic for the Tokyo police.

SHIGEO "SHIGE" SHIBA—A member of the maintenance crew, Shige is Sakaki's second in command. He often serves as an intermediary between the Patlabor pilots and the maintenance division. A whiz at creating new inventions, Shige is highly skilled at handling both the hardware and software of the Special Vehicle's Patlabor force.

KEIICHI GOTO—Commander of SV2, Second Unit, Goto has to struggle daily to keep his ragtag team in line. Beneath his calmly droll exterior is one of the sharpest minds on the police force, and it has been rumored that Goto was assigned such an unglamorous position because he knew too much and asked too many questions.

SHINOBU NAGUMO—Commander of SV2, First Unit, Nagumo exudes a more confident air of command than Goto, her counterpart in the Second Unit. Her tendency to operate by the book contrasts as well with Goto's laxer attitude toward those under him. A scandalous relationship in her past, explored in the second *Patlabor* film, may explain why she has not advanced in rank as quickly as she should have.

DETECTIVE MATSUI—An inspector with the police Investigations Division, Matsui is introduced in the third of the original OVA episodes. Although not officially affiliated with Goto or

SV2, Matsui assists the Patlabor group from time to time out of respect for their captain.

(Note: In the text, I refer to the characters by the names they are called most often by the other characters. For example, Noa, Asuma, and Kanuka are all generally referred to by their given names, while Ohta and Goto are called by their surnames.)

SYNOPSIS AND ANALYSIS OF THE FIRST *PATLABOR* OVAS

The seven episodes of the first *Patlabor* OVAs serve as an introduction to the world of *Patlabor* and set the stage for much of what is to come. The characters in these OVAs sometimes do not seem as fully fleshed out as those in the later television series. Captain Goto in particular is a bit less quirky than he becomes in the TV series. The characters in the OVAs are animated in an exaggerated manner, suggesting the comedic animation style of *Urusei Yatsura* rather than the more serious, realistic style of Oshii's later films. However, in a relatively short time, Oshii manages to develop these characters, illustrating their humanity. *Patlabor* is about more than just the Labor mecha. It is about the characters and how they interact with each other and the larger cultural and political world. Said Naoyuki Yoshinaga, who would direct the *Patlabor* television series, "Oshii's *Patlabor* is a story where the group is the focus. . . . It's a strong ensemble piece right from the start."[15]

The first OVA episode, titled "Second Unit, Move Out!" ("Dai-ni Shoutai Shutsudouseyo!"), is indicative of the attitude of the entire world of Patlabor: The SV2 is finally going to receive brand-new Patlabors and a fresh team to command them, but the machines never arrive at the base because they are stuck in the dense Tokyo traffic. Noa, Asuma, Ohta, Shinshi, and Yamazaki explore the grounds of the Special Vehicles base, familiarizing themselves with each other and their surroundings. Later that evening, although they have yet to receive their new Patlabors, the SV2 receives the call that an unknown Labor is rampaging in Tokyo. After rendezvousing with their still traffic-bound Patlabors, Noa and Ohta proceed to corner the Labor in Ueno Park. They manage to subdue the criminal Labor, but not before it destroys a fleet of police cars, rips an arm from Noa's Patlabor, and decapitates Ohta's mecha.

The second OVA episode ("Longshot") introduces the character of Kanuka Clancy, a sergeant from the New York Police Department in Tokyo to provide security for the visiting mayor of New York. The episode also paints a broader picture of the world in which *Patlabor* takes place, introducing both the Babylon Project and the extremist groups that are using violence to try to stop its construction. Thinking that the Beach House, an anti–Babylon Project group, may try to attack the mayor during his visit, the special police and the Special Vehicles division provide tight security. When Asuma discovers an automatic rocket launcher planted in plain view in front of City Hall, he, Noa, and Kanuka rush to the scene. After a standard bomb disarming "Which wire do I cut now?" moment of tension, Asuma and Kanuka barely manage to disarm the launcher in time to stop it from firing its destructive cargo.

Patlabor OVA episode 3, "The 450 Million Year Old Trap" ("Yon-oku Gosenman-nen no Wana"), is more humorous in attitude, assuming some of the aspects of a bad monster film. This episode also introduces Detective Matsui, a minor but recurring character in the OVAs and TV series. (Oshii makes more use of him in his two *Patlabor* films.) Matsui asks Shige to help him because Shige is one of the few people who knows how to pilot the small submersible Matsui has borrowed to investigate a series of mysterious occurrences in Tokyo Bay. However, when they dive to investigate, their sub is severely damaged by an unseen attacker. The newspapers speculate that there is a gigantic sea creature in Tokyo Bay, and the SV2 continues to investigate. Noa and Asuma encounter a rogue scientist who says he has proof that life on Earth originated on other planets. After performing genetic experiments on a cell he found in a meteorite from 450 million years ago, the scientist panicked when the new creature began to evolve too rapidly, and he dumped it into Tokyo Bay. The SV2 decides it must attack the creature before it is able to spawn and create more havoc. After a number of different plans, including using electricity, sound waves, and emotional appeals to the creature, Shige appears and tries unsuccessfully to destroy the creature with a device he has constructed. The monster soon rises up from the bay, bearing a striking resemblance to Patlabor team member Yamazaki. The creature and Yamazaki stare into one another's eyes for a long while, then the monster turns around and leaves, never to return.

"The Tragedy of L" ("L no Higeki"), the fourth *Patlabor* OVA episode, is another pulp homage, this time in the genre of supernatural horror rather than science fiction monsters. After a major public relations fiasco brought about by Ohta's rash actions, the team is sent away for further training to the camp where they had trained as cadets. As the men bathe, Asuma and Shinshi turn around to find Ohta floating facedown in the water, which has turned bloodred. They soon discover that the water's color came from the red dye used in the large-caliber paintballs used by Labors in practice. (Ohta had fainted because he thought it was blood.) Later that evening Ohta looks out the window and sees a ghostly woman repeating "Don't shoot." The other men look out a different window and see a hulking form walking across the grounds. The next day Asuma and Noa play hooky from training to try to figure out what is going on. A local shopkeeper tells them about an incident that occurred right after Asuma's class graduated—during a practice exercise, a young woman spectator was accidentally killed by a paintball that was misfired when one of the Labors fell. The shooter, however, was the woman's brother. In a fit of grief, he picked up her body with his Labor and walked into the lake, never to be seen again. Later during practice, a Labor falls in the exact same way as described in the story, and the team wonders if ghosts or a curse is at work. Asuma investigates and discovers that the "ghost" is really the dead woman's younger sister, trying to get the team to think harder about the meaning and responsibility of being armed policemen. However, their fellow team member Kanuka has figured the ruse out even more fully, discovering that the deadly accident never really happened, that the entire scenario was a series of lies fed to the team by those they thought they could trust, including Goto, Nagumo, and the shopkeeper. However, Asuma was correct about the intent: to make the team think more fully about their actions and not act so rashly.

Patlabor OVA episodes 5 and 6 constitute two halves of the same story. Called "The SV2's Longest Day" ("Nika no Ichiban Nagai Hi"), the story serves as a dry run for the events Oshii would later expand on in the second *Patlabor* film. SV2 has gone on vacation, and while Goto stays around to help out Shinobu's section, the rest of the team members go back to their families and hometowns, from Yamazaki down in Okinawa to Noa up in Hokkaido (with Asuma following soon behind). At the same time, the Japanese Self Defense Forces (JSDF) are participating in joint war games with the United States. When a suspicious truck trailer runs a routine police checkpoint on the highway, it is revealed that the truck is carrying a JSDF military Labor. In the station in Hokkaido waiting for Noa to pick him up, Asuma encounters a mysterious hawk-faced man in a noodle shop. Back at SV2 headquarters, Goto reveals that one of the reasons he stayed at the base is that security men have been surveying it for the last few days. On a hunch, he decides to send one of the Patlabors back to the manufacturer, despite the protests of the mechanics. He later tells Nagumo that he fears something big may be about to happen, and that the rogue SDF Labor may have something to do with it. Goto is soon proven correct—members of the military begin a siege of Tokyo, and thanks to Goto's quick thinking, Nagumo is able to confront them at the entrance to police headquarters. This is fortuitous because the military forces commandeer the SV2 base, holding the remaining Labors and mechanics captive. In this high-stakes game, Goto realizes he is playing against Kai, a man he knew from his college days, and Kai realizes his new opponent is Goto. As news of the siege spreads throughout the country, the members of the SV2 race back to Tokyo.

At the beginning of the second OVA of "The SV2's Longest Day," a news report reveals that the JSDF members currently occupying a section of Tokyo have been declared renegades from the official Self Defense Forces. However, it is learned that the rebel forces, led by Kai, have stolen a nuclear weapon that the U. S. military had brought into the country through Yokota Air Force Base. Nagumo is ordered to abandon police headquarters without engaging the enemy, for fear of provoking them. When Nagumo, who knows that all of Japan is watching them, refuses to follow orders, her superiors try to place her under arrest, but she escapes and begins acting independently. Goto figures out that Kai plans to launch the nuke from a ship at sea. When Kai issues his far-reaching ultimatum that the Diet be dissolved, political parties be banned, and the constitution be suspended—conditions to which the Japanese government would never agree—Goto decides that his team must act before Kai launches his attack. Taking a big gamble and using a new prototype Labor donated from Shinohara Industries, Yamazaki is launched from a submarine into the air. He lands on the deck of one of the ships and destroys the missile before Kai can launch it. Noa and her Patlabor are flown in by helicopter; she takes command of the situation and places Kai under arrest.

In seven short OVA episodes, the members of Headgear manage to create a remarkably rich and detailed world within which they tell a variety of stories. (I have described only six episodes; a seventh OVA of the original *Patlabor* series, named "SV Units, Go North" ["Tokushatai Kita E"], is the only one of the original *Patlabor* episodes on which Oshii did no work.) One of the series' main strengths is its flexibility and character-driven verisimilitude—in just seven episodes, it jumps from realistic science fiction, to comedic takes on B-grade monster and horror films, to serious political thriller. This genre mixing is brought even more to the fore in the *Patlabor* TV series and second OVA series; in the two *Patlabor* films, Oshii would take the characters in a much more serious direction.

One of the hallmarks of *Patlabor* is its self-awareness as product of Japanese popular culture. For example, Asuma begins the self-referential discussion of pop culture in the first OVA episode as soon as he steps from the bus, saying that the base before him reminds him of something out of a war film, "one of those movies without a single woman in it." This comment also serves to highlight the strong female component of the Patlabor force: Noa, Nagumo, Kanuka, and, later in the television series, Takeo Kumagami. The second OVA episode begins with Noa dreaming about a Patlabor that can fly, in the process referencing many of the standard tropes of mecha animation. Giant robots from anime also are mentioned in the fourth OVA episode when

Goto chastises the rest of his team by asking, "What do you think you're piloting? Great Mazinger? Dangaio?" (the names of two famous robot mecha). It is in these first *Patlabor* OVA episodes that the members of Headgear allow their pulp sci-fi influences to shine through; for example, in episode 3, Shige's attempt to destroy the monster is a direct parody of the ending of the original *Godzilla* film. As Asuma says in that episode, undoubtedly mirroring the thoughts of *Patlabor*'s creators: "Are these cool times we're living in, or what? We've got giant robots walking around [and] sea monsters popping up." Headgear member Kazunori Itō, who wrote many of the scripts for the *Patlabor* OVAs and episodes, would go on to write scripts for the new trio of *Gamera* films in the 1990s. These films were helmed by "a pack of fans-turned-pros, who grew up pledging allegiance to giant monster movies," and Itō's contribution in particular "pushes the old monster-on-the-loose clichés—the high level meeting of important personages, for instance—into new territories of self-awareness."[16] A similar statement could be made about the creative staff of *Patlabor.*

In these OVA episodes, Oshii combines some of the comedy of *Urusei Yatsura* with an increasingly serious tone. Although the two *Patlabor* films are the highlights of his involvement with the project, there are many aspects in the OVAs that are distinctly Oshii. The base in *Patlabor* is very similar to the apartment building in *Twilight Q 2,* situated on reclaimed land that used to be ocean. The contents of Professor Hirata's office in episode 3 are culled from the artifacts of Oshii's previous films: large fish floating in glass containers, constantly moving water, fossils on the wall, and even a giant egg on a stone pedestal.

Oshii maintains his philosophical predilections in the *Patlabor* OVAs as well. Despite the plot of episode 4 being rather contrived, Kanuka's concluding statements sum up Oshii's system of thought. Although the plot is presented in a lighthearted way, the episode portrays the danger of leading an unexamined life. Rather than question what they have been told, people often construct elaborate fabrications around their lives, boxing themselves into philosophical corners. People cannot make informed decisions if they do not apprehend the true reality of the situation; they cannot draw fitting conclusions from flawed premises. Initially this attitude may seem to contradict the emphasis Oshii places on dreams and dreamlike images. Oshii does not set dreams and reality as two opposite poles, diametrically opposed, but as necessarily related and complementary. In this view, dreams are not falsehoods, but are simply a larger part of what exists in the world. This theme, conveyed pedantically in this *Patlabor* OVA episode, is one to which Oshii will return in later works.

Episode 5 features a very brief taste of the ways in which Oshii would use distorted camera angles in *Patlabor*. It shows a close-up of Asuma's face through a fisheye lens as if through a door's peephole. In this way, Oshii makes explicit the act of looking—by momentarily distorting the visual space, viewers are made conscious of the viewing act. This act is important in Oshii's technologically oriented films because it emphasizes the vagaries of one's perception of the world.

The story "The SV2's Longest Day" is a dry run for the events on which Oshii would elaborate in the second *Patlabor* film. Although the episodes ably set the scene for a military takeover of Tokyo, many aspects of the plot are left unexplored, such as the reasons behind Kai's siege of the city. The OVAs problematize the issue of Japan's involvement in global military affairs that seem to be forbidden by its constitution. They also introduce the theory that there are nuclear weapons present in Japan, introduced through U. S. military bases, even though they are prohibited. The air force base in question, Yokota, appears later in *Blood the Last Vampire* as the locus for vampiric activities.

The success of Oshii's *Patlabor* OVAs prompted interest in continuing the animated *Patlabor* universe. The response generated by the first six OVAs enabled the creators to secure funding for a feature-length *Patlabor* film. It also prompted the hasty creation of a seventh OVA episode to hold the viewing public's interest until the film's release. As he directed the first six OVAs, Oshii helmed the first *Patlabor* film, further developing his themes and ideas through the characters of the SV2. (Note: Because the title of the first *Patlabor* film does not distinguish it from the general name of the series, I refer to it in the following text alternately as "the first *Patlabor* film" or *Patlabor 1* [its name on release in the United States.])

SYNOPSIS OF THE FIRST *PATLABOR* FILM

A lone figure stands silently atop a large structure, petting a large black bird and then letting it fly free. Slowly, as others look on in horror, trying in vain to stop him, the man casts himself into the darkness below. As he begins his agonizingly slow descent, a faint smile creeps across the man's face.

In a subsequent scene, a giant red multilegged tank runs amok through a forest until a battalion of heavily armed military Labors is able to bring it to a standstill. However, when the cockpit of the tank opens, it is revealed that no one had been piloting it.

Noa and Asuma are on their way to the Ark, a special Labor manufacturing facility for the Babylon Project, to escort Captain Nagumo back to base (and to sneak a glimpse at the new proto-type Patlabor Nagumo has been testing). The second unit of the SV2 has been on constant duty while the first unit has been testing the prototype, and there has been a sharp spike in the number of seemingly inexplicable Labor rampages in Tokyo in the previous two months. The two captains, Goto and Nagumo, are informed about the rampaging robot tank and are told that it had been undergoing testing in a wind tunnel when it went berserk. After moving out to stop another Labor on the warpath, Asuma takes it on himself to figure out why the Labors are malfunctioning.

After much work, Asuma discovers that the rampages must be due to the new operating system—HOS, or Hyper Operating System—that has been installed in nearly every Labor in the country. The HOS was the brainchild of a genius named Eiichi Hoba, the man who jumped into darkness one month earlier. (One hundred workers on the Ark saw him fall, yet no body ever surfaced.) Asuma and Sakaki go to investigate Shinohara Heavy Industries, the originators of the HOS; its president happens to be Asuma's father. While looking at some files, Asuma comes across the master disk for HOS, but when he tries the password "E.HOBA," a virus begins to spread: The screen displays "Go to, let us go down, and there confound their language, that they may not understand one another's speech" (from Genesis 11: 7), after which all the computer screens in the manufacturing complex begin to flash red, repeating the word "Babel." Asuma and Sakaki beat a hasty retreat.

While the Special Vehicles Unit is trying to discover the flaw in the new Labor operating system, Detective Matsui and his partner search every place Hoba has lived in the past two years—twenty-six in all. Half of the rooms have been deserted, while the rest have already been demolished. Every room the detectives are able to see is run down, barren save for empty birdcages hanging from the ceilings and lining the floors. (Matsui even steps on a birdcage while looking through the ruins of one of the old houses.) The search eventually culminates at Hoba's family home, which is filled with birdcages, feathers, and dust. The detectives find a calendar for the year 1999, behind which, written on the wall, is the line "He bowed the heavens also, and came down; and darkness was under his feet" (from 2 Samuel 22: 10 and Psalms 18: 9).

When Asuma takes Noa out on a date, he asks her if she has had any problems with her Patlabor, after which he notices a dog acting strangely. Noa says that dogs are able to hear different noises from humans and that the dog probably just hears the wind. In a flash, Asuma realizes what is happening: Certain buildings in Tokyo are acting as giant whistles, generating noises that trigger a preprogrammed rampaging response in the Labors with the HOS system installed. Further investigation of resonance reveals Hoba's final plan: If wind blows through the Ark fast enough, enough buildings will resonate to make all the Labors in Tokyo, possibly all the Labors in Japan, go berserk. A typhoon is approaching Tokyo that would create such a resonance. The Patlabor group decides to destroy the Ark by telling its computer to drop all of the floors of the structure, thus changing the building's resonance. However, to accomplish this, Division 2 is forced to fight their way into the Ark past the security robots.

Before the SV2 can drop the floors of the Ark, a scan reveals that there is still one employee left in the facility. The computer gives the identity as "E. Hoba," with an ID number of 666. Asuma sends Noa up to investigate. When she arrives, she finds a room filled with birds of various sorts, all with their eyes glowing red. One bird seems to be central, with an identification tag attached to its leg bearing the number 666; it gives one loud, menacing squawk as Noa approaches.

Asuma discovers that the virus that Hoba put into the HOS also has infected the main computer of the Ark, and when the virus is triggered, Division 2 can no longer use the main computer to drop the Ark's floors. Additionally, all the other Labors on board start up on their own and begin to run amok. Luckily, in Noa's vicinity there is a manual switch to drop the floors, which she is able to trigger successfully. Finally, Noa has to fight one last Labor—one of the new Patlabors Division 1 had been testing. She manages to climb onto the back of the opposing Patlabor's neck and shoot out its memory. The film ends with a team of rescue helicopters flying across the clear, bright sky to rescue Division 2 from the sagging hulk of the Ark.

COMMENTARY AND ANALYSIS OF THE FIRST *PATLABOR* FILM

Some of the *Patlabor* creators have stated that the first *Patlabor* film was not as intellectually challenging as some of Oshii's previous films. Said Headgear member Izubuchi, "In some ways, the first *Patlabor* movie was intended as nothing more ambitious than a work of mere entertainment."[17] Even Oshii has described this film as "a proper pop entertainment movie."[18] However, in it Oshii manages to bring to the fore a discussion of religion and power through his own unique style.

The first scene of Hoba plunging from the top of the Ark, which ends with the sound of fluttering bird wings, seems incongruous until later in the film; birds, wings, and feathers are tropes that Oshii commonly uses (seen in both *Patlabor* films as well as *Ghost in the Shell*) to suggest the freedom of flight and an escape from containment. For example, Kusanagi's introductory plunge in *Ghost in the Shell* echoes this scene of Hoba's descent.

As in some of his previous films, Oshii's *Patlabor 1* is filled with allusions to the Bible. From the beginning of the *Patlabor* story, there have been such references, especially in the form of the Babylon Project, but they occur more often in this film. Noa's name takes on special significance when the Ark, a critical part of the Babylon Project, is introduced. (In the subtitles of the U.S. version of the film, her name is even romanized as "Noah.") In the original biblical story, God told Noah to construct an ark to save himself and his family from the great flood God was preparing to unleash on the sinful people of the world. In *Patlabor*, the Ark is a factory producing creatures of a different sort—giant mechanical robots designed to make life easier for humanity. In this sense, the human-built Ark, although it carries robots and not humans, serves as the source from which humankind's continued progress will spring. Another biblical allusion is the reference to Hoba as "E. Hoba," which when pronounced in Japanese sounds like the word "Jehovah." This is further illustrative of Hoba's megalomaniacal complex; he has even assumed the very name of God.

Related to this allusion to religion is Oshii's use of numbers. Three different numbers can enhance understanding of the film. Although this use of numbers may seem at first tangential and coincidental, and the numbers have their roots in Western biblical culture, in Japanese popular culture numbers can be viewed as significant.[19] The first and most obvious number is that most infamous of biblical numbers, 666. In the book of Revelation in the Bible, this number is said to be the number of "the beast," although its exact meaning is a subject of much debate. In popular culture, the number 666 often is used to identify the Devil or the Antichrist. In *Patlabor 1*, it is used as Hoba's identification number given in the Ark and the number on the tag of the bird Noa finds at the top of the Ark, perhaps suggesting that Hoba and the bird are conceptually related. According to Oshii, the bird, "was an apostle of Hoba. It was an angel."[20]

Another related biblical allusion is that the critical wind speed for the Labors to go berserk is 40 kilometers per second; in the original biblical story, Noah's ark was adrift for forty days and forty nights. Other appearances of the number forty in the Bible include the number of days and nights Moses stayed on Mount Sinai and the number of days Jesus fasted in the desert while being tempted by the devil. The film also brings a lesser-known number, 26, into the fold as the number of places in which Hoba has lived in Tokyo. In the numerological system of the Hebrew gematria, this number can spell YHWH, the name of God.[21] Oshii uses these numbers to create a more richly layered story, adding some insight into Hoba's madness. Hoba's use of the numbers 26 and 40 demonstrates his self-identification with a god, but one whose vengeance will smite the works of man. The use of 666 provides the opposite identification—that of the Antichrist. This numerology provides a brief glimpse into Hoba's conflicted and conflicting way of thinking.

Patlabor 1 also contains references to the biblical story of the Tower of Babel, a tale that has been fodder for a number of science fiction stories, such as Neal Stephenson's *Snow Crash* (1992) and the anime film *Metropolis* (2001). The Tower of Babel allusion often is made to highlight the hubris of humans in an undertaking viewed as immoral or unnatural. In *Patlabor,* such perceived hubris is mankind's technological arrogance of creating the Labors and reclaiming land from Tokyo Bay. The attempt to bring humankind away from the arrogance comes not from a vengeful god, but another human, Hoba, who is arrogant in his own way. Oshii's version of the Bible story twists the story of Babel; the Babylon Project is not actually destroyed in the end, but rather is saved by the men and women of Division 2. However, in order to do so, they must sacrifice a tower of their own, namely, the Labor manufacturing station, the Ark. The destruction of the Ark is an action symbolic of Oshii's own deconstruction of Christian mythology, systematically tearing down the structure when necessary.

The revolt of the Labors that occurs in the film is not terribly surprising given customary science fiction tropes. In fact, the very first time the word "robot" was used dramatically, in Karel Capek's play *Rossum's Universal Robots* (1920), involved mechanical beings rising up against their human masters. According to philosopher Jean Baudrillard, "The robot, like the slave, is both good and perfidious: good as a captive force; perfidious as a force that may break its chains. Like the sorcerer's apprentice, man has every reason to fear the resurrection of this force which he has exorcized and bound to his own image."[22] This fear of the Labor running amok is at the heart of the *Patlabor* universe; the SV2 was created specifically to combat the use of Labors for crimes. Oshii utilizes these themes of technology against man, but technology is only the intermediary: Hoba sees himself as a messianic figure whose duty it is to bring his version of knowledge to the people of Japan.

In the film, Oshii shows religion to be a malleable pawn for those who would use it to control others or themselves. The quote from Genesis about going down to confound the language of man shows Hoba posturing as God, scattering the languages of the world by destroying the Tower of Babel. The second biblical quote portrays a similar mind-set; in context, the line from 2 Samuel talks about God coming down from the heavens to smite his enemies after one has put one's faith in him. Hoba must have felt that God required some assistance. He took these biblical verses to heart and took it upon himself to deliver the swift wrath of God's vengeance against the citizens of modern-day Tokyo. His skewed interpretation of Christianity portrays a religion fully centered on the self and the ego, and Oshii demonstrates how this can blind people to their social and spiritual sides. Through the character of Hoba, Oshii demonstrates the danger of megalomania and the cult of personality that all too often manifests itself in modern religious movements. Oshii reconceptualizes the passages from the Bible just mentioned to demonstrate how dangerous blind faith can be.

Oshii closely links Hoba's spiritual degeneracy to the technological chaos he causes. Hoba is the source of all of the biblical references in the film, from the inscription behind his calendar to his ID number of 666, as well as all of the computerized mayhem as designer of the faulty Hyper Operating System and the viruses contained within. By giving such effects one common source, Oshii is equating and problematizing the misapplication of both technology and spirituality. This is one of the aspects of power Oshii is trying to get people to realize—in the wrong hands, spirituality can be as dangerous as technology.

Stylistically, Oshii uses a number of distorted shots to achieve a sense of otherworldliness. Two of these shots center around Asuma. The first shot, which lasts for only a couple of seconds, is immediately after he triggers the "Babel" virus at Shinohara Industries. The shot rotates around Asuma's head, showing the banks of computer monitors flashing red in the background. This disorienting shot represents both Asuma's confusion and the chaos begun by the virus; it is a visual illustration of the Bible verse from

Genesis about confusing the languages of the world. The second, and more experimental, shot is when Asuma is arguing with the police chief about his punishment for leaving the base to pursue his own line of investigation. The sequence begins with the distorted faces of Asuma and the chief, viewed as through a fisheye lens (one of Oshii's favorite distorted shots), moving on to rapidly moving close-ups of a police uniform and insignia. As Asuma and the chief yell at each other, the confusing forms represent their anger visually. The brief scene ends in a shot of a single police emblem, representing the final triumph of the authoritarian police hierarchy in which Asuma has no choice but to accept the punishment meted out to him. Another visual technique Oshii employs is when the Patlabor team is storming the Ark; the view is from the front of the command car, and the audience can see only that which the front headlights have illuminated. Oshii also uses this technique in *Urusei Yatsura 2: Beautiful Dreamer,* when Mendou's car is lost, trying to find its way out of the maze. Although used only for a few seconds, the technique heightens the tension by showing what the characters see, not knowing what will appear around the next corner. Oshii brings much of his stylistic force to bear during this final battle onboard the Ark. In another allusion to the Great Flood that occurs in the Bible's book of Genesis, the surging typhoon creates dark skies and a torrent of rain, not unlike the atmosphere of *Angel's Egg.*

Although Oshii's fascination with technology, especially military technology, has been evident from his directorial debut, in this first *Patlabor* film he begins to explore how technology alters how one perceives the world. The mediation of one's experiences through computers and video monitors relates directly to the physical confinement of the Labor mecha themselves. Through the world he portrays, Oshii shows how people in modern society have become almost too dependent on computers as arbiters of how we perceive our lives. This dependency is detailed through the predictable disaster scenario at the heart of *Patlabor 1,* in which overreliance on technology threatens to destroy Tokyo.

On the other hand, through Noa's interactions with her Patlabor Oshii portrays technology as comfortable and familiar. One can interact with technology in almost the same way as a family pet. (In fact, the Patlabor named Alphonse is the third in the Alphonse lineage; the first two were a dog and a cat Noa had when she was younger.) It is an animal's reaction to sound that provides the key clue for Asuma to discover the trigger for the Labor rampages. Knowing Oshii's affinity for pets, especially dogs, the power of this attraction to technology has great meaning. Although frequently dystopian in tone, Oshii's technology-related films are not totally pessimistic in their outlook on the integration of the human and the machine. Oshii has even said that he would not object to putting his brain in a robot body one day: "My eyesight is becoming bad, my hearing has always been bad, and recently I've been having stomach problems. So my body is wearing down. I wouldn't mind becoming a cyborg."[23]

Presaging his analysis of gender, sex, and technology in *Ghost in the Shell,* in the first *Patlabor* film Oshii shows a strong link between femininity and the Labors themselves. Although Ohta, the main male Patlabor pilot, does appear, his role is much reduced when compared to those of Noa and Kanuka. In performing his police duty, Ohta is shown as somewhat bumbling, creating quite a disturbance as he tries to apprehend a runaway Labor. This contrasts with the climactic Labor battle between Noa and the prototype Patlabor, which has gone berserk with Kanuka inside. Here Noa displays great piloting skill, performing complicated maneuvers that speak to her symbiosis with her machine. Femininity and the Labors have additional associations with the Patlabor prototype itself. Early in the film, Captain Nagumo is shown testing the new Patlabor; this is the first time she has been seen in a Labor. (Previously she has been shown in command outside of the Labor's robotic confines.) The design of the prototype also is associated with typically feminine attributes—it is less bulky and more agile than the older Patlabors used by the SV2, and its main method of combat is not a gun but a lithe, extendable arm that can cut through opponents' armor. Although it is taken over by Hoba's Babel virus (foreshadowed by Noa's initial comment that she thinks the new Labor looks "evil"), the prototype demonstrates itself to be more capable in combat than the older Patlabors, at least within the crowded confines of the Ark. The mecha as feminine force is an idea later executed more fully (and obviously) in Hideaki Anno's groundbreaking television series *Neon Genesis Evangelion.*

In spite of the richness of many of its themes, *Patlabor 1*'s plot sports a few shortcomings. Hoba is made too mysterious; viewers have little context in which to understand his desire to cause the Labors to rampage. As in the first *Urusei Yatsura* film, Oshii allows each character to have at least a little screen time. Thus, plot contrivances entail bringing Kanuka all the way from her post in New York to participate in the final assault on the Ark. (Yet her brief exchange with an airport immigration official interjects a spot of sorely needed levity.) The final scene of the incoming rescue helicopters underscores the fact that this film is a "pop entertainment movie." With the impending threat on the city of Tokyo resolved, the typhoon clears and the sun returns to the sky. The sunny ending is almost too perfect—much of the meaning behind Hoba's assault on the city remains unexplored. *Patlabor 1* can be viewed as one of Oshii's springboard films; many of its themes and messages are more fully developed in the second *Patlabor* film.

PATLABOR ON TELEVISION AND THE SECOND *PATLABOR* OVAS

In October 1989, three months after the first *Patlabor* film opened in theaters, the *Patlabor* television series began airing. Many members of Headgear reprised key roles in the new series (with Kazunori Itō as planner, Akemi Takada as character designer, and Yutaka Izubuchi as mecha designer), but Mamoru Oshii turned the directorial reins over to Naoyuki Yoshinaga. (Like Oshii, Yoshinaga had previously worked on the *Urusei Yatsura* television series, serving as chief animator. Yoshinaga later directed another adaptation of a Rumiko Takahashi manga, the domestic comedy *Maison Ikkoku.* Originally Yoshinaga had been brought into the *Patlabor* fold to work on the hastily produced seventh episode of the OVA series.) However, Oshii was screenplay writer for five of the forty-eight episodes in the *Patlabor* TV series. The episodes he wrote are as diverse as the *Patlabor* series itself, running the gamut from stories that go into character development, to political intrigue, to comedy.

Episode 3, the simply titled "Special Vehicles Section 2" ("Kochira Tokushanika"), was the first of the Oshii-scripted episodes, chronicling an average day in the life of the SV2. The episode shows what the team members do while they are waiting for an emergency call to come in, activities such as cutting the seitaka around the base and fishing for dinner. The climax of the episode is not an emergency call; rather, the division's speedboat, which the crew appropriates for deep-sea fishing, has run aground and must be rescued by the Labors without chief mechanic Sakaki finding out. In a way, the episode idealizes the simplicity of the SV2's off-duty time, yet also marks them as outcasts. Because their base is located so far from downtown Tokyo, the team members often have to fend for themselves, especially where food is concerned, having to fish, keep chickens, and grow their own tomatoes. Thus, in addition to being disciplinary misfits, the SV2 is located geographically apart from the rest of Tokyo and symbolically apart from the rest of Japanese society. A couple of times in the episode, Asuma compares SV2 to a pack of stray dogs. Oshii emphasizes such a point of view because it allows him more readily to critique Japanese politics and culture in later episodes and in the second *Patlabor* film. This view, along with the dog references, emphasizes Oshii's own personal identification with the members of the Second Division.

The emphasis on food occurs again in another *Patlabor* television episode Oshii wrote (and as a motif in *The Red Spectacles* and *Avalon*). In episode 29, "The Destruction of the Special Vehicles, Second Section" ("Tokushanika Kaimetsusu!"), Kumagai recounts the events that led to the temporary crippling of the SV2. One day Noa goes around to the entire crew getting their lunch orders for Shanghai Restaurant, the only local place that will deliver to the base. When she calls to place the order, she promptly forgets what everyone told her and has to make the rounds again. She calls in the order again, but it never arrives and Ohta yells at the restaurant staff, saying they will never order from them again. The crew's culinary backups—the convenience store, the fishing, the henhouse, and the tomato plants—all end up failing them as well. In the late afternoon, after Ohta apologizes, Shanghai Restaurant agrees to make them more food, but cannot deliver it as their delivery boy never came back. Ohta and Shinshi drive off to pick up the food, but do not return. Goto, Noa, and Asuma go to find them; as soon as they leave the base, Shige gets a mysterious phone call from Shinshi warning them not to come. Concerned, the mechanics all head out for Shanghai Restaurant and do not return, leaving Kumagami the only person left at the base. What happened was that the delivery boy, out of spite for having to work hard to deliver the Patlabor team's food, decided to give their first order to a pack of stray dogs. The restaurant owner found the empty bowls, but did not have time to wash them before filling them with the SV2's second order. When Ohta and Shinshi arrived at the restaurant, they ate their food but quickly succumbed to food poisoning. Terrified, the restaurant owner fled. Goto, Asuma, and Noa arrived and took Ohta and Shinshi to the hospital. The mechanics reached the restaurant after the SV2 team had left and ate the rest of the food that had been prepared, which gave every mechanic food poisoning and lead to SV2's "destruction." Like some of his work on *Urusei Yatsura,* this episode is an example of Oshii's idea of comedy, in which small events build logically on one another until the story reaches the point of ridiculousness. Oshii uses part of this episode to parody the student turmoil of the 1960s, with the Shanghai Restaurant standing for the establishment and the Patlabor crew, the exploited students. The crew's seemingly simple demands—the delivery of the food they ordered—becomes increasingly politicized as the hours pass. Thus, the Patlabor crew becomes increasingly militant in its attitude toward the restaurant. Had both sides communicated calmly and clearly from the outset, Oshii seems to be saying, the crisis situation could have been averted. Here Oshii distances himself from the tactics employed by groups of the student protest era to illustrate the necessity of rational dialogue. Oshii would reexamine the ideals and situations of the Japanese student movement in an episode written for the second *Patlabor* OVA series, as well as the film *Jin-Roh.*

Other episodes of the *Patlabor* television series for which Oshii wrote the script examine politics, the necessity of teamwork, and the shared urban myth of alligators in the sewers. Episode 9,

"Red Labor Landing" ("Jōriku Akai Labor"), involves the suspected theft of a Soviet military Labor by a terrorist, in which the SV2 members discover they have been set up by Japan's public security forces. Although it ends in farce, the episode highlights Oshii's distrust of the internal politics of police and governmental bureaucracies evident in *Patlabor 2* and *Jin-Roh*. In episode 14, "You Win!" ("Anata no Kachi!"), Captain Goto notices that friction has been building among his team members. To quell the bad feelings that are beginning to ferment, Goto takes them all out drinking so they can begin opening up to each other. Although his plan works in this regard, the next day the entire team is hung over on duty (except for Noa who, the true daughter of a bartender, feels great). Episode 38, "The Underground Mystery Tour" ("Chika Meikyū Bukken"), begins with the strange disappearance of a variety of foodstuffs from around the base. After discovering a series of underground tunnels, installed when the artificial island on which SV2 is based was constructed, the Patlabor crew members descend into the darkness to solve the mystery. While looking for the culprit, who ends up being a worker on the original construction of the area who moved into the tunnels permanently, the SV2 members encounter many frights, not the least of which is a giant albino alligator. The episode takes a comedic look at such events, eschewing many of Oshii's themes in exchange for some lighthearted fun. However, a more literal translation of its title is "Underground Labyrinth Objects," again alluding to Oshii's use of the labyrinth motif by using nearly the same title as the subtitle of the *Twilight Q 2* OVA.

Following the television series, another OVA series was begun that continued the storytelling arc of the television episodes. Oshii did not direct, although he did script four episodes of the series, most of which were in a humorous or parodic vein. The most noteworthy of these new episodes was "The Seven Days of Fire" ("Hi no Nanokakan"). When Chief Sakaki discovers a treasure trove of pornography in the mechanics' living quarters, he decides their discipline is too lax and institutes new, stricter rules and regulations (described in Asuma's voice-over narration as "Cromwellian"). In response, a black market trafficking in pornography and certain prohibited foods develops among the members of the maintenance crew. Although Shige initially wants to go easy on the men, after a dinner during which Sakaki praises his talent and future, Shige forms a special squad to enforce discipline (with uniforms modeled on those of the German SS). This in turn fosters the growth of subversive groups, plotting in secret against Shige's reign of terror. However, this resistance quickly fractures into three main factions and eleven subfactions that disagree mostly on how Sakaki should be viewed. In the end, after seven days of strife and infighting, Sakaki manages to bring everyone back under control. Summing up Oshii's philosophies, the episode ends with Asuma's statement: "If anything is to be learned from this useless fight, it is to never put our faith in higher powers. They're just as messed up as we are." Here Oshii again parodies his own background in the student uprisings of the 1960s. (He also throws in a parody of the anime film *Akira* and an allusion to his own film *The Red Spectacles* for good measure.) While the mechanics' revolt is initially a reasonable reaction to the sudden imposition of harsher rules and regulations, it quickly devolves into personal grievances and power struggles, much like the real student movement in Japan in the 1960s. In the process, Oshii's comedic structure is played out, slowly building absurdity in logical steps from a normal premise. The portrayal of the splintering of factions would be more of a parody if it were not overshadowed by what actually happened: for example, in the student movement "The original Zengakuren [the nationwide organization of smaller college and university self-government associations] has produced at least thirty-two separately named factions—and just one of these factions, the New Left Kyousandou, has spawned fifty-four distinct factions of its own."[24]

In the episode "Black Trinary" ("Kuroi Sanrensei"), the members of the SV2 encounter a member of the Public Security bureau unconscious in the street. When he awakens, the man tells them he was just chasing a serial bomber who had been hitting Labor factories for the past week. After tracking the bomber to the same public bath where they were headed and sending Noa to headquarters for backup, the male SV2 members begin to look for the bomber based on the only clue the Public Security man could give them: the suspect has three moles in his right armpit. When they don't find the bomb the suspect is said to be carrying (which has been appropriately stashed in locker 666), the men of the SV2 begin to try to surreptitiously search the armpits of every man in the public bath. After much hilariously odd behavior and naked fighting, the Patlabor team comes to the realization that the bomber must be a woman, and she is apprehended by the police who come to surround the bath.

The episode "It's Called Amnesia" ("Sono na wa Amnesia") begins with a dream of Ohta's in which he is forced to shoot people who look strikingly like his SV2 teammates. (The dream is an obvious homage to the film *Blade Runner* [1982] with Ohta in the Rick Deckard role.) However, when Ohta wakes up he cannot remember who he is, and Shinshi, Asuma, Yamazaki, and Shige are strewn about the room, looking as if they have been killed violently. Ohta, who cannot remember who he is or what he had been doing, runs terrified from the apartment and begins to wander the city. Noa, Kumagami, and some of the maintenance crew comb the city, trying to find him before he becomes permanently lost in the crowd. Ohta wanders alone in the rain, pausing to speak with a convenience store clerk who remembers him as the "psycho cop" who set him straight from a life of petty noodle-stand crime. When Ohta pauses at a construction site, a sudden explosion traps one of the worker's Labors. Ohta commandeers one of the still-functioning construction Labors in order to save him, and gets knocked unconscious in the process. With Ohta in the hospital with a mild concussion, Asuma (who is not dead after all) reveals what happened. Shinshi's wife was out of town, so the men of the SV2 decided to have a party and ended up watching one of Shinshi's home movies of his smiling wife. When Ohta insulted the video, Shinshi hit him over the head with a sake bottle, knocking him unconscious. The rest then decided to play a practical joke on him, and disguised themselves with fake blood. However, they had not anticipated that Ohta would have amnesia when he awoke and would flee. When Ohta awakens in the hospital, he has regained his memory and is as temperamental as ever. This episode contains strains of Oshii's previous films and *Patlabor* episodes. Ohta is a loner with no memory, wandering a forbidding city, much like the characters in *Angel's Egg* and *Twilight Q 2*. The story also has a structure similar to these previous works; the episode seems mysterious until the denouement, when the events begin to make sense with a kind of twisted logic.

Finally, in "The Dungeon Again" ("Dungeon Futatabi"), the albino alligator first encountered in "The Underground Mystery Tour" returns. Now in captivity, the alligator has laid a pearl (actually a urethral stone) valued at over $2 million. Fantasizing about what they would be able to do with the money, three of the mechanics break open the seal that had been put on the tunnels and descend to see if there are any more "pearls" in the dark depths. The SV2 goes down after them, more prepared than they were the first time they made the descent. As they do so, Goto receives a call from Detective Matsui, who informs him that Tadayama, the man who had been living in the tunnels and stealing from the SV2, recently escaped from the hospital in which he was held, vowing vengeance. While searching for the missing mechanics, the SV2 members encounter surprise traps set by Tadayama, including falling rocks, feral cats, and a fusillade of arrows. When they find Tadayama's dwelling again, they break in to find the three missing mechanics having noodles with him; they had been rescued by Tadayama after they got lost in the tunnels. However, when Tadayama says he saw a room filled with the pearls a short distance away, the team is ready to press on and retrieve them. They quickly discover that the white spheres are not pearls at all, but albino alligator eggs, which quickly hatch and attract the attention of three giant adult albino alligators. Another chase in the tunnels ensues, ending with everyone barricaded in Tadayama's underground sanctuary. Another lighthearted episode from Oshii, it quickly turns into a rehash of the previous alligator story, creating a (possibly unintentional) labyrinth of its own, from which there is little hope of the viewer escaping.

This last *Patlabor* OVA episode scripted by Oshii serves as a stark contrast with the second *Patlabor* film. Much more serious in tone, this film gives more emphasis to the political machinations within the *Patlabor* world, focusing less on the interactions among the characters that had been developing in the previous episodes. It is much more meditative and philosophical than anything that had been produced in *Patlabor* before, questioning

Japan's role in the modern world and examining the city of Tokyo.

SYNOPSIS OF THE SECOND *PATLABOR* FILM

In an introduction very similar to that of the first *Patlabor* film, the viewer is thrown into a battle. Military mecha with Japanese pilots and bearing United Nations insignia make their way through a dense Southeast Asian forest in the year 1999. When they detect enemy troops who begin to fire at them, the Japanese forces request permission to engage them in combat. The response is negative; UN troops from Canada will arrive soon to handle the fighting. As the Japanese troops begin to take heavy damage, they continually ask for the authorization to return fire. Finally the commander of the Japanese mecha force decides to fire back; he is able to destroy the enemy, but all of the soldiers under his command are killed.

The story then flashes forward to the year 2002. Much has changed for the SV2. All of the members are older and many are more advanced in rank. Shinshi is now a division chief, and Ohta serves as an instructor to new recruits into the Patlabor program. Even Noa has become more serious with the passage of time, no longer harboring an attachment to her Patlabor nicknamed "Alphonse," which she has not piloted in over a year. Newly promoted Nagumo, after giving a presentation on the spread of Labors and Patlabors throughout Japan, is invited to a reunion of the Tsuge group. Tsuge and his team were pioneers in the field of Labor technology. Nagumo was Tsuge's star pupil, but it is implied that she was romantically involved with him as well. Tsuge disappeared shortly after he got back to Japan from a UN mission three years earlier.

On her way back to the SV2 base, Shinobu encounters a traffic jam because there has been a bomb threat made on the Yokohama Bay Bridge. As a combat airplane flies stealthily through Japanese airspace, it fires a missile at the now-abandoned bridge, destroying a large portion of it. Subsequently, the film presents a montage of various evening news programs, in both Japanese and English, all talking about the attack. From an amateur video, the silhouette of a Japanese fighter plane can be seen on the periphery of the explosion, flying away from the attack. At the behest of Captain Goto, Detective Matsui contacts a professional company that was filming around the bridge at the time of the attack, but someone else posing as a police officer has already absconded with the only copy of the tape.

A mysterious man named Mr. Arakawa, from the Japan Ground Defense Force, Special Investigations, visits Captains Goto and Nagumo in their office. He brings to them a videotape of footage filmed around the bridge at the time of the attack. However, the image of the plane in this video is unlike that which has been showing on the major news programs; this plane has a stealth-style wing shape and a new type of engine nozzle. Arakawa says that there is no such plane like this in all of the Japanese Self Defense Force (JSDF). At his invitation, Goto and Nagumo go for a ride in Arakawa's car so he can speak with them more privately.

During the drive, Arakawa tells them that before the attack on the bridge, a U.S. fighter plane disappeared from an American base in Japan. He explains that although it was a U.S. plane that attacked, neither the American military nor the pilot himself were culpable. Arakawa's Special Investigations unit has been keeping an eye on the National Defense Family, a group of U.S. military advisors and defense contractors who, by attacking the bridge, were attempting to sow the seeds of paranoia and, in turn, sell more weapons to an increasingly militarized Japan. He reveals that one of the group's founders was Yukihito Tsuge, the man with whom Nagumo once studied and was romantically linked. Unfortunately, Arakawa has little concrete evidence. He is turning to the Patlabor team for help because of Goto's many contacts and because of SV2's characteristically perceived disregard for regulations. After Arakawa receives a telephone call in his car, he begins to speed up, telling the captains that three Japanese fighter planes have just launched and should reach Tokyo in twenty minutes.

In the JSDF air control center, the crew members scramble to make sense of what is going on, but they cannot establish communication with any of the other bases. Interceptor fighters are launched to combat the potential menace, but when the air control center finally manages to contact the air base from which the renegade aircraft are supposed to have launched, the base says that nothing has taken off from there. As one group of interceptor fighters disappears from the screen and another closes in on the target, civilian air controllers at Narita Airport become worried about a possible attack, canceling all outbound flights and rerouting all inbound ones. Just as the mysterious aircraft are about to enter Tokyo airspace, they disappear from the screen. Contact is reestablished with the missing interceptor fighters, which had been experiencing heavy communications jamming.

Later, meeting at an aquarium, Arakawa explains the situation to Goto, saying that the JSDF computers were hacked through their connections to the American military base computers. Arakawa theorizes that one of the software programmers worked for the National Defense Family, providing an easy point of access to the Japanese defense mainframe. Arakawa goes on to discuss Tsuge's background as one of the early proponents of Labors in military combat situations. However, a scandal involving the married Tsuge and his protégée, the young Nagumo, although it was quietly covered up, derailed her career plans. Goto asks if Tsuge is trying to start his own little war, to which Arakawa responds that Tsuge may already have succeeded.

Boarding a boat bound for headquarters, Goto ruminates on the conversation he and Arakawa just had. Arakawa talked of the nature of Japan's postwar peace, saying that the country has profited from the violence and unrest in other parts of the globe by ignoring it. Goto responded that they still must protect peace, as an unjust peace is more desirable than a just war. Arakawa said that the line between the two is subtle and hazy and that sometimes peace is not to be trusted. Someday, he says, their punishment for ignoring the course of world events will be meted out. When Goto asks if God will be delivering this punishment, Arakawa responds that modern technology can enable anyone to become like a god.

Arriving back at SV2 headquarters, Goto learns that orders have been issued for the Patlabor units to surround the JSDF's Nerima Air Base the next morning. In theory, the mobilization is to preempt a possible coup by the JSDF, but Goto, seeing it as nothing more than political posturing by his superiors in the police force, disagrees with the idea of the police provoking the JSDF at such a critical time. When Goto suggests to Nagumo that they boycott the order to move out, she becomes irritated and storms out of their shared office, prompting Goto to change his mind.

The next day the situation is tense as the police and the JSDF forces stand off against one another at the airbase in an intimidating display. Goto's division is present, but their Labors are still reclining on their trailers; Goto has refused to stand them up, telling his superiors that they are malfunctioning. Goto receives a call in his car from Arakawa, who tells him about the situation on the JSDF side—the top military commanders have resigned in disgust, leaving the civilian leaders (who are planning to use the police as scapegoats) in charge. Arakawa reminds Goto that Tsuge's force in Southeast Asia was decimated while under civilian command and suggests that Tsuge is trying to replicate the same circumstances in Japan.

Later in the evening, the JSDF are ordered to mobilize, deploying throughout Tokyo because the police have not been able to handle the tense situation adequately. Hearing the news, the SV2 prepares for the worst, buying out all food from the nearby convenience store and preparing the Patlabors for deployment. Meanwhile, the JSDF vehicles and tanks roll out through the streets of Japan's capital city. The next day is a surreal montage of the citizens of Tokyo going about their routine business against the backdrop of tanks and soldiers on every corner, the city seemingly under martial law.

In the interim, Detective Matsui has been pursuing his own leads in the case against Tsuge, which have brought him to an airship company. The company, which Arakawa said has financial ties to Tsuge, has been flying a fleet of three blimps around Tokyo. (They were evident in the backgrounds of previous scenes.) In tracing the company's funds, Matsui discovers a recent purchase of three items from America. These items are theorized to be nuclear weapons, one for each blimp, smuggled through nearby Yokota Air Force Base. To uncover more information, Matsui breaks into the airship company offices and palms a computer disk. He is apprehended on his way out of the building, but escapes.

Nagumo receives a telephone call from Tsuge at her mother's house and agrees to meet him. At a river landing, she boards a boat sent by Tsuge. Nagumo cruises quietly down the river, under a series of bridge overpasses, and as the snow falls around her she pulls next to Tsuge's boat. They gaze at each other for only a short time until police speedboats arrive, bearing Arakawa and Goto, who had been tipped off by Nagumo's mother. Tsuge's own boat rushes away into the darkness.

In the morning, attack helicopters with JSDF markings emerge from hidden cargo containers as the three blimps, laden with their unknown cargo, ascend into the skies of Tokyo. One of the first stops for the helicopters is the SV2 base; their massive machine guns destroy all the Labors in the hangar, catching the Patlabor crew seemingly unawares. As Goto and Nagumo sit before a police board and argue about the dire situation and who is at fault, other attack helicopters blow up bridges and communications towers around the city. To throw Tokyo into further chaos, Tsuge begins systematically jamming all civilian, military, and police communications frequencies. In the confusion, the two Patlabor captains, who were about to be relieved of duty, manage to escape police headquarters, commandeering a patrol car to facilitate their getaway.

As he and Nagumo hide out at Chief Sakaki's house, Goto finally understands Tsuge's plans. Tsuge is not trying to stage a real coup d'etat, using the attacks as a means to a political end; rather his goal is the sowing of confusion itself. He aims to give Tokyo a taste of what a real war is like. The members of the SV2 have not yet been defeated, however, and prepare to strike back, recruiting everyone they can into their fold (by humorously insistent force, in the case of Shinshi).

When the police shoot at one of Tsuge's blimps (discovered to be unmanned, running on autopilot), a special program is triggered, causing the airship to dive into the city. On impact, the blimp releases a large cloud of yellow gas, sending the soldiers in the streets scattering for fresh air. Luckily, the gas turns out to be just colored smoke, ultimately harmless; however, the blimp did have poison gas onboard, which suggests that the other blimps also may carry poison gas. Thus the city is effectively held hostage.

Arakawa shows Goto a satellite photograph of an island in Tokyo Bay from which he believes Tsuge is controlling the blimps, saying that they must resolve the situation quickly, as the U.S. military has threatened to step in if Japan cannot solve its own problems by the next morning.

The SV2 prepares their Patlabors for an assault on the small island through a subterranean access tunnel. (The Patlabors had not, in fact, been destroyed by the helicopter gunship at SV2 head-quarters; due to Goto's foresight, they had been moved to a different location.) When Asuma and Shinshi decode the data disk Matsui stole from the airship building, it reveals a passage from the New Testament. As the SV2, under Nagumo's command, leaves for the island, Goto and Matsui arrest Arakawa as Tsuge's accomplice. Arakawa had wanted to stage a political action, but Tsuge had set about creating his own little war, betraying Arakawa.

After fighting their way through a tough pair of sentry robots, the SV2 are able to get Nagumo to the shaft elevator that will take her to the surface of the island. Topside, as Nagumo dismounts from her battered Patlabor, she spies a man at the crest of a hill, surrounded by flocks of birds, gazing through binoculars into the distance. Tsuge's first words to Nagumo are that from where he is standing, Tokyo looks like a mirage in the distance. He says that when he returned from his UN mission, he lived for a time in that mirage, but he felt impelled to expose the illusion. Nagumo places Tsuge under arrest, and he acquiesces quietly, gently holding her hand before she finishes handcuffing herself to him. On the helicopter back to the mainland, Matsui asks Tsuge why he did not kill himself after he set his plan in motion. Tsuge responds that he wanted to see a little more of the city's future.

COMMENTARY AND ANALYSIS OF THE SECOND *PATLABOR* FILM

Film critic Tony Rayns has called *Patlabor 2* Oshii's "first unequivocally great film."[25] To be sure, the film marks the beginning of Oshii's more mature and serious approach to filmmaking, melding his interests in technology, religion, and politics to create a suspenseful thriller that continues to be relevant to modern life not only in Japan, but around the world. The idea of an attack on Tokyo took on an eerie prescience in 1995 (two years after the film's release) when the apocalyptic Aum Shinrikyo cult released sarin gas on the city's subway. The subway attack was similar enough to some of the events in the film that the Japanese police interrogated Oshii during the course of their investigation.[26] Certain images in the film are also likely to be unsettling to many Americans in the wake of the September 11, 2001 terrorist attacks on Washington, D.C. and New York City.

The film's introductory scene is key to understanding the motivations behind the series of attacks on Tokyo staged by Tsuge. As the lone survivor of a UN peacekeeping force, Tsuge feels that he must bring the lessons of the battlefield to the ordinary citizens of Tokyo. His squad in Southeast Asia was decimated due to Japan's ambivalence toward military warfare in the post–World War II era. In the film, Japan wanted to be part of the international community by contributing personnel to the operation (the details of which are never fully explained), yet did not want the troops to engage in actual combat. To try to teach the rest of Japan the lessons he had learned so harshly, Tsuge engages in a campaign to systematically terrorize Tokyo's inhabitants. That his campaign is an extension of his failed UN mission is highlighted by the fact that during the siege of Tokyo, Tsuge uses the same personal call sign as he did in Southeast Asia.

Although Tsuge is the antagonist of the film, and his actions are not to be emulated, Oshii expresses sympathy for and identifies with his political views. Said Oshii, "Tsuge is the other self of Mamoru Oshii. Tsuge's political thoughts and opinions, if there are any, are all mine."[27] Oshii also has expressed a solidarity with Tsuge's goals in trying to get people to wake up from the illusion of modern daily life, saying "If people were really capable of realizing those dangers, I wouldn't have to make my films." Oshii went on to say that he agrees with the assessment that people are still not "waking up to reality."[28] His use of dogs in the film highlights this statement. *Patlabor 2* is the first time Oshii uses the basset hound, which would become one of his trademarks, in anime. The dog is on a small boat and is the first living creature to notice that

Tsuge's helicopters are emerging from their crates. This recognition imbues the dog with special meaning—while people may be misled about what is going on in the world, animals like dogs are more readily able to perceive the truth. Two different shots of dogs during the montage sequence of the occupation of Tokyo illustrate that the actions of humans influence more than just the human world, but impact all living beings.

As the opening credits roll, the viewer is introduced to a visual theme that will be omnipresent throughout the film—that of mediation of perception through technology. In other words, the modern world is viewed continually through a filter of television cameras, video displays, and computer screens. During the credits, Noa and Asuma are testing a new Labor piloting system. As the system starts up, an entire city materializes in the simulation Noa views through her visor. This projected city is complete with obstacles such as people and cats running across the road. The Labor piloting simulation parallels the use of media in the rest of the film. By using technological mass media communications, we project a world around us that may not really exist. Where Oshii's previous films dealt with the issues of dreams and reality, in his later films technology substitutes for dreams.

In the process of telling the story of the bridge explosion, Oshii offers several examples of how the media can shape perceptions of reality. For instance, the aftermath of the explosion is conveyed to viewers through a montage of television news clips. Later Detective Matsui begins his quest to find a videotape that may be able to provide more detail about the incident. He hopes the tape can at least corroborate the events suggested by the amateur footage garnering repeated airplay throughout the media, but he soon discovers that such evidence is easily falsified. The question becomes how we can truly know what is real in our mediated world.[29]

The use of technology is sometimes played for humorous effect in the film. When Mr. Arakawa shows Goto and Nagumo the tape, the camera angle is as if the viewer is behind the television screen, looking out at the characters. Goto says he knows the words to the song on the tape, and offers to sing it karaoke-style. (As another humorous intertextual joke, the video says the song's music and arrangement are by Kenji Kawai, the actual composer for the *Patlabor* films.) The location of the important video shot is discussed in relation to the insidiously vapid lyrics, delivered in a comedically deadpan tone. Also, in order to get a better look at the detail Arakawa is trying to point out to Goto and Nagumo, their faces begin to crowd the screen, assuming comical visages in extreme close-up. Although there certainly is less comedy in this second *Patlabor* film, scenes such as this show that the characters are still able to maintain their humanity, portrayed through humor, in the face of technology.

One direct reference from the Bible appears in *Patlabor 2.* The quote is from Luke 12: 51–53 (and in a more condensed form in Matthew 10: 34–35) and appears in English a number of times toward the end of the film. Viewers first see it briefly on a computer screen, decoded from a computer disk Matsui steals. (The decoding process shows it materializing out of randomness, like the introductory credit sequences in both *Ghost in the Shell* and *Avalon.*) This Bible quotation also ends up being the shutoff code for the blimps. Nagumo recites it during her final confrontation with Tsuge, and in that conversation we learn that the quote made up the content of the last letter he had written to her. The quotation is:

> Suppose ye that I am come to give peace on earth?
> I tell you, Nay; but rather division:
> For from henceforth there shall be five in one house divided,
> three against two, and two against three.
> The father shall be divided against the son,
> and the son against the father; the mother against the daughter,
> and the daughter against the mother;
> the mother-in-law against her daughter-in-law,
> and the daughter-in-law against her mother-in-law.

This quote serves to illustrate the reasons behind Tsuge's actions, which are more political than spiritual. Writer Michael Fisch views Tsuge's use of the quote as illustrative of a specific political message in favor of Japanese unity: "Just as Jesus is speaking [in the passage] against the Pharisees' collaboration with the Romans, Tsuge is criticizing Japan's collaboration with America."[30] It is

Japan's postwar waffling on the issue of using force that killed the rest of Tsuge's unit when they were in Southeast Asia. Tsuge wants to create chaos and confusion in Tokyo, but it is not purposeless chaos. Jesus knew that the message he was preaching was going to be problematic for the people who would believe it, causing rips in the social fabric of the time. Similarly, Tsuge wants to show how his view of a stronger and more active Japan will cause conflict both within the nation and in its relations with other countries.

Patlabor 2 contains another reference to myth that is not directly related to the Bible or Christian mythology, but to the idea of gods more generally. After meeting with Arakawa, Goto meditates on the theme of how technology can make humankind godlike because magic and advanced technology are often indistinguishable. In this sense, Tsuge can be seen as even more of a messianic figure because he wields not only the words of Jesus, but also powerful technology. It is appropriate then that the blimps Tsuge uses to hold the city hostage are marked with the words "Ultima Ratio" ("final argument"). This is very close to the phrase "Ultima Ratio Regum," or "the final argument of kings," that Louis XIV of France ordered to be stamped on all French cannons as a testament to his military might. The use of these words on the blimps likewise identifies Tsuge as full of a sense of his own arrogant power.

As in the first *Patlabor* film, in *Patlabor 2* there is a connection between the results of abusing technology and spirituality. Although the details are different, and the second film unfolds in a different manner from the first, in this aspect Tsuge can be substituted for Hoba. Again, Oshii is trying to get people to realize the problems of technology (represented by the Labors and other military equipment, broadcast media), mythology (through the portrayal of a religious justification for Tsuge's antisocial actions), and hierarchy (the infighting between the different police and the military, the imposition of martial law for the good of the people).

The two *Patlabor* films are remarkably similar in theme and tone, although the second one is much more sophisticated in its execution. Both films involve antagonists who are for the most part unseen and whose goals can only be guessed at, adding to the effectiveness of their terror. Hoba and Tsuge both use verses from the Bible to justify and explain their actions, and in doing so both characters see themselves in the role of Jesus, bringing down a way of right thinking from God. Interestingly, Oshii does not seem wholly opposed to the goals of the antagonists, as he believes that a check on the collective ego of humankind is necessary. Hoba, in the first *Patlabor* film, agitates against Japan's constant construction projects and overexpansion, while Tsuge, in the second film, advocates a rethinking of postwar politics in which Japan is complicit in violence around the world. Oshii shares the antagonists' remorse at the vanishing of old Tokyo and their wariness at the headlong rushing of technological "progress." It is the methods Hoba and Tsuge employ to accomplish their goals to which Oshii is opposed, a fact mirrored in Oshii's critique of how they use religious scripture to validate their actions. Oshii is cautioning his viewers about the justification that religion all too often seems to provide for those who choose to misinterpret it.

In both films, the main human antagonists are hardly present as physical entities, but are rather virtual foes, having made a minion of technology. In the first *Patlabor* film, what the police fight is not a person but a computer virus. The ability of the virus to carry out commands based on the reactions of the Patlabor police who are trying to stop it shows that the virus is observing, watching. Such a form of technological paranoia is probably one of the most common elements in modern science fiction. It is another form of the robot that rises up to kill its masters. Yet Oshii amplifies the paranoia by showing how easily the virus can spread to new systems. It is important to note that the virus was not originally something external that a computer somehow "caught"; rather, it was a part of the original program Hoba incorporated into a new operating system for the Labors. Throughout the terrorist attacks on Tokyo in the second *Patlabor* film, Tsuge constantly observes through various technological means the havoc he is inflicting on the city. When we finally see Tsuge, he is looking at the city through a pair of binoculars, symbolic of his more technologically sophisticated monitoring of the responses to his terrorist actions. In these ways the antagonists of the *Patlabor* films are shown as being mediated through their use of surveillance systems.

For all its bracing critique of technology and the direction modern Japan is taking, *Patlabor 2* is still primarily about the characters and how they grow and change over the course of events. The film marks the conclusion of the events set in the *Patlabor* universe; accordingly, Oshii was careful to involve all of the major characters in the story without making it feel forced (in contrast to some of his previous efforts). Noa in particular has changed greatly over the course of the OVAs, television series, and films. The opening credit scene of the first OVA series introduces Noa and her amusingly technophilic lust for her Patlabor. As the SV2 prepares for their confrontation with Tsuge toward the end of the second Patlabor film, Noa impresses on Asuma that she is prepared to go ahead, saying that she is more than just "a girl who likes Labors" and that perhaps it is time for her to move on. The film also tries to resolve Goto's unrequited love for Nagumo. However, her reaction to the Tsuge incident demonstrates to Goto that some part of her is still in love with the man who tried to destroy the city. Goto sees that he can never be to Nagumo what Tsuge was, and the film ends on this melancholic note.

The two *Patlabor* films can be viewed as companion pieces to Oshii's earlier *Angel's Egg* in regard to the systematic breaking down of religious dogmatism. Yet Oshii feels that there is some truth to religion. In his next film, *Ghost in the Shell,* we see him further exploring religion and mythology while still maintaining his critiques of institutional systems of power.

MINIPATO

After a nearly ten-year hiatus from *Patlabor,* in 2002 Oshii returned with a unique project: *MiniPato,* a comedic look at the world of *Patlabor. MiniPato* was a series of three shorts, the first of which was screened in Japanese theaters before *Patlabor WXIII,* the most recent theatrical release in the series. (Oshii had nothing to do with the third *Patlabor* film other than his original role as a member of Headgear. *Patlabor WXIII* has a much different feel from the previous film excursions in the Patlabor world, omitting much of the philosophical and political depth of Oshii's works, and it plays out like nothing more than a well-executed monster movie.) While Oshii's feature-length directorial work has been becoming increasingly serious, *MiniPato* is a throwback to some of his work on the *Urusei Yatsura* series.

MiniPato came about as the result of a series of illustrations by *Jin-Roh* character designer Tetsuya Nishio, who had made a set of caricatures as promotional materials for the Production I.G. web page. The caricatures of the *Jin-Roh* characters had a unique style and feel to them, particularly because of Nishio's use of the brush pen, instead of the more common animation markers. Bandai liked the illustrations so much that they spoke with Nishio about turning it into an animation project. As the project progressed, Oshii and Kenji Kamiyama (animation director for *Jin-Roh*, scriptwriter for *Blood the Last Vampire*) came on board, and it changed from caricatures of the cast of *Jin-Roh* to those of the *Patlabor* crew.

The most striking aspect of *MiniPato* is its style of animation, a mix of paper cutouts and sophisticated computer graphics for a style that the animators called "3-D CG pata-pata [flip-flop] animation." Although he did not direct the *MiniPato* shorts, Oshii was the screenwriter and came up with the general idea for animation techniques they would use. Said Oshii, "I've been wanting to do three-dimensional flip-flop stuff like tissue paper for several years, and I thought this would be perfect. Both designs and materials would fit in it. Besides, I thought that *MiniPato* would be accepted even if it was a little silly."[31]

The three *MiniPato* episodes demonstrate Oshii's guiding influence. The first episode, "Roar! Revolver Cannon!" ("Hoero Riborubā Kanon!"), consists of Goto lecturing the viewer on the arms of *Patlabor*. Although this episode can be humorous, occasionally it strays too far into a serious analysis of weapons and ballistics. The second episode, "Ah, Victorious 98 Model AV" ("Ah, Eikō no 98-Shiki AV"), is narrated by Shige and is a humorous look at the Patlabor robots themselves. This episode both situates Patlabor within the mecha genre of Japanese animation and pokes fun at the concepts behind mecha anime in general. The third and final episode, "The Secret of SV2" ("Tokushanika no Himitsu"), details a moneymaking scheme carried out by the members of SV2 to mass-produce dried goby fish. Director Kenji

Kamiyama developed the general idea of *MiniPato* as providing background for the *Patlabor* universe, but Oshii was still able to serve up some of his characteristic confusion. Said Kamiyama, "I was blown away by the third one. Both Nishio and I dropped our jaws. We were like, 'What do we do with this material?' I thought Mr. Oshii got me again. I just didn't get it at first."[32]

Not only do the *MiniPato* episodes parody the characters of *Patlabor* in general, they also parody specific scenes from the films. The second episode ends with Shige installing a new operating system on a Labor, causing it to go crazy in an homage to the Babel virus of the first *Patlabor* film. The third episode consists of a monologue by Nagumo, during which select scenes from the first two *Patlabor* films are shown as redrawn in the *MiniPato* style, even recreating some of the image distortion Oshii employed in the originals. Additionally, Kenji Kawai reworked some of the Patlabor pieces he had scored, creating a new soundtrack that sounds very familiar. The *MiniPato* episodes even feature a caricature of Oshii drawn as a dog.

Parody is a large part of the anime and manga experience, and many fans and budding artists produce *dōjinshi,* or amateur comics. Quite a few of the dōjinshi parody already existing anime of manga series, occasionally adding an element of sexuality to the stories. It is unusual, however, for an anime or manga creator to parody his or her own characters in such a public forum as Oshii has done with *MiniPato.* That he does so displays a willingness to experiment in the creation of his craft and a fondness for the characters of *Patlabor.* Additionally, it is heartening to see that Oshii has not lost his comic touch—many of the films in his mature directorial period do not display the same sense of humor that marks his earlier works.

In Oshii's next project after *Patlabor 2,* Oshii goes on to explore the meaning of humanity and the nature of personhood, issues he had touched on in the film. However, *Ghost in the Shell* is much more serious than his previous works, containing few of the glimpses of humor visible in even *Patlabor 2.* Moving away from a central ensemble cast like that of *Urusei Yatsura* and *Patlabor,* in *Ghost in the Shell* Oshii focuses on the journey of a single individual.

Lum holds Ataru in her electric embrace in Urusei Yatsura: Only You.

Ataru runs away from the crowd chasing him at the end of Urusei Yatsura: Only You.

Ataru sees himself reflected infinitely in the transformed Tomobiki High School in Urusei Yatsura 2: Beautiful Dreamer.

Alluding to the myth of Urashima Taro, the town of Tomobiki rides on the back of a giant turtle in Urusei Yatsura 2: Beautiful Dreamer.

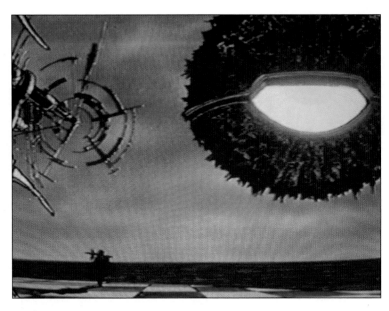

A giant orb descends upon the surreal landscape as a lone figure watches in Angel's Egg.

The girl discovers her precious egg is broken in Angel's Egg.

The large man, the little girl, and a fish in the mysterious apartment in Twilight Q 2.

The detective ponders the meaning of his predicament in Twilight Q 2.

Asuma gets angry in one of Oshii's exaggerated shots in the first Patlabor *film.*

Noa looks out upon the crashing waves as the Patlabor team sets off to destroy the Ark in the first Patlabor *film.*

A blimp crashes in Patlabor 2, *sending a cloud of colored gas through the city of Tokyo.*

Tsuge watches events unfold across the bay in Patlabor 2.

Goto talks to the audience about the weapons of Patlabor in MiniPato. *Note the dog on the left, which is supposed to be a caricature of Oshii.*

A shot in MiniPato *that parodies a scene in the first* Patlabor *film.*

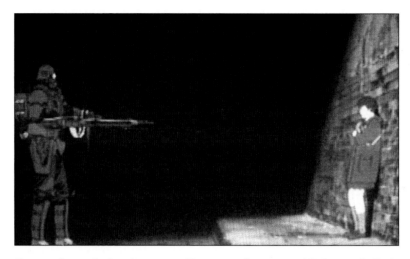

Fuse confronts the bomb-carrying Nanami in the sewers of Tokyo in Jin-Roh.

Kei and Fuse share one final embrace in Jin-Roh.

Saya attacks one of the vampires during a school dance in Blood the Last Vampire.

Saya looks with pity upon her vanquished foe in Blood the Last Vampire.

Kusanagi engages her thermoptic camouflage after the assassination at the beginning of Ghost in the Shell.

Batou sets up the connections for Kusanagi to interface with the Puppet Master in Ghost in the Shell.

Ash commandeers a tank within the game of Avalon in Avalon.

Ash, in "Class Real," has her final confrontation with Murphy in Avalon.

The author in the lobby of Production I.G. next to a replica of the Kerberos armor from Stray Dog: Kerberos Panzer Cops *and* The Red Spectacles. *Photo by Hiroharu Ikemura.*

CHAPTER 6

GHOST IN THE SHELL (1995)

ALTHOUGH OSHII'S REPUTATION AS A VISIONARY director continued to grow through the early 1990s, he was still unmistakably a part of the commercial anime industry. Specifically, he worked closely with the company Bandai, whose various subsidiaries produce video games, toys, and animation. Oshii had been working on another anime project for Bandai between the two *Patlabor* films, but the company suddenly canceled it. Said Oshii, "I was so upset that I asked Bandai if I could direct something else, and they said 'Do whatever you want.'"[1] With Bandai's blessing, Oshii directed *Talking Head* (1992), his personal meditation on the art and industry of film and animation. Although the film sometimes is billed as a mix of live action and anime, the animation does not occupy very much screen time (and only a very small bit of animation at the beginning is in what has come to be accepted as the anime style). Like Oshii's other live action films before *Avalon* (*The Red Spectacles* and *Stray Dog: Kerberos Panzer Cops,* which are discussed briefly in chapter 7), the style of *Talking Head* is very different from that of his animated films. *Talking Head* takes on an obvious staged form, drawing from both Japanese and Western styles, with most of the action taking place as if in a play. In true Oshii fashion, the end reveals that most of the film's events had been dreamed by the main character.

Bandai also was responsible for Oshii's involvement in *Ghost in the Shell,* the film for which the director became best known around the world. After completing work on *Patlabor 2,* Oshii consulted with Bandai Visual about what direction to take with his next project. Originally he was planning to direct an OVA series based on his manga *Kenroh Densetsu* (released by Dark Horse Comics in English as *Hellhounds: Panzer Cops*), set in the same universe as his previous live-action films *The Red Spectacles* (1987) and *Stray Dog: Kerberos Panzer Cops* (1991). Instead, Bandai suggested that Oshii next work on their proposed adaptation of the manga *Ghost in the Shell.* His work on the two *Patlabor* films situated him perfectly to work on this film, as the plot coincided with many of the themes he had been pursuing. Although he had not created the story on which the film was based, Oshii managed to make the work his own; original manga author Masamune Shirow gave him permission to reformulate the plot as he saw fit. Oshii said that he was given the license to direct the film "in my own style, with my own ideas. . . . I had the freedom to put *Ghost* into my world, without having to further ask his [Shirow's] approval."[2] With its mix of concerns about technology and the nature of reality, the *Ghost in the Shell* manga was perfect for adaptation by Oshii. Although largely excised from the film version, the original manga contained a good deal of political critique, and dialogue like "Emphasizing a lifestyle based on consumption is the *ultimate* violence against poor countries"[3] made the source material a good thematic fit with Oshii's previous work in *Patlabor 2.*

As a manga artist, *Ghost in the Shell* creator Shirow is unique in both style and production. Many manga titles are drawn quickly to meet tight deadlines. In contrast, Shirow's manga is very detailed, with complex lines and an equally complex plot. Unlike other manga artists, many of whom employ a stable of staffers to meet publication demands, Shirow draws all of his art himself. In fact, he is something of an enigma; no publicity pictures of the artist exist, and his name is a pseudonym. He made his debut in

1983 with the serialization in a fanzine of his manga *Black Magic,* which was later reissued by a professional publisher; this again sets Shirow apart from most manga artists, who often make their professional debuts through a system of serialization in manga magazines, rather than a repackaging of their amateur work. Shirow also works from his studio in Kobe, rather than the cultural and publishing capital of Tokyo, where most manga artists are based. Like Oshii, Shirow trained at college to become an art teacher, but unlike the film director, Shirow taught at the high school level before he devoted himself to his manga career full time. Shirow's manga display a love of sleek technology and beautiful women. One of the most common motifs in his manga, and especially in his illustration work, is that of sexy women (often youthful and scantily clad) posing with futuristic military weaponry. However, the fetishized feminine forms of his artwork belie the detailed and intelligent plots of his manga.

One of the highlights of the film version of *Ghost in the Shell* is its extensive use of computer graphics, emphasizing the trend of pushing the animation of the unreal in more realistic directions. Said animation director Toshihiko Nishikubo, "*Ghost in the Shell* was the first in animation to explore reality to the limit. We aimed to create animation that is more real than life."[4] Hiroyuki Yamaga, director of the anime *The Wings of Honneamise* (*Oneamisu no Tsubasa,* 1987), has suggested that his film actually began the trend in realistic animation which was later picked up by directors such as Katsuhiro Ōtomo (dir. *Akira,* 1988) and Oshii.[5] By making animation behave more like live cinema, these recent trends in anime serve to make the realities of the directors' imagined worlds more believable. Additionally, the sophisticated computer graphics used in the production of a film like *Ghost in the Shell* mirror the story's commentary on how the increasing use of technology is impacting our everyday lives.

Although *Ghost in the Shell* reportedly played for only four weeks after opening in Tokyo, the film did substantially better in the United States, rising to the number-one position on the Billboard sales charts after a moderately successful art house theatrical run.[6] At the time, it garnered more attention in the Western media than any previous anime film, save perhaps *Akira. Ghost in the Shell* has become one of the most analyzed anime films by Western academics. For better or for worse it has become an ambassador abroad for Japanese animated film.

CHARACTERS

MAJOR MOTOKO KUSANAGI—The main character of *Ghost in the Shell,* Kusanagi is a government operative in a secretive branch called Section 9. She is a cyborg and very feminine in appearance; her body is almost entirely artificial, yet there remains, in theory, an organic core of brain matter in her skull. The main plot of the film involves Kusanagi's pursuit of the mysterious entity known as the Puppet Master.

THE PUPPET MASTER—Also known as Project 2501, the Puppet Master is an artificial life-form that evolved on the Net from a government program. It seeks out Kusanagi as a kindred being, as it is searching for a way to evolve and needs Kusanagi's assistance to do so.

BATOU—Another member of Section 9, Batou is a large, masculine cyborg. Not only Kusanagi's work associate, he is also her only friend, showing genuine concern for her well-being even outside of the work environment.

ARAMAKI—"Old man" Aramaki is the chief of Section 9, and as such is involved in the internal politics of subterfuge that are inherent in such a governmental position. He is Kusanagi's direct supervisor.

SYNOPSIS

A lone figure crouches atop a large skyscraper, the fluorescent city teeming with life below her. Motoko Kusanagi and the rest of her team in the special government division of Section 9 are in the process of assassinating a visiting foreign official. To pull off the hit, Kusanagi secures herself to the top of the high-rise in which the dignitary is covertly meeting with a secretive computer programmer. Kusanagi removes most of her clothing (she still wears a skintight flesh-colored suit) and lets herself fall down the side of the building. In a suite inside, the official and computer programmer are discussing something called Project 2501. Police burst into the room from the main part of the building, at which point the diplomat claims immunity and tries to talk his way out of his predicament. Kusanagi's secured cord stops her at just the right floor. She opens fire with a high-powered machine gun and the official's body explodes in a haze of blood. As Kusanagi continues her descent toward the ground, she activates her "thermoptic camouflage," slowly fading into the background of the city below until nothing more can be seen of her.

After the opening credits, during which the audience is shown a montage detailing the assembly of the cyborg Kusanagi, it is learned that the prime minister's translator has been "ghost hacked." (The film never explains what a "ghost" is, but it seems to be akin to the concept of the soul, although it is something physical that can be detected in a computer scan.) This ghost can be accessed through the electronic lines of data connectivity that serve to link nearly everyone and everything in this future world. The hacking is believed to be the work of the Puppet Master, a cyberterrorist who has caused chaos throughout the world, and Kusanagi and the rest of the members of Section 9 are sent to track him down. After a pursuit involving a garbage truck and a foot chase through crowded city streets, the culprit turns out to be a mere pawn of the Puppet Master. The Puppet Master had erased the man's memory and implanted false memories; even with the advanced medical technology of the time, the implantation of such memories is irreversible.

Taking some personal time off, Kusanagi goes diving in the ocean, an experience that she says always conjures many different emotions in her. As she and her partner Batou sit on the deck of their small boat drinking beer, they both hear the same voice, saying "For now we see through a glass, darkly" (a biblical quote from the book of Corinthians). Although they try to dismiss what they both think they heard, the mysterious voice haunts them. Kusanagi begins to talk about the things that give rise to her concept of self.

She says that such things as a face, a voice, "memories of child-hood," "feelings for the future," and "the extent of the data net," while components of self, also "simultaneously confine [her] within set limits." Although she is a powerful cyborg, she is constrained by the structures of power around her; even though stating she is free to quit Section 9 at any time she chooses, she would be forced to return her cyborg body and the memories contained within. (In this way, the film asserts that Kusanagi is more than just a mental "ghost" inhabiting her mechanical cyborg shell and says that the mind is inexorably linked with the body.)

On a dark, rainy evening, a nude female cyborg torso is brought into Section 9. The conditions surrounding its arrival are highly suspect: A cyborg-producing factory had started up on its own and produced just one body, which got up and left the factory, but subsequently was hit by a truck on the highway and severely damaged. The operatives of Section 9 discover that the inhabitant of the artificial body is none other than the Puppet Master, who claims to be an artificial entity created from a government pro-gram on the Net. Because it has achieved sentience, it is now a fugitive from the government and requests political asylum. How-ever, before a decision can be made or a statement taken, other government agents attack Section 9 and abscond with the cyborg torso. Kusanagi and the other Section 9 members follow the cap-tors, yet Kusanagi alone attempts to retrieve the torso. Her goal is not to bring the torso back to Section 9, but rather to "dive" into it, to communicate freely and deeply with the Puppet Master, whom she believes holds the key to her understanding of self be-cause it is a self-evolved being.

Kusanagi tracks the abductors to a museumlike structure in a crumbling, flooded part of the city, in which she finds a multi-legged armored tank. To get to the Puppet Master she has to try to defeat the tank by herself, playing a game of cat-and-mouse among the pillars of the building. As it tracks Kusanagi, the tank's guns rake across skeletal images of what appear to be large ancient fish on the walls, obliterating them into large pockmarks and shrapnel. One of the most striking scenes of the film is when the tank's fir-ing guns follow Kusanagi up a staircase and continue going up the image at the top of the stairs, a picture of a tree of life painted on the museum walls. The holes in the image continue to climb until the tank runs out of ammunition just shy of the pinnacle of the tree, labeled with the Latin word "hominis."

Kusanagi scrambles atop the tank and tries to force the hatch open, but she ends up ripping her cybernetic body apart in the process. Just as one of the tank's arms has her in a death grip, Batou arrives with an antitank rifle, which stops the hulking machine. As there are no current threats, Kusanagi decides to interface directly with the Puppet Master's cyberbrain. With Batou's help, she is connected to the intelligence residing within the hijacked cyborg torso, and she begins a dialogue with it. As they converse, unmarked helicopters fly toward their location, carrying snipers intent on destroying both the Puppet Master and Kusanagi.

The Puppet Master tells Kusanagi that it has been watching her for a long time and that it needs to try to evolve by merging with her. As an artificial life-form, the Puppet Master lacks the capability for the type of reproduction that engenders variation and serves as protection from extinction. Both of them will change, the Puppet Master says, but such change is necessary for survival. He tells Kusanagi, "Your desire to remain as you are is what ultimately limits you." As Kusanagi sees what appears to be the silhouette of an angel descending from the sky, the snipers on the helicopters are able to target both her and the Puppet Master's body. The Puppet Master is destroyed, but Batou is able to save Kusanagi's head from the incoming fire, although it is blown clear from the rest of her body. As Section 9's helicopters chase away the unknown, Batou rushes to salvage Kusanagi's functioning remains.

In Batou's personal safe house, Kusanagi wakes up in the mechanical body of a young girl. Batou apologizes for the body, saying it was all he could find on the black market with such short notice. He goes on to explain that the situation has been officially covered up but that the foreign minister has been forced to resign and the event has ended in a political stalemate. Smiling, Batou says that the only thing the government does not know is what happened to Kusanagi's cyberbrain. As Kusanagi gets up to leave, she mentions the biblical quote she and Batou had heard the other evening, saying that the preceding lines were "When I was a child,

I spake as a child. I understood as a child, I thought as a child. But when I became a man, I put away childish things." Kusanagi says she is now neither the Puppet Master nor the same woman who used to be known as Kusanagi. As she walks out into the night, she looks out over the city, wondering to where she should now go, concluding "The Net is vast and limitless."

COMMENTARY AND ANALYSIS

Patlabor 2 questioned the nature of reality through an analysis of the ways in which it is constantly mediated, examining many ideas typical of the cyberpunk genre of literature and film. Not until *Ghost in the Shell* did Oshii create a film that fully fleshed out many of these ideas. His film is a meditation on the nature of the self in the digital age, depicting how we may in the future (and to some extent do now) construct our personal identities.

As science fiction writer Bruce Sterling stated, "[c]ertain central themes spring up repeatedly in cyberpunk. The theme of body invasion: prosthetic limbs, implanted circuitry, cosmetic surgery, genetic alteration. The even more powerful theme of mind invasion: brain-computer interfaces, artificial intelligence, neurochemistry—techniques radically defining the nature of humanity, the nature of the self."[7] Such cyberpunk themes are present as crucial visual elements in *Ghost in the Shell*. Although cyberpunk originally was a mid-1980s Western literary movement, its ideas spread rather quickly through Japan, and the novels of genre archetype-setter William Gibson were especially popular.[8] The Japanese interest in cyberpunk is an intriguing cultural reversal, as many American cyberpunk authors incorporated Japanese words or cultural concepts in their works, most notably Gibson in his book *Neuromancer* (1984), one of the best representatives of the cyberpunk literary genre. By incorporating such references, Japan was made to be the battleground on which the conflict between antiquated tradition and technological modernity would play out in the popular consciousness. In his film Oshii is able to use this idea of a technologized Asia to his advantage.

The world of *Ghost in the Shell* is international in scope, an aspect inherent in the original manga and one that corresponds with trends in cyberpunk fiction. (Japan loomed large in the minds of many cyberpunk writers, but it was far from the only locale.) Manga artist Shirow said his original work can "transcend national boundaries. Even native speakers may have different reactions to the multiple meanings I've built into the story through the Japanese characters."[9] The story itself, and the production of the film, reflect its international nature. *Ghost in the Shell* was partially financed by the American-based Manga Entertainment and, according to Manga CEO Marvin Gleicher, was the first Japanese anime film to be partially funded from outside Japan.[10] Additionally, the crew traveled to Guam to study the firing characteristics of machine guns and other heavy arms. (Such weapons are illegal in Japan.) The urban locale at the heart of the story was transposed from the fictional Japanese metropolis of Newport City in the manga to an unnamed East Asian sprawl in the film version that bears a striking resemblance to Hong Kong. At the same time, though, Oshii has downplayed the international scope of *Ghost in the Shell,* and anime in general, saying, "I doubt if there's ever been a Japanese animation produced with the Western audience in mind. I certainly never directed any of my animations thinking about how these might be received in the West."[11]

Cyberpunk and East Asia have not always had an easy relationship. Beginning with *Neuromancer,* cyberpunk literature has tended to fetishize Asia, and Japan in particular. One plausible explanation is that in the latter half of the twentieth century, Japan became the locus for all things high tech. For example, the September 2001 issue of the technology and cyberculture magazine *Wired* bore the image of a computer-generated cute female image—perhaps Kusanagi by way of Sanrio—with technological accoutrements such as cell phone, headset, and a suit that looked like it was made of liquid metal. Bearing the statement "Japan Rocks" superimposed on the technofemale image, the issue contained a special section on Japan whose key question, posed in the title for the introduction to the section, was "Is Japan still the future?" Headlining the section is a piece by William Gibson examining whether Tokyo is still the "futurologically sexy" place about which he wrote in his cyberpunk novels of the 1980s.[12] A subsequent piece, entitled "Ten Reasons Why the Sun Still Rises in the East," briefly details how such things as industrial design, architecture, robotics, comics, videogames, erotica, and game shows make Japan a global pop culture trendsetter.[13] Such articles show how in modern media the idea of Japan is closely tied into the idea of futuristic technology. In the early 1990s David Morley and Kevin Robins wrote that "[t]he association of technology and Japaneseness now serves to reinforce the image of a culture that is cold, impersonal and machine-like, an authoritarian culture lacking emotional connection to the rest of the world."[14] The Orientalism of old was an exoticizing and totalizing mind-set, viewing Japan solely in terms of manifestations like Zen and tea ceremony; this new Orientalism, or Techno-Orientalism, involves Japan's relation to the products and processes of technology. According to Toshiya Ueno, a frequent commentator on Techno-Orientalism and anime, "In Techno-Orientalism, Japan is not only located geographically, as Jean Baudrillard once said, as a satellite in orbit, but also projected chronologically by being located in the future of technology."[15] Techno-Orientalism is the West's fetishization of an imagined technological Japan.

In analyzing *Ghost in the Shell,* it is especially important to keep the ideas of Orientalism and Techno-Orientalism in mind. Because Oshii's films address the intertwined issues of the spirit and technology, some may misinterpret a discussion of these films as falling into a Techno-Orientalist trap. For example, Ueno says of Antonia Levi's book on Japanese animation, *Samurai from Outer Space:* "Her analysis implies that *anime* is more interesting for 'western' people than for the Japanese because of its cultural specificity. The Orientalism reappears when she insists that in Japanese animation, traditional or ancient mythology is very significant, so that *anime* is assumed to be closely connected to cultural identity in Japan."[16] Here Ueno asserts that by closely examining how religion is referenced and reformulated in anime, one is necessarily expressing an Orientalist mind-set; I do not believe this to be the case. By analogy, some people might perceive my present discussion of Oshii's films as being part of the Orientalist and Techno-Orientalist strains of thought. However, the converse of Ueno's criticism of Levi is that mythology is not significant in anime, an odd assertion given the extensive mythological references in anime. Similarly, mythology must be viewed as significant in Oshii's films because he refers to it so extensively. To ignore the culturally specific tropes in anime is to omit completely an entire level of meaning.

Such critiques also miss how the Japanese are responsible for the propagation of Techno-Orientalist formulations of themselves in the West. The Japanese government's White Paper for the year 2000, called "Japanese Government Policies in Education, Science, Sports and Culture," states that "Japanese animation is a fine and unique form of expression due to the techniques of Japanese artists, and there are high expectations for it in the future."[17] Thus, the Japanese government is promulgating anime as a representation of Japan to the world and a cultural export of note. If, as Ueno suggests, anime "is defined by the stereotype of Japan as . . . an image of the future,"[18] then the Japanese government is complicit in perpetuating such stereotypes. This Japan-originated Techno-Orientalism also can be seen through the book *Inside the Robot Kingdom: Japan, Mechatronics, and the Coming Robotopia* by Frederik L. Schodt, an author who has, not coincidentally, written some of the best English-language resources on Japanese comics. Early in the book, Schodt comments, "The Japanese people often refer to their nation as *robotto okoku,* or 'the Robot Kingdom,'"[19] implying that at least certain elements of Techno-Orientalism are of Japanese construction. It is also telling that the publisher of Schodt's investigation of the Japanese robot was Kodansha, a Japanese publishing house. It could be argued that because of his emphasis on technology, Oshii is contributing to formulations of Techno-Orientalism. Many of his films contain a high level of technical detail; for example, the crew of *Ghost in the Shell* took firearms training in Guam in order to more realistically animate the functioning and firing of such weapons. Some of Oshii's films, as we have seen, are set in a not-too-distant future and contain many examples of futuristic technology such as giant robots, cyborgs, artificial life, and virtual reality. However, these films thoroughly question and problematize the presence of such technology. For a Japanese director investigating questions of technology in society, the specter of Techno-Orientalism threatens to overshadow the work at hand.

It must be admitted, though, that examining this fictionalized Japan can provide insights into how we can and should relate to technology in our daily lives. In *Ghost in the Shell,* Oshii provides many symbolic examples of such technological interactions. In the film's look and feel, he is returning to the rich imagery of the film *Angel's Egg* he created nearly ten years earlier. Oshii incorporated some of the visuals and themes of *Angel's Egg* into his adaptation of *Ghost in the Shell.* Although *Ghost in the Shell* is a more technologically sophisticated film, many of the core elements remain the same. *Ghost in the Shell* uses Christian imagery and quotations from the Bible to question the meaning of individual identity and of reality. Perhaps most striking are the similarities in the setting of the climaxes of both films. Both occur in a mysterious building containing the skeletal remains of giant creatures. Also present in both films is a large stylized tree on one interior wall of the building. In *Angel's Egg* the tree makes the soldier remember the great, terrible bird he thinks he once saw, in *Ghost in the Shell* the tree symbolizes the evolution of life itself.

Toward the climax of *Ghost in the Shell,* the use of sophisticated weaponry that destroys both the images of the skeletal fish and the tree in the museum is symbolic of a sense of loss created by the encroachment of technology. If the tank had more ammunition, it would have destroyed the "hominis" label on the tree as well, alluding to the fact that we modern humans are more than capable of orchestrating our own destruction. This scene is illustrative of Oshii's problematization of technology—in one way, we are killing ourselves and our past through technology's sheer drive forward, but in another way (as we shall see), successful negotiation of relationships with technology can potentially open powerful avenues of freedom.

Another allegorical scene in *Ghost in the Shell* is the opening, in which Kusanagi is ordered to assassinate a diplomat. The scene is not long, yet it introduces many of the key issues explored throughout the film. When the diplomat's body explodes, we can see, in addition to the expected internal organs and spinal column, a network of cords and plugs, showing in the brief flash that the man was in fact a cyborg. He may look like a "normal" human on the surface, but he is in fact an amalgam, a merger of blood and microchips. We also can see, as Kusanagi shoots, that the giant fish tank in the room was not real either but merely a hologram; as Kusanagi's bullets shatter the wall, what appeared to be a fish tank does not explode and shower the room with water, but rather goes black like a dead television and fractures like glass. In an attempt to hit Kusanagi, the police in the room shoot out the rest of the fish tank screens in the room, ruining the remainder of the illusion. In less than ten seconds, we are shown that both the man and the fish, whose presence we did not question, owed their existences to technology.

This first scene shows Oshii playing with ideas of mediated knowledge and structures of power. In the *Patlabor* films, he often showed the distortion and alteration of points of view by depicting scenes through various camera lenses and monitors. The world of *Ghost in the Shell* is even more mediated than that of *Patlabor,* and Oshii shows that with the increasing prevalence of technology, even a "direct" apprehension of the world is subject to illusions, such as the holographic fish tank, the cyborg nature of the diplomat, and Kusanagi's thermoptic camouflage. Such mediation of the visual image is indicative of an apparent domination of reality by the forces that control such media structures. In the case of Kusanagi, the system of control is the government for which she works. She is portrayed as being very powerful, but she can use the power only at the behest of her employer, not for her own freedom.

That Kusanagi is subject to control is shown during the credit sequence, which illustrates her assembly. The process of constructing Kusanagi indicates her confinement within her own body. Her organic brain is scanned and placed into a casing that is in turn enclosed by a mechanical skull. Her artificial musculature is covered by a metal skin and coated with a synthetic epidermis. Finally (although this is not explicitly shown), she is inserted into a hierarchy in which she has little choice but to participate, as the government can use her body against her as a prison for her mind. However, Kusanagi is able to find release, not by overcoming the confines of the body, but rather through the further blurring of the mind/body and organic/artificial dichotomies.

The original manga written by Masamune Shirow differs in a number of respects from Oshii's film. The plot involving the Puppet Master was not the only story in the manga, although it was a pivotal one; Oshii chose to focus on this one particular story arc to give the film a better-defined focus than the sprawling manga. Oshii's Kusanagi is a much lonelier character than the one in the manga. She is given to long periods of solitary contemplation, often in conjunction with images of water, such as diving in the harbor. Oshii also uses the film to further his use of the basset hound as a visual trope; it was not a part of the original manga. The dog first appears when Kusanagi and Batou are chasing the man who had been trying to ghost-hack the translator—the man runs in front of a wall mosaicked with posters featuring a basset hound. Later, as the police debrief the hacker, the camera transitions to a television commercial involving the same dog that had been on the posters. The police then show the man the photograph he had been trying to show his partner of his wife and kids; it turns out it is a photo of him with a dog—again a basset hound. The image of the lonely and contemplative Kusanagi and the basset hound are brought together later during a canal cruise. As Kusanagi looks around, observing the detritus of the city, she sees a basset hound on a pedestrian walkway above her, looking down at the water. In a world nearly devoid of friendly human interaction, the recurring basset hound is a reassuring reminder of the foundation of human existence.

Additionally, the film places less emphasis on forthright sexuality than the manga. In the manga, Kusanagi is given a "cuter" character design, with frequent emphasis on the curves of her body. Character designer and key animation supervisor Hiroyuki Okiura says of the film version of Kusanagi that she "is a cyborg. Therefore her body is very strong and youthful. However, her human mentality is considerably older than she looks. I tried to depict this maturity in her character instead of making her younger like the original girl created by Masamune Shirow."[20] Kusanagi has a boyfriend in the original manga and is seen (in a segment edited out of the U.S. release) participating in a virtual lesbian orgy. Although the film version of *Ghost in the Shell* retains a number of instances of female nudity, it is not as exploitative as the original, and actually serves to foster Oshii's mythic ideas.

A number of writings on *Ghost in the Shell,* from both academic and nonacademic sources, have commented on the apparent nudity present in the film. Although Kusanagi is a very powerful female character, this use of nudity has been viewed as weakening her by depicting her body in a sexualized fashion. Author Carl Silvio postulates that the film "appears at first sight to subvert radically the power dynamics inherent in dominant structures of gender and sexual difference, while covertly reinscribing them."[21] Thus an examination of nudity in the film is essential because the use of sexualized images of the body is one way that strong female protagonists have sometimes been subverted in popular cinema. The body is an important unit of control, and by observing Kusanagi as both an erotic figure and a mother figure, her body becomes a personalized form of control within herself.

According to Silvio's analysis, any look at the female body is both eroticized and undermining. For example, he describes the scene on the boat in which Kusanagi removes her wetsuit as "Botau [*sic*], with mouth agape, looking at her, followed by a quick reverse shot back to Kusanagi, the object of his gaze."[22] This account is a mischaracterization of the scene, however, as Batou does not actively look at Kusanagi, but instead turns away when he notices she is changing. Silvio also takes issue with Kusanagi's creation scene during the opening credits and her use of thermoptic camouflage, calling the film's attention to her body "obsessive objectification."[23] One reason for this attitude may be the misperception of Kusanagi as being nude in a number of scenes in which she is actually wearing the flesh-tone bodysuit that serves as a blank canvas for her thermoptic camouflage. The only instances of nudity in the film are in Kusanagi's creation scene, when looking at the torso of the embodied Puppet Master, and at the very end, when Kusanagi's bodysuit has been torn away. This nudity stems not from a position of weakness, but rather serves to mark such scenes as periods of transition in Kusanagi's life. The first scene shows the process of Kusanagi's creation and details her "birth." Nudity in such a context should not be interpreted as necessarily being sexual, but rather portrays the cyborg Kusanagi as more human. The nude scene at the end of the film brings the creation metaphor full circle; she is exiting her life (or rather that period of her life as

"Major Kusanagi") in the same state in which she entered it. Also, Kusanagi's nudity here is appropriate; it can be seen as an outward sign of her intimacy with the nude torso of the Puppet Master. Thus, Oshii's use of nudity subverts the sexuality of the original manga, which presented the sexualized fetishization of the female body.

Another critique of Kusanagi's representation in the film is that she is weakened by her depiction as a maternal being. In *Technologies of the Gendered Body,* Anne Balsamo analyzes a *LIFE* magazine article that details the possible artificial replacement parts for the body of the future. The image of this future person, however, is obviously gendered as male, complete with artificial nonfunctional testicle and lacking any reference to one of the few prostheses that actually was available at the time, the breast implant. Balsamo goes on to say that "[i]n this future vision, the male body is marked by the sign of a full-bodied person whereas the female body is marked only by an artificial uterus; such significations offer an ominous warning about the imaginary place of women in the technological future."[24] Thus, the coding of Kusanagi as an "artificial uterus" of sorts, bearing the Puppet Master's offspring into the Net, must initially be regarded with suspicion.

In her analysis of the female in Japanese religion, Yuko Nakano writes that "[m]any Japanese men have what could almost be called a kind of religious feeling about motherhood, or are caught up by the image."[25] This could account for why Oshii, as a man, has the Puppet Master (whose artificial voice certainly sounds masculine) code Kusanagi as the bearer of their offspring when discussing their pending union. This joining of the Puppet Master and Kusanagi has religious overtones as well; it can allude to the "virgin birth" of Christianity as well as a similar belief in Shintō whereby a *kami* (a god) "might possess a pure and holy virgin and that she might become aware of this divine power and give birth to a child of the kami."[26] However, like all elements of control in his films, Oshii does not use this image of the mother in a customary way, but rather subverts it. Kusanagi, while she may in a sense be the "mother" to the new being she becomes, does not take up the standard social role of the mother in society. Instead, at the end of the film, we see Kusanagi contemplating the vastness of the Net, implying that she will be going out into society as she always has done rather than becoming focused on home and family. There is nothing inherently weakening or discriminatory about being a mother; the social role such a person may occupy is, however. Oshii eschews this categorization and in the process shows Kusanagi as liberated from dualistic roles of man/machine and mind/body.

Deepening the themes Oshii conveys in *Ghost in the Shell* are his allusions to many varieties of religion, including Buddhism, Shintō, and Christianity. For example, the lyrics for the main theme song of the film were composed in the ancient Yamato language and speak of a god descending from the heavens. The song displays a strong Shintō influence and can be seen as alluding to the descent of the Japanese sun goddess Amaterasu, who is the mythological source of Japanese civilization.[27] Again, *Ghost in the Shell* depicts the female as being a source of strength, culture, and empowerment.

Another religious metaphor is the use of imagery involving falling, alluding to mankind's initial fall from grace as depicted in the Bible. Susan J. Napier has detailed these falls in *Ghost in the Shell:* They include the fall from the skyscraper at the beginning of the film immediately prior to the assassination attempt, the metaphorical fall involved in diving in the harbor (after which Kusanagi hears the Puppet Master quote a line from the book of Corinthians to her), and finally her fall into the mind of the Puppet Master at the climax of the film.[28] These falls initially may be construed as a biblical "fall from grace," but in fact Oshii uses the idea of the fall in a much more sophisticated way. In his historical analysis of the Bible, Bernard Batto states that the biblical story of the fall "is not a story of a 'fall' from original perfection at all. Quite the contrary, it is a story about *continuously improved* creation."[29] Thus through Kusanagi's series of "falls," we can see her as improving, finally reaching an apogee through her merger with the Puppet Master—another example of Oshii's intertwining of mythology and technology to reach an "awakened" state.

Oshii makes a quite critical deviation from Shirow's original manga when Kusanagi is given a new body after she has merged with the Puppet Master to become a new entity. In the manga, Batou secures a rather androgynous body for Kusanagi, and he is surprised when Kusanagi, in the new body, tells him that the body is actually male. In the film of *Ghost in the Shell,* Kusanagi's new body is that of a young girl. Kusanagi's maintenance of her female sex is important because of the religious connotations inherent in the female body in Japan. Teigo Yoshida shows how women in Japanese religion can be and have been portrayed as alternately polluted or sacred, depending on context.[30] In the film, Oshii plays with these notions of religious femininity. In the very first scene, Kusanagi attributes the static in her thought reception to the fact that she is having her period. The viewer knows that, as Kusanagi is a cyborg, this cannot be the case and she must be joking. Nonetheless, this serves to mark Kusanagi as feminine, as menstruation is a very powerful symbol of womanhood. Blood of any kind is seen as polluting in Japanese Shintō beliefs, and this idea carried over into Japanese Buddhism as well, generating the concept of the Pool of Blood Hell.[31] Pollution is alluded to again in the climax of the film, when Kusanagi symbolically "gives birth" to the offspring that was a result of her merger with the Puppet Master. (The exact details of what constitute these offspring are never made clear in the film.) Giving birth is an activity often viewed as impure in Japanese culture, but as Yoshida indicates, it also can be seen as sacred. The fact that Kusanagi is a cyborg also sets her apart, not necessarily within the world of *Ghost in the Shell,* but within Japanese culture, as there is a strong Shintō-based taboo against scarring the body in any way[32]; Kusanagi's cyborg body is nothing if not altered and scarred. Yet at the end of the film, it is Kusanagi who transcends her previous existence, while still retaining her female sex. In traditional Japanese Buddhism, "[t]he idea that women could not attain buddhahood has been around since ancient times, and so the theory of *henjonanshi* (metamorphosis of woman into man) was created in order to enable women to attain buddhahood by taking on the form of a man."[33] Thus it is important that Kusanagi keep her original sex during her metamorphosis into a different type of being because it goes against the traditional Japanese Buddhist idea that a woman has to be reborn as a man before she can reach enlightenment.

Ideas from Christian theology are central to Kusanagi's quest as well. When the Puppet Master tells her, "For now we see through a glass, darkly," this quotation from Corinthians indicates Kusanagi's impending freedom from the constraints of Section 9. By using such a quote, the Puppet Master is telling Kusanagi that her way will soon become clear and that they will soon see each other "face to face," as the remainder of the quote says. The chapter of Paul's first epistle to the Corinthians from which the quotation is taken is on God's gift of love, and by using it the Puppet Master is professing its own love for Kusanagi. The Corinthians chapter ends with the words, "There are in the end three things that last: faith, hope, and love, and the greatest of these is love." The Puppet Master's gift of love enables Kusanagi to extricate herself from her bonds as a cyborg worker and to mature as an individual. As she leaves Batou's safe house, Kusanagi tells him what preceded the Puppet Master's original quote. Through the odd manifestation of the Puppet Master's love for her, Kusanagi is able to put behind her the "childish" governmental infighting she dealt with as an operative of Section 9, freeing her to explore more philosophical issues concerning the nature of self.

Kusanagi's merger with the Puppet Master helps her free herself from the hierarchy of Section 9 and the confinement of her previous body. The presence of this hierarchy is shown as being essential to Kusanagi's concept of self as well as its potential downfall through her cyborg body. Although Kusanagi "inhabits" her body, it belongs to the government, thereby ensuring her obedience. Her body serves as her own prison, ensnared by the constant potential for observation. Yet she does not fight directly against this force, but rather discovers a way around it, a way to subvert it. By merging with the Puppet Master, Kusanagi discards the need for her previous, government-owned body and is free to pursue whatever course of action or existential quest on which she may choose to embark.

Thus, through the concept of the cyborg, Oshii can critique the nature of work in the modern capitalist society. Such critiques are not new in cyberpunk science fiction—questions about the nature of work form the backbone of Gibson's *Neuromancer*. Says Heather Hicks, "William Gibson's novels are full of cyborgs whose technological components have transformed their lives into pure work. . . . they have passed from an existence in which they live, to one in which they function—in which they *work*."[34] In *Patlabor,* the robot Labors did the actual work of constructing engineering marvels like the Babylon Project. However, in *Ghost in the Shell,* the worker has moved from inside the machine (contained, yet still separate) to becoming the machine itself. At the same time, one's very existence (at least for those like Kusanagi and Batou) entails being forced to perform work about which one has no choice. The meaning of life has become the meaning of work. This idea continues to mirror previous thoughts in science fiction cyborg films. As Hicks points out: "The very euphemisms for cyborg death in *Bladerunner* [*sic*] and the *Terminator* films imply living is the equivalent of working in the ontology of the cyborg. If to be 'retired' or 'terminated' is to die, must not working be the entire extent of life?"[35] Oshii's solution to this central problem is not to divorce technology from the body, however, but to rethink the relationships between the two. The new Kusanagi at the end of *Ghost in the Shell* still has a cyborg body; however, she has slipped the bonds that previously held her in place, tying her to the government and Section 9.

The idea of the cyborg—the fusion of the body and technology in both real and conceptual ways—has become central in some modern academic thought. Beginning with Donna Haraway's seminal essay "A Cyborg Manifesto," the idea of the cyborg as a potentially liberating force has sparked much debate. Says Haraway: "Cyborg imagery can suggest a way out of the maze of dualisms in which we have explained our bodies and our tools to ourselves. This is a dream not of a common language, but of a powerful infidel heteroglossia."[36] While an in-depth discussion of cyborg theory is beyond the scope of this book, the concept of the cyborg as a radical method to find freedom from domination is one that resonates throughout *Ghost in the Shell.* Through the diversity of life created by the merger of Kusanagi and the Puppet Master, the two beings are trying to create something akin to the "powerful infidel heteroglossia." (This idea is also portrayed in more symbolic form in the destruction of the towering Ark of the Babylon Project in the first *Patlabor* film.) Although Kusanagi's cyborgness initially inscribes her within circles of power beyond her control, had she not been a cyborg, she would not have been able to slip these bonds and the additional restraints of society.

Through Kusanagi's conscious decisions (her quest for a real identity, not one merely assigned to her based on her status in the structure of Section 9, and her choice to merge with the Puppet Master), she creates a new form of life. This being possesses a fuller concept of self than Kusanagi did previously, as she worked solely at the command of the governmental structure. Although she was powerful, she was not powerful for herself, but was rather a pawn of the government and bureaucracy. Kusanagi was confined by the technology of the body, but through the technology of the Puppet Master she is able to slip the shackles of her imprisonment. One can infer that this new life-form will no longer "see through a glass darkly," but finally may be able to see clearly.

As a film, *Ghost in the Shell* occupies an interesting position in the science fiction genre as being a Japanese film that bridges the gap between two Western films, *Blade Runner* (dir. Ridley Scott, 1982) and *The Matrix* (dir. Andy and Larry Wachowski, 1999). *Ghost in the Shell* can be seen as restating a number of the story elements from *Blade Runner,* such as a questioning of the nature of humanity, the fallibility of memory (including the use of photographs to supplant memory), the use of a not-quite human protagonist trying to discover who s/he is while solving a case. As Livia Monnet writes, "[T]he many visual and diagetic correspondences between *Ghost in the Shell* and *Blade Runner* indicate that Oshii's anime has a conscious agenda of remediating Ridley Scott's cult film, and that an intermedial conceptual fusion occurs between the two films."[37] That Oshii would incorporate elements of Scott's work is hardly surprising—in fact, he had already done so in the *Patlabor* OVA episode "It's Called Amnesia" he had written. According to Napier, *Blade Runner* "was important not only to him but has undeniably influenced many Japanese animators."[38] By incorporating such elements, Oshii reformulates and comments on the earlier film, adding an element of history to his already multilayered film. Similarly, *The Matrix* fuses specific elements from *Ghost in the Shell* into its own storyline. This was in fact one of the original goals of the Wachowski brothers when they set out to make their film. Said *Matrix* producer Joel Silver, "The Wachowski brothers showed me *Ghost in the Shell.* They showed me what they wanted to do with that type of action and photography, and try to make it with real people, with real actors. . . ."[39] From the way in which the opening credits were created to specific scenes that were referenced (such as a chase through a marketplace that includes exploding watermelon), *The Matrix* contains many references to Oshii's film, yet succeeds in fashioning its own unique cinematic style.[40] It is appropriate that *Ghost in the Shell* should be an influence on such a landmark American film—after all, modern Japanese animation and comics were originally inspired by the cartoons of Disney and the Fleischer brothers (most famous for their large-eyed creation Betty Boop). Oshii's film thus serves as a link in the continual fashioning and refashioning of global popular culture.

Since the *Ghost in the Shell* film was released, more media have explored its world. A related video game for the PlayStation system, directed by Hiroyuki Kitakubo of Production I.G. (director of *Blood the Last Vampire*), was released in 1997. Masamune Shirow wrote a sequel to his original manga titled *Ghost in the Shell 2: Manmachine Interface,* and with his assistance, Production I.G. also produced a television series called *Ghost in the Shell: Stand Alone Complex,* which began airing in 2002. As of this writing, Oshii is working on the sequel to his film. Called *Innocence,* the film will continue to explore the boundaries of technology and human interaction. Says Oshii on the plot of *Innocence:* "It's a story about Motoko [Kusanagi] and Batou. Batou is gradually replacing his real body with robotics, while Motoko has fused with the network and is bodiless. So it's a love story between a man who doesn't have a real body and a woman who's lost her body."[41] Using the latest in computer animation technology, *Innocence* promises to expand Oshii's reputation for creating complex and visually interesting films.

Like Kusanagi, Oshii was able to find his own form of freedom through the film. The international acclaim of *Ghost in the Shell* boosted his reputation as a director, allowing him more choice and flexibility in pursuing his artistic visions. According to Oshii, thanks to the international success of the film, "It's much easier to get money for projects now. As for myself, I haven't changed at all. Just like always, I make the things I want to make."[42]

CHAPTER 7

JIN-ROH (2000) AND
BLOOD THE LAST VAMPIRE (2000)

FOLLOWING THE SUCCESS OF *GHOST IN THE SHELL,* Mamoru Oshii took a break from directing to focus his energies on other film projects. During this time, he became involved in two films in which he did not serve as director, but was nonetheless a major creative force. The two films, *Jin-Roh* and *Blood the Last Vampire,* are fascinating companion pieces because they are nearly polar opposites in terms of approach and style.

Jin-Roh, with a script by Oshii, is a thoughtful and complex thriller that assumes the pacing characteristic of one his films. The debut film for director Hiroyuki Okiura, *Jin-Roh* demonstrated his ability to depict a truly believable tale of a Japan that could have been. Okiura had worked closely with Oshii on the computer graphics–intensive *Ghost in the Shell,* but decided to forgo the general use of computer graphics effects in *Jin-Roh*; almost all of the scenes were created using hand-drawn cels, one of the few recent films to be animated in this way.

Blood the Last Vampire, on the other hand, demonstrated what sophisticated computer graphics can do for an anime film. With Oshii as supervising producer, the film was directed by veteran director Hiroyuki Kitakubo, whose directing credits include the *Golden Boy* OVA series (1995), *Roujin Z* (1991), a chapter of the animated omnibus *Robot Carnival* (1987), and *Black Magic M–66* (1987) (which, like *Ghost in the Shell,* was an adaptation of a Masamune Shirow manga, and featured the animation talents of a young Hiroyuki Okiura). At a running time of around 45 minutes, *Blood the Last Vampire* is less than half as long as *Jin-Roh.*

Despite the differing approaches by each film's director, both *Blood* and *Jin-Roh* demonstrate Oshii's ultimate influence on each, expanding on themes he had developed in his previous works. Both films are set in alternate Japans of the 1960s, and both films question Japan's involvement with military conflicts as well as the political direction in which the country is heading. Even *Blood the Last Vampire,* a supposedly nonpolitical film, cannot help but be influenced by Oshii's brand of political consciousness.

JIN-ROH

As mentioned in the last chapter, before *Ghost in the Shell* Oshii originally had wanted to direct a short animated series based on his *Kenroh Densetsu* manga. The general scenario for the world Oshii envisioned is that, at the end of World War II, Japan was defeated and occupied by Germany rather than America (although this premise is never stated explicitly). Japan begins to recover both economically and spiritually from the devastation of war, but it faces high crime and violence brought about by widespread poverty. Additionally, armed revolutionary forces on the streets pose a severe challenge to the police. In response, the government creates the Capital Police, a paramilitary force to ensure the security of Tokyo. The armed guerrillas eventually coalesce into a single group called The Sect, which frequently fights pitched battles with the elite Special Unit of the Capital Police, known as Kerberos.

Oshii had explored this Kerberos universe before in his live-action films *The Red Spectacles* (1987) and *Stray Dog: Kerberos Panzer Cops* (1991). However, neither film fully captures the essence of the politically complex postwar world he had crafted around the Kerberos soldiers. Both films focus much more on the main characters as individuals rather than as soldiers; in fact, the fearsome Kerberos armor worn by the Capital Police appears only briefly in the films, which take place after the Kerberos units have been officially disbanded. Like *Talking Head*, Oshii's live-action film discussed in the last chapter, the two live-action Kerberos works are stylistically distinct from much of his anime work. The films often seem very theatrical, with their exaggerated vocalizations and surprising bouts of broad physical comedy. (Much of the force of *The Red Spectacles, Stray Dog,* and *Talking Head* stems from the acting of Shigeru Chiba, who had worked with Oshii as a voice actor as far back as the *Urusei Yatsura* TV series.) None of Oshii's live action films before *Avalon,* however, succeed in the intelligent and thought-provoking ways his animated films do. These films are far from unwatchable, but they project an unevenness of vision that is surprising given Oshii's great successes in the animation medium.

As the Kerberos anime project evolved, the series Oshii originally envisioned gradually evolved into a feature-length film, which was seen by the producers as being more marketable. Both Bandai Visual and Production I.G. saw the proposed film as ideal for the directing debut of Hiroyuki Okiura, who had worked as character designer and chief animator on *Ghost in the Shell.* Bandai originally had wanted frequent Oshii collaborator Kazunori Itō to write the script for *Jin-Roh,* but he did not want the job, and, as Oshii said, "[T]hey reluctantly asked me. You see, I never wanted to do a script-only project, but I figured that if Okiura was going to direct, I could do it."[1] Although Okiura was initially hesitant to direct a film so closely connected to his mentor, he agreed to do it on the condition that the story be an original romance between a man and a woman, not found in the *Kenroh Densetsu* manga. Thus, *Jin-Roh* became the first animated foray into the world of Kerberos.

CHARACTERS OF *JIN-ROH*

NANAMI—A young girl who is working for the terrorist organization The Sect, Nanami functions as a courier, one of the many
Little Red Riding Hoods the group employs to ferry explo-
sives from one part of town to the other. When confronted by
Kazuki Fuse in the sewers, she detonates the bomb she is carrying in an act of self-sacrifice that makes Kazuki Fuse begin
to question his motivations as a member of the Capital Police.

KAZUKI FUSE—As a member of the Special Unit of the Capital Police, Fuse is a constable in part of an elite antiterrorism unit.
After witnessing Nanami blow herself up, he begins to be
filled with self-doubt. Nanami's suicide also leads Fuse into a
relationship with her sister, Kei. (Interestingly, Fuse is voiced
by Yoshikatsu Fujiki, who played the live-action lead in *Stray
Dog*.)

KEI—A seemingly sweet girl a number of years Fuse's junior, Kei
first meets the Kerberos policeman at her sister Nanami's
grave. Fuse is initially struck by how similar Kei looks to
Nanami, prompting in him feelings of remorse and duty. Although wary at first, Kei begins to become romantically involved with Fuse.

ATSUSHI HENMI—An old friend of Fuse's from the police academy, Henmi is now in the Public Security branch of government. He furnishes Fuse with information about what is
occurring in other parts of the police organization and the
government in general. However, Henmi's motives in helping his friend may not be as simple as they appear.

HACHIRO TOBE—Fuse's former training instructor, Tobe takes a
special interest in Fuse's welfare after his encounter with
Nanami. Like Henmi, Tobe's concern for Fuse may be moti-
vated by deeper political connections.

SYNOPSIS OF *JIN-ROH*

The preliminary titles set the tone for the film, stating: "This
thing is like a wolf; this thing is a wolf; thus, it is a thing to be ban-

ished." Unrest rages at night on the streets of Tokyo as the Metropolitan Police and the Capital Police try to keep the rock-throwing protestors in line. A young girl named Nanami, clad in a red cloak, maneuvers through the crowd, carrying a shoulder bag to give to a Sect contact. This man takes the bag to the front lines of the protest and hurls it at the police, where it explodes with great force, prompting the police to charge the mob and beat the protestors with their clubs and shields. Nanami steals away into the underground network of sewers to escape the approaching police, where she encounters other Sect members, who give her another satchel charge to take to a different part of the confrontation. Running through the underground maze, Nanami sees a band of heavily armed and armored Kerberos police approaching. She manages to hide while they kill the other Sect members in a bloody barrage of gunfire, then tries to flee the sewers, but before she can escape she is confronted by a lone policeman in armor. Looking into her eyes, the policeman cannot bring himself to kill the young girl, yet the girl panics and detonates the bomb she is carrying.

Constable Kazuki Fuse is exercising alone in the yard in front of police headquarters, while his superiors inside are discussing his performance and the internal political problems the police divisions are facing. Fuse, the policeman who had been unable to shoot Nanami in the sewers, is recovering from his wounds from the bomb, which had been relatively minor to his body but seemed more damaging to his psyche. Fuse's superiors agree that he be brought before a board of inquiry, where he is ordered to report back to the police academy for retraining.

While at the academy, Fuse goes to meet his friend Henmi at a natural history museum on his day off. Conversing in front of an exhibit on wolves, Henmi gives Fuse information on the girl Nanami and tells him not to dwell on her death. Using Henmi's information, Fuse visits the mausoleum where Nanami's ashes are kept. As he walks through the rows of family vaults, he sees a woman in a red cloak who bears a striking resemblance to Nanami. She turns out to be Kei, the dead girl's elder sister. The two walk through the city together and talk about Nanami. Kei says that she does not blame Fuse for her sister's death, as they were both just doing their jobs. Kei then gives Fuse a copy of "Rotkappchen," the

German version of Little Red Riding Hood, which she says she had been planning to put in the vault with Nanami's ashes.

Back at the police academy, Fuse reads "Rotkappchen" while recalling the events that occurred in the sewers. He cannot get the images of Nanami and Kei out of his mind during a practice exercise, which ends in him getting "killed" in the mock battle. Henmi seems concerned for his friend, and discusses Fuse's poor performance with Tobe, Fuse's commanding officer, who is carefully watching Fuse as well.

Kei sees Fuse on more of his days off; although he seems emotionally distant, they do things couples typically do together, such as going to a playground and an amusement park atop a downtown department store. Looking out over the city, Kei expresses her desire to be free, to be able to go somewhere else and reinvent herself. While on the roof, Fuse has a hallucinatory flashback of Nanami running through the tunnels again. As he chases after her, wolves begin to emerge from the tunnels with Fuse at the head of the pack. After he finally reaches her, the girl becomes Kei and continues walking away. When he tries to talk with her, the wolves rush forward and tear into her flesh, with Fuse unable to stop them. Images of him shooting a machine gun into Kei at point-blank range and Fuse with a pack of wolves in a snow-swept wilderness flash through his mind.

Secretly meeting at a junkyard, some police officials devise a politically expedient plan to restore peace to Tokyo. Signaling a move away from armed conflict in favor of counterintelligence efforts, the various security forces plan to merge their structures into a unified organization. This restructuring carries with it one condition—the disbanding of the Special Unit of the Capital Police. To accomplish this goal, Henmi has been betraying Fuse by maneuvering him into his current relationship with Kei, who used to be a terrorist like Nanami but is now working for the police. Henmi plans to reveal their romance when the time is right, creating a shocking public scandal that will discredit the already reviled Special Unit. Henmi tells Kei to not feel bad because she is not betraying a human being, but rather an animal. Back at the Special Unit headquarters, however, they already know about the plan; the unit has obtained photographs of Henmi meeting with Kei, which Fuse's superiors share with him.

One evening Fuse receives a call from a panicked Kei, who says that strange men have been following her and asks him to meet her. After pulling a semiautomatic pistol from a hollowed-out copy of *Tristan und Isolde* in his barracks, Fuse rushes to the natural history museum at which Kei said they would meet. As Kei waits in front of the wolf exhibit, armed policemen lurk in the shadows, ready to leap on Fuse. Anticipating the trap, Fuse diverts them and reaches Kei, who quickly summarizes the plan to frame him. After stealing one of the unmarked police cars in front of the museum, Fuse and Kei speed away as the government men shoot at them.

Fuse gives Kei the chance to go her own way, but she decided to stay with him, and they break into the department store they had gone to previously, surveying the city at night from the amusement park atop its roof. There Kei confesses to Fuse that their meeting was prearranged and that she is not really Nanami's sister; it was an elaborate plot to discredit the Special Unit. However, Kei says that she still has feelings for Fuse, despite the politics of the situation. Fuse is about to suggest that they run away together, an idea of which Kei is much in favor, yet reconsiders, saying there is still business yet to be completed.

Going into the sewers, Fuse and Kei are met by a group of people coming out of the shadows, bearing bags and cases containing pieces of a Kerberos armored suit. Tobe is one of these people, and he explains to Kei, as Fuse is putting on the special armor, that the Special Unit had known about the plot to disgrace them all along. Tobe says he and Fuse are not men, but wolves disguised as men. They are part of an underground faction of the Special Unit only rumored to exist—Jin-Roh, or the Wolf Brigade. As Henmi and his men from Public Security pursue their quarry into the sewers, led by a tracking device planted on Kei, they are surprised to find Fuse and the others waiting for them. Henmi and his men become the pursued, and are killed in a series of gun battles through the mazelike sewers.

In a desolate junkyard, the Jin-Roh team cleans and stows their equipment. Tobe tells Fuse that in order for Public Security to believe that Kei is in their hands and still alive, she must be killed so that her body is never found. After placing a pistol in

Fuse's hand, Tobe walks to the one building in the distance. The panic rising in her voice, Kei begins to recite the end of the Red Riding Hood tale as she desperately clings to Fuse. As she does so, Fuse's fight with his inner demons is visible on his face. A single gunshot rings out, and Kei slumps out of Fuse's arms, his hand still clutching the smoking pistol. The film ends with the image of Fuse's copy of "Rotkappchen," discarded in the junkyard.

COMMENTARY AND ANALYSIS OF *JIN-ROH*

Loosely based on the fairy tale of "Little Red Riding Hood," *Jin-Roh* is an unflinching look at an alternate postwar Japan. While Okiura did get his wish that Oshii write an original story, many elements of the *Kenroh Densetsu* manga are incorporated into the final film. For example, the scenes of the protesters' fight with the police and their descent into the sewers of Tokyo are taken directly from the first few pages of the original manga. The conspiratorial meeting in the junkyard in which the bureaucrats discuss the need to be rid of the Special Unit was taken nearly verbatim from a similar scene in *Kenroh Densetsu*. A new recruit in the manga named Inui serves as a prototype for the Fuse character in the film. At the end of the first story in the manga, Inui is killed in the sewer by a terrorist woman who, pretending to be an injured civilian, throws him off balance just long enough to shoot him. Before his death, his superiors call him a "lone wolf" and "an abandoned dog . . . a stray,"[2] drawing the same connections between man and animal that feature so prominently in *Jin-Roh*. These connections are present in Inui's very name, as *inu* means "dog" in Japanese. (Inui was also the name of the unrelated main character in *Stray Dog.*) Although *Kenroh Densetsu*'s Inui meets a pathetic end befitting a neglected stray, Oshii obviously identified with the character in the manga enough to recast him as a much stronger presence in the film.

    Jin-Roh not only looks back at an older period of Japanese history, it also reenvisions the landmark anime film *Akira*. Premiering in 1988, *Akira* focused world attention on the Japanese animation industry, demonstrating that anime can be cinema. As is wont to happen to successful films, *Akira* influenced many other films and inspired a number of parodies. One such parody can be seen in the "Seven Days of Fire" *Patlabor* OVA episode Oshii scripted. Even some drawings by manga artist Kamui Fujiwara in the original *Kenroh Densetsu* manga are reminiscent of Katsuhiro Ōtomo's work on his groundbreaking *Akira* manga. Both *Akira* and *Jin-Roh* begin with riotous crowd scenes swarming with antigovernment protestors. Said *Jin-Roh* character designer Tetsuya Nishio about the film's protest scene: "I want to make it as good if not better than the one from *Akira.*"[3] Although *Akira* goes on to tell the story of a gang of teenage bikers and the monstrous power they discover, *Jin-Roh* is a down-to-earth political tale that follows the tragic journey of outcasts of a different stripe. The overall framework of both films differs, but themes of political disenchantment and disenfranchisement run through both *Akira* and *Jin-Roh,* which are set in alternate worlds controlled by a corrupt bureaucracy.

Although the *Jin-Roh* script was written by Oshii, Okiura made many changes. According to Mitsuhisa Ishikawa, one of the founders of Production I.G., Okiura greatly modified one of Oshii's favorite scenes: "The only date sequence between Fuse and Kei that Oshii wrote into the script was a trip to the planetarium in which the two of them gaze at the constellations. They focus on one of a dog and spend something like ten minutes talking about the constellation of the dog. Oshii likes it so much and he thought that those were the best lines in the script, this metaphorical dialogue about dogs. Okiura hated that scene. He was like, 'What the hell! This is not a love scene!' So without telling Oshii, Okiura completely cut that out of the script, and instead added a whole new scene with the couple at a rooftop carnival looking up at the sky."[4]

Oshii was upset that Okiura changed the scene, but he appreciated and understood the film director's prerogative to alter a script to meet his needs. Oshii has said that the story is about the relationship between man and beast, the beast within, more than the relationship between man and woman. By altering such scenes, Okiura recast the script as more of a love story. Of course, being so heavily invested in the *Jin-Roh* project, Oshii felt personally attached to it, especially because it is based in the world he created and explored in manga and two previous films. Although he admired Okiura's approach to directing the film, Oshii could not help but envision how his version of the story would have turned out: "[I]f I had done it, it wouldn't have been the same film," said Oshii. "[S]peaking as a director I have to admit that I regret not having directed it myself."[5]

True to his past works, Oshii used allusions to Western myths and legends to add further depth and detail to his story. He incorporated the tale of "Little Red Riding Hood" into the script because it struck the compromise for which he was looking between a story about a man and a woman and a story about man and beast. Oshii said: "'Little Red Riding Hood' is a very standard tale in Japan and one could say that it is even more popular than our own Japanese folk tales and legends. Also one of the reasons why I chose it is because we do not have many tales concerning wolves in Japan."[6] The version of the story to which the film refers is the German one called "Rotkappchen," which translates to "Little Red Cap." Oshii uses the tale as a political allegory of modern Japan. This is not a novel role for the fairy tale; folklorist Jack Zipes theorized that the Grimm brothers' version of "Rotkappchen" from the early 1800s was partially intended as "a commentary on the French invasion of the Rhineland during the Napoleonic Wars."[7] In the politicized interpretation of the tale, Zipes says that the wolf is a symbol of France as both liberator and oppressor; that "'Little Red Cap' symbolized the innocent German youth who is at first drawn by revolutionary enthusiasm to the French and is then repulsed by the actual cruelty and barbarism of the Revolution."[8] This combination of attraction and revulsion inherent in the story can be seen in the romance between Kei and Fuse. Perhaps not coincidentally, "Rotkappchen" was also the name of a World War II–era German missile. Thus, there is historical precedent for the concept of a militarized "Red Riding Hood" story as in *Jin-Roh*.

The film's first allusion to the folktale is when Nanami picks up the satchel from another Sect member, who describes the bag to her as "a gift for your granny." Both Nanami and Kei wear dark red cloaks, further alluding to the eponymous garment of the tale. Kei later gives Fuse a copy of "Rotkappchen," which had ostensibly belonged to Nanami. However, the version of the tale Fuse reads in the book is different from most traditional versions. Most stories are a variation of Red Riding Hood needing to take food to her grandmother's house, encountering a wolf that rushes ahead to eat the grandmother and later impersonate her to Red Riding Hood, who is either able to escape or is eaten (depending on the version). In *Jin-Roh*'s version of "Rotkappchen," a young girl who has not seen her mother in seven years is forced to wear iron clothes. She is told she cannot se her mother until she has been able to tear them. When she is able to do so, she sets out for her mother's house with a basket of food. The encounter with the wolf remains unchanged, and he races ahead and devours her mother. The wolf then tricks the girl into eating her mother's flesh (an element present in some versions of the story).

In the way the "Little Red Riding Hood" folktale is constructed in *Jin-Roh,* it is not immediately apparent who is innocent and who is the predatory wolf. The most obvious explanation is that Kei is *Jin-Roh*'s version of Little Red Riding Hood, while Fuse plays the role of the wolf. This explanation takes into consideration Kei's seeming vulnerability and her former role as a courier for The Sect, as well as Fuse's ferociousness and his position in the secretive Wolf Brigade. In various places throughout the film, Fuse is compared to a wild animal, and Fuse's commander foreshadows the tragic end midway through the film when he says that relations between beasts and humans always end badly. In the end, Fuse does not want to harm Kei; when all pretenses have been dropped, he still has feelings for her. However, as in his dream at the amusement park, Fuse is like the head of a pack of hungry wolves. He has led them right to her, and there is little he can do to stop them.

While this interpretation of the relationship between *Jin-Roh* and the "Little Red Riding Hood" tale may be the most obvious, it is not the only one possible. The version of "Rotkappchen" recounted in the film mentions the girl having to wear iron clothes. When coupled with the image of Fuse in his Kerberos armor, this allusion could point to Fuse as Little Red Riding Hood. We learn that, prior to the time portrayed in the film, Fuse had been lured into the Wolf Brigade, which had taken all that the young man had to give: his loyalty, his honor, and his soul. The only time Fuse shows any real emotion is when he is forced to shoot Kei at the end of the film; the wolves led him into a trap from which not even love could escape.

Another allusion to myth and legend in the film is the name given to the Special Unit of the Capital Police: Kerberos. The word "Kerberos" is a Japanese version of the word "Cerberus," a creature from Greek mythology that stood guard at the gates of hell. Appropriately enough for Oshii, this creature is a three-headed dog. This mythological allusion is indicative of both the ferocity of the Special Unit and an indictment of Japanese society. As the original Cerberus stood watch over hell, so does the Kerberos unit stand ready to protect society; Oshii is drawing parallels between hell and the maelstrom of confusion and political infighting that marks Japanese society in the story.

Perhaps the most poignant allusion occurs when Fuse, on his way to rescue Kei at the museum, pulls his pistol from a hollowed-out copy of *Tristan und Isolde* by Gottfried von Strassburg. Based on a medieval myth of mainly Irish origin, *Tristan* details the tragic love between the two title characters. The use of this title, evident only briefly on the cover of Fuse's book, foreshadows the tragic demise of the love between Fuse and Kei. This use of the Tristan legend also prefigures Oshii's use of Arthurian lore in *Avalon*. (The Tristan tale, although originally separate from the tales of King Arthur, was merged with them and is often considered a part of Arthurian legend.)

Oshii's concern for the city of Tokyo also appears in *Jin-Roh,* as it did in the *Patlabor* films. Sitting in a playground, Kei and Fuse look at the remains of a demolished structure on a street corner; they cannot remember what had been there before. Kei laments how quickly they forget such things, if they indeed ever noticed them. Although Oshii's criticism of the rapidly changing landscape of urban Japan is nothing new, it assumes a renewed edge when delivered in *Jin-Roh,* set in the late 1950s to early 1960s. Oshii shows that the vicious cycle of building and destruction is not merely a function of late–twentieth century attitudes, but may be symptomatic of a general postwar system of thought, of an almost conscious need to forget the past.

Jin-Roh was created as an animated feature due to this forgetfulness. The film has been criticized for being anime when it should have been live action, as were Oshii's previous efforts set in the Kerberos world. Such a critique makes two erroneous assumptions, however. The first assumption is that live action is the default format in which a film should be created. This way of thinking is indicative of a belief that the director needs a specific reason to make an animated film and should somehow justify his choice through the visual materials he chooses for the film. The second assumption is that Okiura could have made *Jin-Roh* in a live-action version if he had wanted to do so, that there was no reason for it to have been animated. In fact, however, recreating a realistic world of the type detailed in the film would have been very difficult, and certainly beyond the film's budget. Japan's continuous system of tearing down what is old and building anew forced *Jin-Roh* to be animated rather than live action. Okiura would not have been able to film such an expanse of buildings dating from the requisite mid-century time period anywhere in the country. The animated medium of *Jin-Roh* serves as a warning to viewers not to forget the lessons of the past, lest we be forced to survive on simulacra.

As in the second *Patlabor* film, *Jin-Roh* critiques Japan's postwar politics of peace. The film explicitly states that the ungainly policing situation on the streets of Tokyo is due to the government officials' desire to not violate Article 9 of the new constitution. (See chapter 5 for a further discussion of the peace clause of Japan's postwar constitution.) Thus, in *Jin-Roh* the Japan Self Defense Forces (JSDF) cannot intervene in the antigovernment unrest on the streets. As Oshii critiqued a constitution that interfered with Japan participating in international peacekeeping operations, in *Jin-Roh* he critiques a constitution that allows for the creation of such a paramilitary police force. From the events of *Patlabor 2,* it is clear that Oshii is not advocating that the JSDF maintain a presence on the streets of Japan. Rather, he is attacking the hypocrisy that allows for the existence of the Wolf Brigade, a group that violates the spirit but not the letter of Article 9.

Oshii is also highly critical of institutionalized agents of governmental authority such as the police. In previous works, such as the two *Patlabor* films and *Ghost in the Shell,* Oshii tried to depict how people function within overarching systems of control. This theme comes to the fore in *Jin-Roh.* At the beginning of the film, one of Fuse's superiors says that The Sect members are not mere thugs, but rather committed individuals who "don't see themselves as the criminals they are." Through the parallels Oshii draws between The Sect and the authorities, he shows that the statement is equally applicable to the Special Unit of the Capital Police. Said Oshii, "I don't like the police. I've never liked the police, and even now I hate the police."[9] Oshii goes on to explain in part why he feels this way, drawing further parallels between the criminals and the authorities in his films: "The country—or the police/military—commit[s] terrorist acts that are accepted by the government. The laws of the police force or the wars of the military are all approved by the government. They are all committing acts of terrorism with public sanction. . . . We are told that these things are necessary. In those terms, it's the same with the terrorists. They feel they have to do what they do. Terrorists say they are at war. It's just that the rest of the world does not accept their war. The actions of the government, by the police or the military, are accepted. But they are all using violence as a means to an end."[10] Far from idealizing authority, Oshii is trying to show how people can find freedom from such seemingly impenetrable systems.

Jin-Roh also offers a glimpse of the politics involved in the release and distribution of anime, and Japanese films in general. Like Akira Kurosawa's *Rashomon* fifty years earlier, *Jin-Roh* did not gain popularity until it was shown abroad. In fact, *Jin-Roh* was shown in France before the film was released in Japan. According to anime critic Takashi Oshiguchi, as "in Japan, there is a tendency not to resist a film's release if it was regarded favorably abroad," the long domestic distribution run of *Jin-Roh* in Japan was "based on the acclaim that it got from playing in one theater in France."[11] Ironically, this early debut in France eventually disqualified *Jin-Roh* as a nominee for the first Academy Award for Best Animated Feature at the Seventy-Fourth Annual Oscars in 2002.

BLOOD THE LAST VAMPIRE

At the heart of *Blood the Last Vampire* is a group known as Oshii Juku, or Team Oshii.[12] Oshii coached this small group of writers and animators in how to pitch ideas for animated shows. Said Oshii, "[Production I.G. founder] Ishikawa asked me to make a project team of young creators, that could be the center of film making in I.G. I accepted since I owed him so much."[13] The study group would write stories based on assigned ideas, such as "under-sea stories" or "vampires," and then would gather each week to critique one another's work. The story elements of *Blood the Last Vampire* came together from a number of different ideas pitched at these Team Oshii meetings.

The general atmosphere of *Blood*—one of gruesome foreboding—came about because of director Hiroyuki Kitakubo's encounter with the American film *Se7en* (dir. David Fincher, 2000). Production I.G. head Ishikawa frequently got tickets to press showings of films, and he often took staff members along with him. According to American animator Scott Frazier, who was working at Production I.G. at the time, he, Ishikawa, and Kitakubo went to a press screening of *Se7en*. A tale about a serial killer who dispatches his victims in particularly original and nasty ways, *Se7en* contains an admirable mix of atmospheric chills and nausea-inducing gore. Said Frazier: "We went and saw *Se7en*, and we didn't know what it was, we just walked in cold. . . . [The film] just blew [Kitakubo's] mind. That totally fixated him on doing something with an atmosphere [like that of *Se7en*], so he had that in his mind and he said 'I'm going to do that with *Blood*.'"[14]

Although he is only in his late thirties, Kitakubo has worked in the animation industry for over twenty years. At age fifteen, while still in junior high school, Kitakubo got a part-time job at an animation studio. Among his other films, Kitakubo collaborated with Yūji Moriyama (*Project A-ko*) on an episode of the *Cream Lemon* OVA series called "Pop Chaser," which features "interstellar Wild-West lesbian antics inside a giant robot suit."[15] Some of Kitakubo's more notable projects have involved *Akira* director Katsuhiro Ōtomo, namely *Robot Carnival* and *Roujin Z*. Immediately before his work on *Blood,* Kitakubo had worked with Production I.G. on its video game version of *Ghost in the Shell,* directing the game's animated segments.

CHARACTERS OF *BLOOD THE LAST VAMPIRE*

SAYA—The last remaining "original," Saya works for a mysterious organization, hunting and killing the vampires that have infiltrated human society. Although her age is indeterminate, she looks like a young woman. (Interestingly, the word *vampire* does not appear until the end of the film. Instead, the word used to describe the vampiric creatures is *chiropteran,* meaning "bat.")

THE NURSE—Working at Yokota High School, the school nurse is one of the first people Saya encounters on her first day. Her position and ill fortune bring her into direct contact with the vampires infesting the school, and she ends up fighting for her life alongside Saya.

DAVID—As Saya's commanding officer, David oversees and supports her actions as she tries to rid Japan of the chiropteran menace.

SHARON AND LINDA—Students at Yokota High School, Sharon and Linda seem to be normal American girls, although Linda does have an ill pallor because of her "anemia." However, the girls are hiding a deadly secret, one that brings them into direct contact with Saya.

SYNOPSIS OF *BLOOD THE LAST VAMPIRE*

At night in Tokyo, two figures are the only remaining passengers in a car on a nearly deserted subway train heading to Asakusa. A sullen-looking girl warily eyes the man at the other end of the car, who seems to be an exhausted, rumpled businessman. As the train speeds along, the lights in the car suddenly go out, and the girl leaps up, charging at the man. As he scrambles to open the door to flee into the next car, the man is cut down by the sword the girl suddenly draws, and he collapses.

In Asakusa, two Americans rush to the train platform, looking for the girl, who has stuffed the body of the dead man in the space between two subway cars. David and Lewis, the American men, speak with Saya, the girl, about what just happened. Saya complains that her sword is getting too dull and asks David to get her a new one. As they speak, Lewis boards the train to investigate, and is disturbed by the dead man, who looks human, not like the monstrous form of a "chiropterate." Lewis's behavior infuriates Saya who, although substantially smaller, grabs his head and lifts him off the ground. David manages to calm her down, sending her off with her new mission to hunt and destroy other vampires. After Saya leaves, David yells at Lewis, telling him to not anger Saya anymore, because, as the last remaining "original," she is essential to their operations.

On her way to her new assignment the next day, Saya pauses to look at a pair of Japanese swords on display at an antique store. Saya, dressed in the sailor suit uniform typical of Japanese schoolgirls, arrives at the high school on Yokota Air Force Base and, after a brief exchange with the school nurse in the hall, meets with the principal. David is already in the principal's office and makes the necessary introductions, having explained that Saya wants to see what classes at the base school are like. The principal warns Saya that the classes probably will not be doing much work due to preparations for the Halloween party the next day. After David and Saya leave, the nurse asks the principal if continuing with the party is such a good idea, given the recent mysterious suicide at the school; the principal dismisses her concerns as frivolous. David and Saya know they must act quickly, as more corpses have been turning up in the vicinity of the base. At the school after hours, Saya sifts through the student records and searches the infirmary, which her senses tell her to be the vampires' "dining room."

After school the next day, during the Halloween party, Saya follows Sharon and Linda, two girls she has noticed from her classes, to the infirmary. As Linda is about to pounce on the school nurse, Saya rushes in with her sword drawn, killing Linda in a violent splatter of blood. Sharon escapes the room, her face now monstrously contorted, and manages to break Saya's sword and flee down the hall. Saya runs to the nearby antique store, takes one of the Japanese swords, and hurries back to the school. Confused about what she has seen, the nurse follows the blood trail to the dance hall, where the now fully inhuman Sharon vampire, cloaked partially by a long banner wrapped around her body, lies in wait. Saya tries to kill the monster, but her new sword turns out to be a fake; when she tries to use it to attack, it merely bends. The creature then grabs the nurse and, still drawing little attention from the surrounding crowd, walks out of the building with her. David, newly arrived to give Saya backup, is faced with another crisis: A second vampire is slowly advancing toward the base.

Outside, Saya manages to distract the Sharon vampire enough that she lets the nurse go. Running away, the nurse encounters a genial security guard who tries to reassure her, but is soon eviscerated by one of the monsters. Saya drives the creature away and arrives just in time to save the nurse from a similar fate. Pausing only to pick up the security guard's gun, they begin to run.

The two women search a supply hangar for something to use as a weapon that will make the vampire, which Saya describes as an *oni* (demon), lose enough blood in one blow to kill it. However, the Sharon vampire locks them inside the building and drops in though the skylight. David chases the other vampire to the hangar in which the women are now trapped. As Saya fends off the vampire inside the building, she tells the nurse to use one of the jeeps as a battering ram against the doors. After the nurse knocks the doors away, David rushes in and throws Saya a new sword, which she quickly unsheathes and uses to kill the Sharon vampire.

The vampire David had been pursuing stands on the roof, sprout wings, and takes off. David and Saya place the now-unconscious nurse on a strip of grass and drive the jeep toward the runway, after the creature. The vampire flies low and close to a cargo airplane, ready to grab onto it. David drives Saya close enough to it that she can slash it out of the air with one stroke. As it lies dying on the runway, though, Saya runs to it and give it a few drops of her own blood, easing its pain.

After the confusing events of the evening, the nurse is debriefed by military personnel. In the process, they show the nurse a picture of a young girl and ask if it is the same one she saw the previous night. Although in period dress, the circled face in the photograph is unmistakably Saya's. Two notes on the photo add to the nurse's confusion: One says "AD1892," and the other reads "vampire." She returns to the infirmary to ruminate on the mysterious events, wondering if Saya will continue to kill the creatures just as humans kill each other. As another plane takes off from the base, a radio news report talks of renewed fighting in Vietnam. The ending credits roll atop distorted live-action images from the Vietnam War.

COMMENTARY AND ANALYSIS OF BLOOD THE LAST VAMPIRE

For all its carnage, *Blood the Last Vampire* is a startlingly beautiful amalgam of traditional-looking animated characters and computer-generated sets and backgrounds. Its producers have called *Blood* the "first digital theater animation," meaning that it was the first theatrically released anime film created using digital computer animation rather than traditional cel animation. The time-intensive animation technique accounts for the relatively short running time of *Blood the Last Vampire,* and director Kitakubo has cited software and hardware issues as the reason why the film could not be longer.[16] In the film, the story serves to showcase the advanced animation techniques, rather than using the animation as a way of telling a story.

It is interesting that for his Team Oshii teaching project, Oshii guided his team to create a film that is unlike anything he has ever directed himself. While *Jin-Roh* possesses a number of the hallmarks of an Oshii film, *Blood the Last Vampire* contains very few; in fact, the two films are diametrically opposed, which is striking given that they were produced by the same studio at around the same time. The basis of *Jin-Roh* is the politically complicated machinations within the bureaucracy; the tale of killing menacing vampires in *Blood* is relatively simple. As mentioned previously, *Blood* was produced entirely digitally, while *Jin-Roh* was created using primarily cel animation (although the end product was a mix of cel and computer technologies, and according to Oshii, three of the shots were completely digital[17]). *Jin-Roh*'s slow, fluid shots make it seem to run longer than its ninety minutes, while *Blood*'s fast-paced action makes it seem shorter than its forty-five minutes. (As an interesting coincidence, the same year *Jin-Roh* was disqualified as an Oscar nominee for debuting too early, *Blood* was removed from consideration for being too short to qualify as a "feature.") Also, the directors of the two features are opposites in

terms of background and experience. *Jin-Roh* was Hiroyuki Okiura's directorial debut, but *Blood*'s Hiroyuki Kitakubo was an experienced anime director, having begun work in the anime
industry in his mid-teens.

One interesting aspect of *Blood* is its use of language. Most
anime films are created with Japanese dialogue, but *Blood* employs a mixture of English and Japanese. One of the few other
anime to use this technique was one of Kitakubo's previous directorial efforts, a segment of the animated compilation *Robot Carnival* titled "Strange Tale of Mechanisms from Meiji Culture: Volume
of the Red Haired Man's Invasion" ("Meiji Karakuri Bunmei
Kitan: Kōmōjin Shūrai no Maki"), better known by its English title
of "Tale of Two Robots." A comedic take on the anime convention
of mecha fighting, the story involves a stalwart crew of young
Japanese trying to thwart the destructive urges of an English-
speaking mad scientist and the giant robot he has built. (Ishikawa
has said that Kitakubo was chosen to direct *Blood* in part due to
the skill he demonstrated in working on this short film, as well as
computer skills.[18]) The scientist's dialogue, delivered in a bad German accent, sounds forced and over the top, adding to the silliness
of the piece. However, while the use of cheesy English enlivened
"Tale of Two Robots," anime and the English language do not
mesh so well in Kitakubo's *Blood*. Many of the English-language
voice actors sound stiff and wooden, a fact not helped by a script
that offers little in the way of originality. Said Scott Frazier, who
wrote the English portions of the script, "What you hear in *Blood*
is my first draft—it's awful. When I saw the staff showing, I was like
'Oh holy shit!' because I never got the chance to rewrite it."[19]

Similarly, the character of Saya is not a unique type for
Japanese animation. She is portrayed as the archetypal "tough
girl." It said in *Blood* that Saya is an "original," implying that the
vampires she hunts are her children or close relatives. (Their precise relationship is never explained in the film.) However, even this
role is not unique to *Blood;* in the animated film *Vampire Hunter
D* (1985), the vampire had to kill his own kind. Saya does not seem
to give her connection to the other creatures much thought in the
film until the very end, when she gives some of her own blood to
the dying vampire to ease its pain. This scene is one of the few in

which Saya loses her fearsome countenance, appearing almost beatific. This image shows Saya to be harboring understandably conflicted feelings about having to kill her kin, although the moment is unexpected, as she had not previously displayed any feelings of kindness or remorse. Ultimately, however, this scene is not enough to save Saya from being a one-dimensional character.

Saya's sartorial choice is worth noting, though. Other than in the first scene on the train, Saya is clad in a sailor suit uniform, which has come to be fetishized by some men in Japanese society. Ishikawa of Production I.G. said that part of Saya's look was a marketing gimmick: "That [use of the sailor suit] was for the otaku [obsessive anime fans]. Otaku like sailor suits and they like girls that are naïve about sex. They're the people that are going to buy the DVD."[20] However, the fact that Saya is shown so often as being fearsome and inhuman (which she in fact is) problematizes her fetishization as a sexual object. In this way, *Blood the Last Vampire* actually subverts a number of assumptions viewers may hold about the depictions of uniform-wearing heroines in Japanese animation. And yet Saya's role in the film fits nicely with other currents in postwar Japanese popular culture. According to sociologist Sharon Kinsella: "Contradicting, faintly, the notion that uniforms foster spiritual uniformity among those wearing them, military uniform in contemporary Japanese culture has been linked to stories with extremely strong characters. Uniformed characters are frequently heroic, tragic, passionate, uncontainable. Overall, the impression given is that Japanese people in uniform have an intense subjective presence."[21] The character of Saya indeed fulfills all of these descriptors. Thus, Saya's schoolgirl uniform has the added feature of setting her apart as a special figure within *Blood*'s narrative. This aspect is reinforced by the fact that she is both the only Japanese student attending the Yokota school and the only one wearing a Japanese-style uniform.

In spite of the film's visual excellence, many of the characters look unreal, more so than in many anime. The smoothly rendered computer graphics and detailed backgrounds highlight the oddity of the characters themselves. Unlike in other anime, in which fanciful characters may participate in an equally fanciful world, the surrounding world of *Blood,* animated in a way that conforms to real life, heightens the audience's expectation to see realistic-looking characters. However, many of the characters look like dolls, with wide, unblinking eyes set below high foreheads. Some, such as the high school principal, with his outrageously coiffured hair, are almost beyond belief in the context of the film. The character designs serve to blur the line between human and inhuman. Just as Lewis questions whether the man Saya killed at the beginning of the film was human or vampire, we are invited to question whether *any* of the characters are truly human. The designs serve to indicate the true theme of the film, which is a questioning of the line that divides human from monster.

There is a strong interplay between light and dark in the film, which again serves the theme of questioning the assumption that light is preferable to darkness. The bulk of the scenes in *Blood* take place at night or in dim lighting. Even the daytime scenes in the school are cast in the long shadows of an autumn afternoon. This pervasive feeling of twilight adds to the overall creepy effect of the film, but also portrays Saya as a creature of the night and inhabitant of the darkness. Thus, in the film, both the hero and her antagonists are associated with darkness. The only time there is brilliant sunlight is at the very end, after the events of the story have been resolved. This light is an illusion, however, because in the midst of such a thankful reprise, a giant bomber takes off from the airbase, on its way to sow further seeds of destruction in Vietnam. Daylight is the realm of the human world, yet the war symbolized by the airbase is just as terrible as the conflict between Saya and her prey. The parallel between the horrors of the previous evening and the dispatch of the bomber indicates that that which is most frightening does not happen only at night.

With its coda alluding to the war in Vietnam, *Blood* has been seen by some as an antiwar film that repudiates Japan's collusion with the United States in that conflict. Such a view would be in line with themes from Oshii's other films, most notably the second *Patlabor* film. However, because *Blood* was directed by Hiroyuki Kitakubo and not Oshii, it is questionable how strong a link was intended to be made between vampires and Vietnam. *Blood* scriptwriter Kenji Kamiyama said he did not believe there was an ideological goal with the ending of the film: "Honestly, we weren't really thinking about making any kind of political statement."[22] This sentiment is echoed by Scott Frazier, who said that the ending "was more to give [the film] atmosphere than anything else. I don't think there was any real intention of making a statement. . . . No, Kitakubo's not really into [making] statements."[23] Production I.G. head Mitsuhisa Ishikawa has a different view of the *Blood*'s ending, however; he theorizes, "The ending theme highlights the nature of Vampires [*sic*] in light of human nature. Vampires kill out of necessity. To live. Humans are far more violent because they're violent for political reasons; they're violent when they don't need to be violent, to make a point. So the question that Hiroyuki [Kitakubo] poses is, 'Are humans more violent than vampires?'"[24] In his essay "Streaks of Red and White: The Long Short Time of the *Blood* Anime," Carl Gustav Horn draws concrete connections between *Blood the Last Vampire* and the events that surrounded the Yokota Air Force Base during the time of the Vietnam War. Ten days before the events of the film, U.S. Secretary of State Dean Rusk had visited Yokota, and President Johnson "himself spent that very Halloween night [of the events of *Blood*] right across the water in South Korea, trying to firm up support for U.S. policy in Vietnam."[25] Even though the events of *Blood* are fictional, their roots lay in a more commonplace, yet perhaps more sinister, act of political vampirism. It is no coincidence that the vampires in the film are clustered around a U. S. airbase—the base itself serves as a form of vampire, taking the Japanese land and sapping its vitality. Yokota has figured in other works by Oshii, most notably as a possible port of entry for nuclear weapons in *Patlabor 2* (as well as, more humorously, the source of Kanuka's illegal pistol in *Mini-Pato*). Thus, for Oshii, Yokota serves as weak point in Japan's landscape, permeable to dangerously imperial imports. Thus, while some of the staff members may not have had a specific agenda in mind, Oshii's influence can be felt in this use of a vampire tale as political allegory.

 Blood the Last Vampire was a success on a purely visual level, but as a cohesive work of film it left much to be desired. Even Oshii was not entirely pleased with the end result. "To tell the truth, I don't really like how it ended up. . . . I think visually, it's magnificent—all the elements in that area are of a very high standard. But movies aren't just about the visuals; it's a balance of direction and other elements. I thought that this balance was lacking in the completed work."[26] However, the overall story of the *Blood* universe is somewhat more complex than what is shown in the film. According to scriptwriter Kenji Kamiyama, what became *Blood* was originally supposed to be the middle installment in a three-part trilogy released to video.[27] Although no other films have been released yet that fill in the gaps left by *Blood the Last Vampire,* additional stories have been told in other media. Two games for the PlayStation system, a novel written by Oshii, and a manga all greatly expand on the story. Of these supplementary media, only the manga by Benkyo Tamaoki has been released in English, under the moniker *Blood 2000.* Continuing the story of Saya in present-day Japan, the manga dispenses with the film's symbolism. *Blood 2000* describes a side of the *Blood* universe that is both sadistic and sexy, which is appropriate given that Tamaoki is best known for drawing pornographic manga. The manga presents a leaner, hungrier story that Horn, who edited its English-language version, describes as "a lot more punk—I like to say that if the anime is Nine Inch Nails, then the manga is the Misfits."[28] It has also been rumored that a full-length follow-up to the *Blood the Last Vampire* film is in the planning stages and that director Ronny Yu (*Freddy vs. Jason, The Bride with White Hair*) is trying to acquire the rights for a live-action remake of the film.

CHAPTER 8

AVALON (2000)

After a five-year hiatus, Oshii returned to feature directing in 2000 with the film *Avalon*. Through his new film, Oshii would revisit many of the characteristic visual themes he had been working on in *Ghost in the Shell*, but this time he would move away from animation and conduct his film in the realm of live action.

I have mentioned that Oshii's *Ghost in the Shell* was a formative influence on *The Matrix*. Although *Avalon* was a project Oshii has said he had been trying to formulate for a number of years, before *The Matrix* was released, the film's execution seems like Oshii's response to the Wachowski brothers cribbing a number of elements from *Ghost in the Shell*. Perhaps *Avalon* was an attempt to compete with *The Matrix* on its own terms, using live actors and scenes heavily manipulated by digital technology. *Avalon* is certainly less flashy than *The Matrix;* Oshii's film lacks the pumping techno soundtrack and kung fu battles, and even tones down the gunplay the Wachowskis referenced in *Ghost in the Shell*.

Like *The Matrix,* though, Oshii incorporates advanced computer graphics into a film with human actors to create an amalgam that is as much animation as it is live action. Although Oshii had tried to make animation more realistic with some of his previous films, especially *Patlabor 2* and *Ghost in the Shell,* with *Avalon* he is trying to make live-action films more animated. When asked about the difference between the two forms of filmmaking, Oshii has predicted that they will merge into a fusion of the two media: "They are the same thing. . . . In the future, there will be no difference [between animation and live action.]"[1]

In *Avalon,* Oshii is trying to steer his science fiction works away from ideas of how the future might look toward commentary on current technological trends. Said Oshii, "There's no relationship between the future described in the film and the real future. If anything, I think I described the present day."[2] Indeed, while the idea that someone can make a living by playing games, as does *Avalon*'s main character, may have seemed ludicrous at one time, game technologies have evolved to enable players to profit from such activities as betting on the online games they play and selling their game information for real-world money.[3] Oshii highlights such technologies not for their own sakes, but to illustrate his deep concern with how they affect human interactions. The look of the virtual worlds in the film may be more sophisticated than any virtual reality currently created, but the film's ideas bear directly on the preponderance of technology in modern society.

CHARACTERS OF *AVALON*

Asʜ—An expert warrior in the game of Avalon, Ash is at first the consummate player, having little time for people outside of the game. She is called Ash because of the white streak through her character's hair when she plays the game. Her only companion is a basset hound she keeps in her apartment, which she feeds better than she feeds herself. A meeting with her old teammate Stunner sets her on a course that takes her to the heart of the Avalon game itself.

Sᴛᴜɴɴᴇʀ—One of Ash's former teammates in the group Wizard, Stunner is still trying to eke out a living by playing the game.

As a thief character in Avalon, Stunner finds it difficult to find other teams to join and nearly impossible to go solo as the warrior Ash has done. When he chances upon her outside her branch of the Avalon gaming center, he tells her about Murphy.

MURPHY—A former member of Wizard, Murphy became a solo player after the group broke up. Murphy had gone after a mysterious character in the game called "the Ghost," a wispy apparition of a girl, to find a special game realm that would enable him to earn many experience points. However, in his quest Murphy became one of the "unreturned," a living vegetable, and Ash decides to find out what really happened.

THE BISHOP—A mysterious man, the Bishop is not known by any name, only by the type of character he plays. He watches Ash from afar both inside Avalon and outside the game.

GAME MASTER—A mysterious older man, the Game Master is only seen on computer monitors. He is one of the few people to whom Ash regularly speaks, but it is unknown if he is, or ever was, a real human being. His constant uniform resembles that of a priest, a black tunic with a white collar.

SYNOPSIS OF *AVALON*

Much like *Ghost in the Shell, Avalon* begins with a textual prologue setting the scene in a near future in which modern young people use an illegal virtual reality war game to "deal with their disillusionment by seeking out illusions of their own." The prologue goes on to warn of the dangers some have experienced, becoming brain-dead in the process of the game, although some players are so skilled they can make a living from playing the game. The prologue even explains the name of the game, Avalon, as "the legendary island where the souls of the departed heroes come to rest."

The film opens on a scene of orange computer graphics and data, dissolving to a sepia-toned war scene of tanks rolling across a grassy plain. This is Avalon, the dangerous virtual reality war game mentioned in the prologue. A figure wearing military equipment and concealing headgear materializes onto the scene, which then changes to that of a crowded city, with more tanks rolling down the center of the street. This figure is a woman, named Ash because of the gray-blond streak through her character's hair. Ash fights with great skill against her enemies in the game and even manages to bring down a heavily armed helicopter by herself. As the helicopter explodes, the words "Mission Complete" flash across the sky, superimposed on the large fireball. As Ash walks away, satisfied with her day's work, we see a mysterious hooded figure observing her from afar.

The film transitions from the simulated world of the game to the "real" world, with viewers seeing Ash sitting by herself in a dimly lit room, full of decrepit-looking machinery and wearing a large helmet that covers most of her face. In spite of her recent victory, her body language does not convey a sense of joy or happiness. In fact, as the camera pans over her, she seems to be a pathetic figure, sitting in the only chair in the room, plugged into the game, her body still. When she removes the helmet, we see that she looks the same as she did in the game, but in real life her hair does not have the streak of blond. She speaks with her gaming representative, a talking head on a video screen, to purchase some ammunition, and then heads to her apartment, stopping to collect the money she earned.

For those like Ash who live in the world of the virtual, the passage of time in the "real" world has little meaning. Through a montage sequence, viewers are shown how repetitive Ash's daily life is; we are left with the impression that time has passed, but we cannot be sure how much. One day when walking out of the Avalon center, Ash runs into Stunner, one of her old teammates. Viewers learn that their team, Wizard, used to be one of the best in Avalon. The game seems to be organized around archetypal character types found in role-playing games. Ash, because she is a Warrior and can function independently, has gone solo since the breakup of Wizard. She learns from Stunner that Murphy, another former member of Wizard, had also gone solo but is now a mental vegetable being cared for in a hospital.

Stunner reveals to Ash that Murphy was in search of a secret level in the game Avalon called "Special A," from which players cannot reset to escape the game, but which earns them many experience points. It is rumored that at certain places in the game a girl called "the Ghost" (the English word is used) appears, and she is the key to accessing this special level. Everyone who has tried to go after the girl has ended up as Murphy has—a living vegetable. Ash goes to the hospital to visit with the living shell that was once Murphy, but on her way out she is again observed by a mysterious bald figure.

After performing a search on the information Stunner gave her, Ash asks the Game Master about the "Nine Sisters," a term she came across in the course of her query. The Game Master tells her the story of how the dying King Arthur was carried across the water to the land of Avalon, where his wounds were tended by Morgan le Fey, one of the nine sisters. Ash relates a similar mythological tale, in which a shipwrecked Odin is carried across the water and given a ring by Morgan that grants him immortality and youth forever. However, he also is given a crown that makes him forget about his home and the entire outside world.

Ash returns home after a mission and begins to prepare a deluxe meal from fresh ingredients, painstakingly chopping the vegetables and slicing the meat. However, the stew she creates is not for herself, but for her dog. After she put the meal in its dish, though, she notices that the dog is not in the room. She looks throughout the apartment and combs the area around her building but is unable to find the dog.

To find out more about what is occurring in the world, Ash goes to a bookstore and purchases some books on King Arthur and Arthurian legend. On the way out of the store, she finds Stunner waiting for her, tempting her with information of how to get into Special A. Over breakfast he tells her what he has heard: Every time the Ghost appears, there is a character of high-level Bishop class in the party. To become a Bishop, Ash would need many more experience points than she currently has as a Warrior; Stunner tells her that he does not think she will be able to get into Special A by herself.

Back at her apartment, Ash receives an unexpected visitor—the mysterious Bishop she had seen ably working his way through Avalon. Walking through the apartment, the Bishop comments on the luxurious contents of her shabby dwelling, such as the expensive food, liquor, cigarettes, and books. However, when the Bishop opens one of the books, the pages inside are completely blank. He goes on to talk about the breakup of Ash's former group, Wizard, saying that many thought the group broke up because she ignored orders and called for a game reset during a critical mission. Ash tells the Bishop that she wants to form a group with him, requiring two additional Warriors, a Thief, and a Mage. The Bishop tells her to meet him in a flak tower inside Avalon the following evening at midnight.

As she waits at the game center for the appointed time to log in, Ash is alone with the branch attendant, who tells her that Special A does not really exist. The attendant cautions Ash to stay away from the Bishop, the mysterious man who accesses the game from his own private terminal. When Ash says that she wants to get to Special A because Murphy is there, the attendant is understanding and opens a game room for her. After the Game Master tells Ash that he would prefer if she did not try to access Special A, Ash logs in. After a brief conversation with the Bishop, in which it is revealed that he is on the side of the game, Stunner arrives to join the party as Thief and they set out.

In what looks to be an abandoned warehouse, the group encounters enemy soldiers and a citadel, a hulking mass of a tank over three stories tall. While the Bishop and the other members of the team (who, except for Ash and Stunner, are computer creations and not real players) divert the tank's attention in the front, Ash sneaks behind it and fires into its engine grille. With the main mission goal (the destruction of the citadel) achieved, Ash and Stunner begin looking around for the ghost girl. Stunner sees her first and begins firing at her, but one of the enemy soldiers who had not yet been killed shoots him. With his last breath, Stunner tells Ash that it was his fault that Wizard broke up, then his body dissolves in a swirling vortex of pixels. Ash chases after the Ghost, who has taken off running. When Ash gets within range, she shoots at the girl, whose body image swirls and pixelates like Stunner's had. Ash walks forward and is engulfed by an unseen portal. Orange letters and numbers swirl about Ash, whose body dissolves into a similar series of alphanumerics.

Ash awakens to a screen reading "Welcome to Class Real." When she removes the virtual reality helmet, she sees that she is not in the Avalon gaming center, but rather in a barren version of her apartment, complete with a dog food bowl on the floor. Ash opens a box in the room and finds a pistol, a clip of ammunition, and a black dress. The Bishop appears on a video monitor in the room and tells her that she is in what they call Class Real, a very technologically advanced level. Ash's sole task is to finish off the "unreturned," meaning Murphy. She will have an unlimited amount of time to complete the task, but only the one pistol, and she cannot harm any of the other characters in the world. The Bishop says that the only way out of Class Real is to complete the mission; if Ash is able to do so, she will become one of the controllers of the game, like him. Hanging on the wall of the room is a poster for a philharmonic concert called "Avalon" that features a large picture of a basset hound; thumbtacked beneath it is a ticket. The Bishop tells Ash to go to the concert, as that is where Murphy will be.

Clad in the black dress and now wearing earrings and a ring on her left hand, Ash walks out of the room and sees that she is in the long hallway of the deserted Avalon gaming center. Opening the door to the outside world, Ash is shocked by what she sees. The world of Class Real looks very different from the rest of Avalon, appearing to be a modern, bustling European city. Ash walks along the street, taken aback by the moving people who notice her, unlike the blank place-holders back in her world. Ash takes the subway to the concert hall, where she encounters Murphy in the lobby.

Walking outside, Ash confronts Murphy about why he left Wizard and why he went in search of Special A. When Ash tells him that he is in a vegetative state back in the real world, Murphy disputes her assessment, asking why he should not fashion the world of Class Real into the real world for himself. Ash argues, saying that Murphy is just running away from reality. Murphy points out that since Ash has been in Class Real, she no longer has the blond streak through her hair she always has in the virtual world.

Murphy forces a confrontation with Ash in which they shoot at each other to see what will happen to the body when the loser dies. Ash manages to shoot Murphy first, who then shows her he had emptied his gun of bullets. Dying, Murphy tells her that Class Real is the world in which she belongs; his body then vanishes in a swirl of light and data.

Although her mission is over, Ash is given no "Mission Complete" signal as she had been given when she played Avalon. Reloading her gun with the bullets she took from Murphy's body, she walks into the now-empty concert hall to see the ghost girl standing onstage. Ash strides forward toward the girl, cocks her gun, and aims up at the stage. The ghostly girl's face breaks into a slight, knowing smile. The ending scene flashes up a monochrome message: "Welcome to Avalon."

COMMENTARY AND ANALYSIS

Avalon is one of the most stunningly gorgeous science fiction films ever to be produced. Through his use of digital technology, Oshii exhibits a masterful control of the overall mise-en-scène of the entire film. In creating the film, Oshii brought his considerable experience at directing anime to the realm of the live-action film. Said Oshii, "[I]n *Avalon* I wanted to create characters in the same way that I do in animation. I did a lot of digital work on Ash's face during the post-production, which went on longer than the actual shoot."[4] Oshii's signature style is evident from the first scene, which shows the movement of the tanks and the firing of their guns in loving detail, as if to say that each ejected bullet casing is a work of art. The overall film has a very cyberpunk feel to it, with its combination of high tech and old grime. Most of the film plays out in a luscious sepia-tinged monochrome, as if viewed through an old computer monitor. In a world in which computers are advanced enough to generate the simulated reality of the Avalon game, the rest of the world seems remarkably low tech. Wires are visible everywhere—along the streets for the train cars, in the elevator shaft in the Murphy's hospital, streaming from the virtual reality headpieces the Avalon players wear. Oshii may be using this monochrome world to represent the dream world—after all, it used to be believed that most people dreamed in black and white. In *Avalon,* Oshii also indulges in his tendency for long, quiet scenes accompanied by languid background music or narration. Another thing noticeable on initial viewing of *Avalon* is how much the actress who plays Ash (Malgorzata Foremniak) resembles Major Motoko Kusanagi from *Ghost in the Shell.* With Oshii's digital tweaking, this similarity seems far from coincidental. In fact, it was Oshii's goal with *Avalon* to "expand the boundaries of anime," even though the film required twice as much time and effort as a standard live-action or anime film.[5]

In one respect, *Avalon* marks the end of an era in Oshii's filmmaking, as he has said it is that last time he will work with scriptwriter Kazunori Itō. Although Itō had been a staff member on *Urusei Yatsura* along with Oshii, their collaborations did not begin in earnest until they became founding members of Headgear for the *Patlabor* project. From *Patlabor* until *Avalon*—1989 to 2000—Oshii used Itō as scriptwriter for nearly all of his projects. However, Oshii has said that they have reached a point in which his work and Itō's work are going in "different directions" and that he found himself rejecting a number of Itō's ideas for *Avalon.*[6] "I do not think we will ever work together again," Oshii said.[7] Interestingly, after *Avalon,* Itō partnered with character designer Yoshiyuki Sadamoto to create the world of *.hack* (pronounced "dot hack"), another fantastic tale set in the world of role-playing games. One of the main conflicts in the world of *.hack,* which encompasses many formats, including console games, anime, and manga, is a mysterious force that is driving players of an online role-playing game into comas. Although there are many differences between the two franchises, it is noteworthy that Itō has continued of many of *Avalon*'s structural themes in *.hack.*

As evident from its title, in *Avalon* Oshii has shifted his emphasis from Christian mythology to Arthurian lore. The name of the film and the eponymous war game is a reference to Arthurian myth, specifically to the site that was King Arthur's final resting place. However, in the legend Arthur did not necessarily go to

Avalon to die, but merely to have his wounds tended and await the day when he would be able to return triumphantly. Reigning over Avalon are the nine sisters, led by Morgan le Fay, and they are the ones who were to have cared for Arthur until he could rise again. However, historically Morgan has been a problematic character for the tellers and retellers of Arthurian legend, alternately portrayed as the healer of Arthur and a temptress out to destroy Arthur's court.[8]

Avalon is a unique way of examining the myth of King Arthur. Many of the more famous aspects of Arthurian lore, such as the legendary Knights of the Round Table, do not appear the film. Raymond H. Thompson, in his analysis of the legend of Arthur in modern English-language fiction, states: "[T]here are very few science fiction novels about King Arthur and his knights[;] attempts to recreate elements of the Arthurian legend in the future have been much more common."[9] It is not uncommon for science fiction stories to involve Arthurian legend peripherally, yet in general there "has been a widespread failure of science fiction and science fantasy to combine more than perfunctory insight into Arthurian tradition."[10] Many Arthurian science fiction stories merely allude to the old myths in order to give the stories an interesting and novel twist. Oshii's *Avalon* actively engages the myth, rather than merely referencing it, although his concern is not with the integrity of Arthurian legend but rather with what one can learn from it and how the myth can take on meaning in the lives of those viewing his films.

Oshii introduces an additional element into the world of *Avalon*—the use of the role-playing game (RPG) as representational trope. Although the RPG in its modern form began in 1974 with the publication of Dungeons & Dragons by Dave Arneson and Gary Gygax, such games have become increasingly popular in Japan, especially RPG video games such as the *Final Fantasy* series.[11] Many of these video game RPGs portray characters and character archetypes as Dungeons & Dragons did,[12] and the game in *Avalon* is no different. Additionally, quite a number of some of the earliest computer games had Arthurian themes and subject matter.[13] Writer Yuji Oniki has discussed filmmaker Mikio Yamazaki's writings on role-playing games in Japan:

Yamazaki is interested not so much in accumulating data as in figuring out how and why we can't help but construct narratives out of the technology we consume every day. In his book *Electric Hero Marches in the Naked Emperor's Dungeon—A Radical Essay for the Sibylline Computer Game Culture,* he is fascinated by the role computer games play in the stories we construct around our daily lives, whether we play the games or not. . . . Instead of pointing out how RPGs encourage fantasies and antisocial behavior, Yamazaki points out how often these games represent real life in Japan: "When you get tired of playing the role of the fighter-hero and try to bow out, the response [from the game] is, 'You fool, you cannot!' No matter how many times you try to quit, it's always the same, 'You fool!' Ugh. This is the same as those times you'd like to quite school but can't, those times you'd like to quit the company but can't. If pachinko is a game that simulates investments and profit returns, the RPGs might be called simulations of contemporary social life cloaked in a narrative of swords and magic."[14]

Oshii is trying to craft a similar representational narrative through his use of RPGs in *Avalon.* Computer-based RPGs are a very Japanese phenomenon. Many of the video RPGs released in the United States are translations of titles originally released in Japan. Computer RPGs simulate the social element in society, and for some players they may serve as a substitute for interactions with real people. For example, in *Avalon,* Ash's life centers on playing the game; she has very little interaction with the "real world." In this way, Oshii shows how the simulation may usurp its role, becoming a replacement for social interaction in which it is "the map that precedes the territory."[15] Thus Oshii's use of the computer RPG as a structure for his story can be viewed as both an allegory for and a simulation of Japanese society.

However, the society that is modeled is an increasingly alienating one. In this way *Avalon* can be read as a treatise on the social isolation that may come about due to the proliferation of modern communication and entertainment technologies. Ash has very little contact with other people in the film. For the most part, she limits her communication to the Game Master, does not speak with her fellow players in the gaming area, and does not even respond when the attendant congratulates her on a good game. The people on the street do not give any indication that they see Ash as she walks past them—they are all mysterious silhouettes. The passengers on Ash's train are equally shadowy, moving very little, giving no indication of life. On subsequent rides, the same passengers are positioned in exactly the same ways, as if they exist only to give the illusion of life but are in fact mere window dressing. The first real emotion Ash shows is when she comes back to her apartment and greets her dog. When she gets back home, she has no new electronic mail, further evidence of a lack of communication. The only characters in *Avalon* who show any signs of life are the dogs and the game players. In the technology of *Avalon,* there exists the ability to reach out, to facilitate one's interactions with others, yet Ash has withdrawn into herself even as she has embraced such technology. Indeed, the Net is wide and vast, as Kusanagi says in *Ghost in the Shell,* but Ash makes little use of its potential. Although she is a success in the game world of Avalon, Ash does not seem to be enjoying the fruits of her simulated combat victories as she sits alone in her apartment smoking cigarettes. The montage scenes at the beginning of the film serve to highlight her isolation from the rest of the world. In an intriguing break in the film's structure, a montage incorporates both flashbacks and new scenes twenty minutes into the film. The sequence juxtaposes Ash in combat with her life outside the game. As the choral music swells in the background, Ash's life assumes a timeless quality free from jarring interruptions. She plays and goes home, with no appreciable contact with the outside world. The sequence stops to show Ash's meeting with Stunner, her first significant interaction with another person, signaling a break from her daily routine and the beginning of her new quest.

Oshii has cited the computer game Wizardry in particular as an influence on the ideas in *Avalon*. The game was designed in the early 1980s by Andy Greenberg and Robert Woodhead (who, coincidentally, is now the CEO of AnimEigo, which distributes the English-language versions of *Urusei Yatsura*). *Avalon* uses many ideas from Wizardry, such as the name of Ash's former party (Wizard), the composition of parties, and the different character classes. Especially notable is the power of the Bishop character class in Wizardry that could be used to gain extra experience points if a special cheating function was performed. In *Avalon,* only with the help of the Bishop is Ash able to trigger a type of "cheat" of her own, enabling her to reach Class Real. Another bridge between the game and the film is the character of Murphy. Wizardry contains an enemy called Murphy's Ghost, which players could defeat repeatedly in order to garner additional experience points. According to Robert Woodhead, the name of this enemy character had no grand significance; rather, it was an homage to "Paul Murphy, a friend of Andy Greenberg's who was one of the playtesters of the original Apple BASIC Wizardry game Andy put together . . . [that] provided a basis for the design of the gameplay in the final Wizardry game."[16] However, with the background information provided by Wizardry, Ash's confrontation with Murphy at the end of *Avalon* can be seen in a different light. Murphy serves as a major obstacle for Ash to overcome on her path to self-development—while he is in a coma, his ghost continues to haunt everything she does. It was Murphy who had made the decision to break up Wizard, causing Ash to become a solo player, and it is Ash's drive to find out what exactly happened to Murphy that fuels most of the events of *Avalon.* In the end, Ash is able to defeat both Murphy and Murphy's ghost when she shoots him in Class Real. She has gained experience, both in the game world and as a human being, and she is able to move on with her life.

This feeling of wholeness is evidenced by Oshii's symbolic repetition of headless statues throughout the film. The first such statue Ash sees is in the Avalon gaming center; it portrays two cherubs, with the one on the left missing its head. Others Ash sees are a headless statue of what looks like a monk carrying a crucifix and one of an angel with a gaping hole where the face should be. Statues also appear within the game world of Avalon itself. At the end of the film, after Ash has shot Murphy, she flashes on an image of the first statue from the gaming center, only this time it has a head. Although Ash's ultimate fate in the film may not be obvious initially, by her actions she has restored a sense of completeness to her life that was sorely lacking.

Like many of Oshii's films, mythology undergirds the structure of the world in *Avalon*. The master narrative of the Avalon game is a straightforward one of success in military skirmishes, yet Ash can overcome the limitations of the game and of her life through her strategic navigation of the Arthurian mythology at the core of the game. She obtains the help of one of the Nine Sisters, who helps to guide her across a chasm of data into a world in which she has the power to effect change. The game of Avalon at first appears to be a totalizing hyperreality, but Oshii demonstrates how it can be subverted and overcome through a counter-hegemonic oppositional reading of his own film text.

It is in this oppositional reading that we find Oshii's modification of the Arthurian myth, which can be read with both a feminist and an anti-imperialist bent. The character of Ash can be likened to the mythological character of Morgan le Fay, the leader of the Nine Sisters. In the film *Avalon,* the Nine Sisters are said to have originally programmed the game Avalon, and the Bishop tells Ash that if she can complete Class Real then she can become one of them. The Bishop had been watching Ash, waiting for the opportunity to give her this chance to take the power. It is the Bishop who acts as Ash's ferryman to the land of Avalon, guiding her to where she knew she must go; this aspect of the film alludes to the Celtic idea that spirits needed to be guided to the land of the departed.[17] In the case of Ash it is not water that blocks her path to this land, but a sea of information generated by the game itself. However, rather than caring for those who have gone over to the mystical land (Class Real), Ash's Morgan is charged with eliminating those who, like Murphy, are unreturned. In this way, Morgan le Fay is no longer conceptualized in a traditional female role of repository of the healing arts and benevolent caretaker, but instead serves to show the unreturned what they have become—virtual beings in a playground of someone else's making. In his conversation with Ash, Murphy defends his choice to stay in the world of Class Real, questioning the nature of reality. In other words, if Class Real is real to Murphy, then why does it matter to Ash that he is a vegetable back in the "real world"? The way Ash cares for her departed lord, for Murphy, is by shooting him, demonstrating her realization of the folly and the futility of trying to live one's life in a world constructed solely of dreams. Ash no longer needs Murphy and the virtual game of Avalon to fulfill her role in life.

On another level, retaining the pointed political commentary Oshii made evident in *Patlabor 2, Avalon* is a critique of the Japanese imperial system. There are of course many references to royalty in Arthurian legend, and these allusions are replicated in *Avalon.* For example, in her search for information on the realm of Special A, Ash encounters the phrase "Hic Jacet Arthurus, Rex Quon Dam Rex Que Futurus," which translates to "Here Lies Arthur, the Once and Future King." These words are said to be inscribed on King Arthur's tombstone in Avalon, the realm of the Nine Sisters. Parallels can be drawn between the idealized kingdom of Camelot in Arthurian mythology and the idealized system of emperor worship that existed in Japan until the end of World War II. In the eyes of some Japanese, during the war the emperor was leading the nation in a holy quest, not unlike the exploits of Arthur. Similarly, the emperor was defeated but not killed, and some right-wing Japanese await the day when he will become mighty again. In a sense, the Japanese emperor currently is dwelling in his own personal Avalon. Oshii, however, deflates this idea of emperor worship, demonstrating how unnecessary its misguided view is. When Ash finally meets Murphy again, she ends up shooting this representation of Arthur, making him vanish in a swirl of pixels, demonstrating Oshii's conception of the emperor: ephemeral and without any real substance. Although Murphy enjoyed his dream in Class Real, in the "real" world he was simply one of the throng of brain-dead masses who had tried to reach Special A. By shooting Murphy, Ash shows that, even though reality may be difficult to face, one cannot live in a dream world.

The idea of the dream world is echoed in another mythological reference Ash makes to the Game Master. She compares the story of Morgan le Fay to a myth of northern Europe in which a shipwrecked Odin is given a ring of eternal youth and a crown of forgetfulness. However, in *Avalon,* Ash has her own versions of these accoutrements. The giant virtual reality helmets the Avalon players are made to don are nothing if not crowns that make wearers forget their own reality. This point is made even more explicit when Ash journeys into Class Real. Along with the black dress and pistol that she wears, one of her accessories is a large silver ring she wears on her left hand. While this detail may seem small, when coupled with Ash's previous telling of the Odin myth Class Real takes on new meaning. In spite of what Murphy says to try to convince her, Class Real is not a true reality, nor is it the ideal world for Ash. Rather, Class Real is another illusion, albeit a seemingly welcome one in which she may have power and immortality. (This may be what the Bishop meant when he said that upon completion of the mission, Ash would become one of them.) Oshii's use of the Odin myth and incorporation of it into the film is very similar to his use of the Urashima Taro myth in *Urusei Yatsura 2: Beautiful Dreamer.* Like Ataru, Ash must strive to wake from an imposed dream that is not her own. Ash recognizes the illusion of the world and makes a conscious decision to leave Class Real.

Oshii's interest in politics manifests itself in the very form the film *Avalon* assumes. Besides the influence of Japanese imperialism, the 1956 uprising in Hungary, in which the Hungarians rose up against the Soviet regime, served as the original idea for *Avalon,* according to Oshii.[18] The scenes of combat at the beginning of *Avalon* certainly bring to mind the urban warfare of that revolution, with a lone Ash fighting against the technologically superior tanks and helicopters of the opposing side. In using the failed Hungarian revolution as a model, Oshii is depicting his characters as freedom fighters squarely on the side of anti-imperialism.

Besides the use of mythological and political allusions, Oshii also incorporates many of his characteristic tropes. Surveillance and observation play a major part of his films. From the beginning, the viewers are shown that Ash is being observed by the Bishop, which prepares viewers for what is to come. The element of looking has been a part of many of Oshii's films, since Mujaki's watchfulness in *Urusei Yatsura 2: Beautiful Dreamer.* Of course the game Avalon has to keep track of what the players are doing, and thus an element of watching is incumbent on the game itself. However, this is coupled with the Bishop character watching over Ash, both in the game and in the real world. Oshii also implements his unusual character-eye views, most notably when Ash is climbing the stairs of the flak tower to meet with the Bishop and the rest of the team. Ash's viewpoint is through a set of night-vision goggles that enable her barely to make out her surroundings. It is a mediated view (through the goggles) of what is already a mediated view of reality (through the game).

Oshii also incorporates his famous love of dogs, especially of basset hounds, in *Avalon*. The soldiers Ash fights in the first combat scenes in the film are later identified on a computer screen as dog soldiers, alluding to the self-identifying dog/wolf fighters in *Jin-Roh* and robot attack dogs of *Dallos*. More important, actual dogs serve as compatriots and signifiers in *Avalon*. At the beginning of the film, Ash keeps a dog in her apartment, but it later disappears. The presence and disappearance of the dog is one of the film's biggest puzzles. Speaking generally, Oshii said, "For me, the women are the second greatest mystery, after the mystery of the dog."[19] In *Avalon,* Oshii decided to turn his idea of the "mystery of the dog" into a very real conundrum. Oshii said, "[F]or the main character, the dog can be considered as the symbol of 'reality' itself. The meaning of the disappearance of the dog is important in this film, but whether or not the dog existed in the first place is an even more important question."[20] Before the dog disappears, Ash comes home and behaves as if she can see the dog, which is not shown onscreen; there are soft sounds and the scratching of claws on the floor as if the dog is still in the apartment. However, after Ash finishes preparing the deluxe meal, the dog is nowhere to be found. Ash then goes outside and hears what sounds like a helicopter from the game—seemingly the noise and the dog's disappearance are related, an example of slippage between the game world and the real world. When the dog vanishes, Ash is beginning to come to some sort of realization about the nature of the world she inhabits. Repeated images of the dog in Class Real serve to strengthen the connections between the two worlds. As Oshii suggests, the dog may not have existed at all—it may simply have been a figment of Ash's imagination or an idea she was able to project into the world. If so, then it would seem to indicate that the world Ash knows as the "real world" is not real at all. Of course, as Murphy's disappearance shows us, Class Real is, in contrast to what its name suggests, not the "real world" either. Aside from his cryptic comment on the nature of the dog, Oshii has not discussed which world is the "real world." Like Ash, it is up to viewers to figure out such complexities for themselves.

At the same time, Oshii questions whether such distinctions such as the "real world" are meaningful. Before she tries to access Special A, Ash asks the Game Master if he is another person accessing the game or if he is a part of the system. The Game Master's answer in noncommittal, saying that it does not matter and that there would be no way for Ash to be able to tell either way. He is saying that his condition makes no difference to the functionality of the game or to Ash's relationship with him. This response summarizes Oshii's attitude toward the dream/reality debate. While a person could be correct (the world must either be the "dream" world or the "real" world), it may not necessarily matter because a person makes the world what it is according to his or her perception of it.

Another one of the striking visual elements in *Avalon* is its depiction of food. If an army travels on its stomach, as Napoléon is reported to have said, perhaps in the world of *Avalon* reality does so as well. Food is inherently related to reality because it is what the physical body needs to survive; in the film, it is used as a way of connecting to what might be "real." It is significant that Ash's main use of food is not for herself but to feed her dog. In a very sensual scene, Ash is shown going to great lengths to purchase and prepare an exquisite meal. When viewers see what Ash and the rest of the humans in the film eat, the disparity between their food and the dog's food is even more striking. Ash's first meeting with Stunner, which takes place in a mess hall where they eat a thin gruel, best illustrates this contrast. However, later, when Ash prepares the dog's meal, the fresh ingredients are shown in color, in contrast to the monochrome of the surrounding world. She prepared the meal with loving care, and the scene is filmed in an equally tender manner. It is quite a shock, then, when we learn that the carefully crafted dish is intended for Ash's dog. Food also is shown in color later when Ash and Stunner later meet for breakfast. Oshii emphasizes Stunner's mannerless eating, showing him stuffing food into his mouth, with every bite of sausage and egg audible. Such scenes of eating were very important to Oshii, who said, "I worked really hard on the food: for instance, getting the yellow of the egg yolk exactly right. Filming Ash preparing the food for her dog took a whole day."[21] Food in *Avalon,* even clumsily eaten, is a link to the body, and emphasizes the utter humanity of the characters in a film that threatens dehumanization through an alienating technology.

The meaning of the film's ending, when Ash points her gun at the ghostly girl and the scene cuts to a shot of a computer screen saying "Welcome to Avalon," is ambiguous. It presents no real resolution of the story, as viewers are unsure exactly what happened. This is, however, exactly the point Oshii is trying to make. Like the end of *Ghost in the Shell,* which concluded with Kusanagi stating the potentiality of the Net is "wide and vast," the explicitly unresolved ending in *Avalon* unlocks horizons of possibility for the protagonist. Perhaps Ash, like Kusanagi, has become something more than she once was—one of the Nine Sisters or perhaps even something more. Perhaps Ash returned to the grimy and dark "real world," determined not to be beholden to the bequest of dreams. Perhaps it is Ash who is assuming the role of Arthur, and now that she has slain the demons of her past she is prepared to return triumphant to the world. Oshii intentionally leaves the conclusion of *Avalon* open-ended to facilitate the dissemination of a multitude of meanings. According to Oshii: "All films are inconclusive. Just like things called 'life' and 'reality.'"[22]

There are a number of distinct similarities between *Avalon* and *Ghost in the Shell.* Both films follow an open-ended yet cyclical structure: In *Ghost in the Shell,* this is shown by Kusanagi's "birth" scene during the opening credits and her "rebirth" at the end; in *Avalon,* the film begins and ends within the computer game of Avalon, bringing Ash full circle. Like Kusanagi in *Ghost in the Shell,* Ash is set apart as potentially impure. She is seen as being a very solitary person, never making contact with other game players. This segregation is due to her perceived failure as an former member of Wizard. Ash carries fewer markers of impurity than does Kusanagi; she is not portrayed as menstruating or as a possible mother figure, and her body is whole and "natural" while Kusanagi's is almost entirely artificial. Perhaps such changes are due to Oshii's choice of locale for *Avalon* and that the same markers would not have the same meanings or resonance with a non-Japanese cast, crew, and audience.

There are a number of similarities between *Avalon* and *The Matrix* as well. Like *The Matrix*, *Avalon* is a sophisticated film that uses production techniques to question the technological nature of reality. Various visual images in *Avalon* are reminiscent of *The Matrix*, such as the camera rotating around the explosions of the tanks in the first combat scene (reminiscent of the Wachowski brothers' "bullet-time" technique) and Ash's opening of the shutters upon waking in Class Real (to reveal a brick wall in a scene similar to one from *The Matrix*). However, Oshii deals with the question of a computer-generated reality in a much more complex way than do the Wachowskis. In *The Matrix*, the "real" world is given obvious preference to the computer-generated one, and those who know the truth but choose to remain in the illusion, or return to it, are seen as weak or branded as traitors to the human cause. *Avalon*'s treatment of the virtual world is much more questioning. Oshii asks what the nature of such a world would be and why the world of flesh and blood is to be preferred over a false world. While I believe Oshii arrives at the same conclusions as the Wachowskis—that people need to wake up to the illusions in their lives and deal with them—he does so in a much less didactic fashion.

In *Avalon*, Oshii reconfigures aspects of classical Arthurian mythology to generate a story that will more closely resonate with modern film viewers. He adapts and incorporates these myths into his own philosophy, giving them a new vibrancy and rendering them more meaningful. This reconceptualization of an older mythology is central to Oshii's message of getting people to "wake up." His message is a call to recognize mediated systems in our own lives and how they serve to control us. Like Ash, we are voluntarily submitting ourselves to the system daily, never aware of how much the world is being interpreted and fed to us without our consent. The system of control that can be realized and negated, if only we know how to view it.

CHAPTER 9

CONCLUSION

ALTHOUGH I END THE ANALYSIS OF MAMORU OSHII'S films with *Avalon,* his most recent full-length theatrical release as of this writing, Oshii has continued to create striking films that are thought-provoking meditations on the position of humans in modern society. Even though his most recent works have been live-action films (*Avalon* and a segment of the live-action compendium *Killers* [2003]) that he directed, Oshii has certainly not abandoned the medium of anime. He is currently at work on the sequel to *Ghost in the Shell,* one of the most eagerly anticipated and technologically sophisticated anime films ever.

Although Oshii works with an international mind-set, his films are not produced with the Western filmgoer explicitly in mind; his main audience is in Japan. The ideas Oshii puts forth must first and foremost be applicable to the lives of the Japanese viewers. However, there is an increasingly international audience for Japanese film, especially Japanese animation like the *Patlabor* films and *Ghost in the Shell.* By the time Oshii was directing such works, anime already had a significant fan base in America. It has been argued that Japanese animation, far from being a solely underground phenomenon, has exerted a strong influence on visual communication in the United States.[1] Additionally, Oshii's rescripting of Western mythologies renders his films accessible to Western as well as Japanese viewers.

In conclusion, it is helpful to examine Oshii's oeuvre in the context of the films of Hayao Miyazaki, Japan's premier director of animated films. Oshii's approach to filmmaking differs from that of Miyazaki (and the related films of his production company, Studio Ghibli), whose films, while similarly international in scope, have some very Japanese elements to them. Miyazaki's films make for a suitable comparison with those of Oshii for a number of reasons. First, Miyazaki is one of the most successful filmmakers, both financially and critically, working in Japan today. His most recent film, *Spirited Away* (2001), broke all box office records in Japan. It is the most financially successful Japanese film ever and won the Japanese Academy Award for best film, the prestigious Golden Bear at the Berlin Film Festival, and an American Academy Award for Best Animated Feature. Before *Spirited Away, Princess Mononoke* (1997), Miyazaki's previous film, had been the most successful Japanese film. It, too, had won the Japanese Academy Award for best film. Miyazaki, like Oshii, works primarily in the medium of anime. Thus, by the nature of their success Miyazaki's films are a useful benchmark by which to judge other Japanese films, especially other animated films.

The two filmmakers certainly differ in their respective presentations of ideology. Oshii has joked in the past about Miyazaki's political leanings, saying that "making a movie [for Studio Ghibli] is still a kind of extension of the union movement."[2] At the same time, Carl Gustav Horn notes Oshii's own involvement in leftist politics, so Oshii's critique of Miyazaki is not necessarily based on a difference of core political beliefs but rather a difference of how one should express and work toward the goals of such beliefs. In general, Oshii's films are less didactic than those of Miyazaki, yet there are a number of similarities in the themes the two filmmakers employ. For example, one phrase Ashitaka repeats almost as a mantra in *Princess Mononoke* is his desire to see things as they are, with "eyes unclouded." While this is not in reference to any specific religious text, it is very similar to the motif in Oshii's films and is alluded to by the reference to the verse of Corinthians in *Ghost in the Shell,* to not see the world "through a glass darkly." Both men share a common desire to see things for what they are, but they approach this desire in radically different ways.

THE TECHNOLOGICAL AND MYTHOLOGICAL *FURUSATO*

The three overarching and overlapping themes in anime described by Susan J. Napier (the carnivalesque, the elegiac, and the apocalyptic) are at work to varying degrees in nearly all Japanese animation.[3] Miyazaki's works frequently contain elements of all three, while Oshii's films usually contain many more elegiac and apocalyptic elements than carnivalesque ones. (This is especially true of his later films, although *Urusei Yatsura* and moments in *Patlabor* contain a high degree of the carnivalesque.) One important component of the elegiac mode is the notion of nostalgia. Nostalgia is tightly connected to the issues of both mythology and the progression of technology. Nostalgia is a longing for times that have passed us by, especially times perceived as being somehow "simpler" or more "authentic." These "simpler times" are often highly mythic as well, in that they exist as a cultural construction. Technology is seen by some as needlessly complicating our daily lives, thus prompting nostalgia for a time when such technology did not exist. Many of Miyazaki's works have an element of nostalgia to them. In discussing *Princess Mononoke,* Japanese literature scholar Melek Ortabasi says, "The film's reexamination of native tradition(s) results not in a legitimizing, coherent vision for Japan's future, but in a fractured place that exudes an unvoiced longing, echoing unconsciously in the minds of those waiting in long lines outside Japanese movie theaters, for a sense of imagined community long since forgotten."[4] Miyazaki's films are filled with a sense of wanting to belong to something that one can no longer have and, more problematically, never truly existed in the first place. As mentioned, Oshii has criticized Miyazaki for being politically backward looking, a charge echoed by the nostalgia in

Miyazaki's films. Although Miyazaki does problematize quite a number of social ills (pollution, sexism, discrimination, just to name a few), in the end the films can be "considered to negotiate an essentially reassuring narrative structure."[5] Oshii's films fit into the elegiac mode of anime as well; however, the key element of nostalgia is conspicuously absent from his films. Central to a Japanese construction of nostalgia is the idea of nature, which Oshii does not address in his films. Save for a brief scene in *Ghost in the Shell* in which Section 9 is staking out the estate of a wealthy potential suspect, there is no greenery in any of the films discussed. (Perhaps this suggests that in modern society the use and enjoyment of green space is a luxury reserved for those who can afford it.) Rather than retreating into nostalgia, Oshii presses forward with his views of technology. This technology is often problematic, Oshii is saying, but it is a problem that must be faced directly.

While both men deal with technology, Miyazaki also explicitly uses the concept of *furusato,* which has a great deal of weight in Japanese culture. The word can be translated roughly as "hometown," but such a definition does not carry the connotations of intimacy that the Japanese word does. The furusato is closely tied to ideas of a return to nature; such concepts are beautifully illustrated in the Studio Ghibli films *My Neighbor Totoro* (*Tonari no Totoro,* 1988) and *Only Yesterday* (*Omohide Poro Poro,* 1991). Anthropologist Marilyn Ivy notes that the notion of furusato is a modern one, implying a "fundamental alienation" from one's feeling of home.[6] In one sense, the term "mythological furusato" I use in the heading of this section is redundant; by its very definition, the furusato is inherently in the realm of the longed-for myth. In another sense, "mythological furusato" refers to the process by which furusato can be created in one's mind through the use and construction of mythologies. The Studio Ghibli films construct their concept of furusato through the use of mythological nostalgia. In his analysis of Japanese women's magazines, Brian Moeran states that "nostalgia involves a rejection of the reader's present life, here and now, and posits instead a quiet, slightly unreal dream world, saturated with emotions from one's past life in which romance for the countryside is very strong."[7] This analysis is equally true for viewers of film and animation.

Oshii suggests that, like other animators, he does not possess a furusato, and in so doing he "seems to be implicitly rejecting another precious cultural construct, the notion of Japan's uniqueness."[8] In short, this furusato is a home to which one is able to return. Animators, then, are rootless in a way, perhaps trying to create their own roots out of what they see around them. Such a perception adds an additional layer of meaning when Oshii calls himself a "stray dog." This phrase connotes a sense of weakness, as dogs usually are pack animals, but also a sense of dangerousness and unpredictability, as there is no pack structure to keep the lone mutt in line. Oshii uses myth to ground his quest, but he is still not sure what it is he is searching for. It is the fact of the searching that matters, not necessarily what can be found. Although viewers may not necessarily know where they are at the end of Oshii's films, they understand that they have progressed in the quest.

NOSTALGIA AND THE ROLE OF THE FEMALE

Both Oshii and Miyazaki are remarkable for their use of strong female protagonists. In nearly every film by Miyazaki, the central character (or at least a major character) is a young girl. Oshii's *Ghost in the Shell* and *Avalon* both feature strong women in what appear to be overwhelmingly masculine worlds. In addition, both *Patlabor* films highlight women in positions of power and authority. Female roles are closely tied into traditional Japanese ideas of the family, or *ie,* which have been very strong in the Japanese consciousness.

Another area in which the films of Oshii and Miyazaki differ is the presence of family or substitutive family structure. In Miyazaki's films, a family structure is available in one way or another. In *Princess Mononoke,* the *tataraba* (the iron works, or "iron town") functions as a de facto family for those working the industry. While it is obvious that Lady Eboshi wields ultimate control over the iron works, she is a very compassionate person, employing women who had formerly worked in brothels and providing both food and work for lepers. (This last point about providing work is especially important. There has been a strong stigma against leprosy in Japan for many years, and only recently has Japan begun to make amends for forcibly confining lepers to isolated colonies as late as the 1990s.) In the family of the tataraba, Eboshi is both maternal caregiver and paternal technological enforcer. In Miyazaki's *Kiki's Delivery Service* (*Majo no Takkyūbin*, 1989), Kiki must leave home to grow both as a witch and as a person. Not long after she has left one family, however, she soon discovers another, in the form of Osono, the woman who gives her a room and employment, and Ursula, a young woman artist who shares her time with Kiki. Family is also at the center of *My Neighbor Totoro*, in which two young girls, with the help of a bear–like tree spirit, try to cope with the grave illness of their mother.

Oshii's films, on the other hand, offer no such glimpse of family life, even that of a surrogate family. One might argue that Division 2 in the *Patlabor* films could function in such a role, as the policemen and policewomen are shown interacting in what is at times a close manner. However, there is no evidence in the films to support this claim; they are merely a good team, and do not display the nurturing inherent in a family structure. In *Ghost in the Shell*, Kusanagi is shown as interacting with very few people, and even then it is mostly in a work environment. The only time we see Kusanagi talking with someone off-duty is when she goes diving and Batou accompanies her on the ship. Even then, their conversation does not betray any sense of family togetherness. Similarly, Ash in *Avalon* speaks with few people, especially outside the confines of her quest. The absence of the traditional family structure in his films shows that Oshii does not subscribe to more traditional Japanese notions of the role of women.

Regarding the character of Motoko Kusanagi in *Ghost in the Shell*, Oshii has said: "[W]omen aren't indecisive about themselves. . . . Rather than portraying Motoko, I wanted to know what it meant to be reborn. What does it mean to become something you are not? I think that is something men cannot understand. I wanted to portray it because it is something I cannot understand. To become a man is different."[9] Although Oshii says that *Ghost in the Shell* is the first time he used a woman as the main character of his films, this is not quite accurate. No single character can be called the "main character" of the *Patlabor* films, but Noa Izumi and Shinobu Nagumo are two very central characters. At the end of *Patlabor 1,* it is Noa who must finally defeat the rampaging Labor; even though the main menace has been thwarted, this single remnant of Hoba's virus still must be eliminated. And Nagumo's relationship with Tsuge forms a very central part of *Patlabor 2.* Both Noa and Nagumo are presented as being very strong and capable, unafraid to fight when they are needed.

In discussing his decision to make the main character of his film *Nausicaä of the Valley of the Wind* (*Kaze no Tani no Naushika,* 1984) a young girl, Miyazaki said that even though "making a young girl the heroine of the film might play into the hands of those who saw animation as antifeminist or simply as another chance to drool over young girls," having a male protagonist would impose "too many conventional ideas on the story."[10] Miyazaki's young heroines occupy the liminal space of the *shōjo,* a term that can be translated simply as "girl" but which connotes an ambiguous period between childhood and womanhood. Such heroines are recurring themes for Miyazaki, appearing in nearly all of his films. Even if it is not the central focus of the story, such heroines usually go through an adolescent crisis of identity in the course of the film.

The representation of women in anime initially may seem to be something of an anomaly within Japanese mass media. In examining how the Japanese media customarily portrays women in the media, Anne Cooper-Chen formulated five principles: (1) Women and men are evaluated differently. (2) Women are objects. (3) Women are subordinate. (4) A woman's ability is low. (5) A woman's place is in the home.[11] Although instances of objectification of the heroines of the films of both Oshii and Miyazaki have been debated,[12] both filmmakers present characters that defy nearly all of the above generalities. In contrast, some other examples of anime feature strong yet overtly sexual female characters, such as the *Bubblegum Crisis* OVA series (1987–91) and the *Cowboy Bebop* television series (1998) and film (2001). Anime can serve as a site of problematization of gender roles and identities within society while simultaneously serving to reinscribe such roles; in this way, anime functions in the same way regarding sex and gender as the world of the all-female cross-dressing Takarazuka theater in anthropologist Jennifer Robertson's account.[13]

In Japanese culture, women traditionally have been seen as being more in touch with the spirit world. The histories of Japan contain many tales of women shamans, especially blind women.[14] In Japan's drive toward "civilization and enlightenment" in the Meiji period, the government worked to eliminate the village shaman as "an obstacle to state control over the folk heart,"[15] and in doing so worked to reinscribe one of the few domains in which the powers of the female held sway.

The shaman was closely connected to untamed wilderness and, as such, associations with the wild were often looked on with suspicion. In fact, one reason for confining a patient to a mental asylum in Japan in the early twentieth century was that she or he would wander into the mountains for long periods of time.[16] In examining the writings of folklorist Kunio Yanagita, historian Gerald Figal states: "In the preponderance of stories that Yanagita relates [in *Yama no jinsei*], the mental transformations that men undergo while in the mountains and their motivations for going are generally characterized as positive, whereas in the case of women both the result and the motivation are generally characterized as negative."[17] Thus the view developed that while going into the mountains was a highly suspicious act for anyone, it was more acceptable for men to do so than it was for women. The mountains are a place where ascetic training is performed,[18] and the state's fear of the power of women contributed to this negative perception of going into the mountains.

In none of Miyazaki's films do his heroines "go to the mountains," that is, purposefully venture alone to a mysterious and unfamiliar zone. In *Kiki's Delivery Service,* Kiki does set off on her own to find out who she is, but she travels to the city and there finds a new sense of community. San, in *Princess Mononoke,* has spent her life in the wilderness, but this means that she is *of* the mountains; she has no wish for an eventual return to human society. And in *Spirited Away,* Sen's travels in a mysterious world are not of her own choosing. However, both Kusanagi in *Ghost in the Shell* and Ash in *Avalon* can be seen as "going to the mountains" in a metaphorical sense. Kusanagi even ends up on top of a mountain at the end of the film, looking down on the expansive city and contemplating her next move.

The problematization of sex roles is closely connected with Oshii's problematization of technology. Oshii utilizes the image of the female to present a vision of the future that is unapologetically unnostalgic for past sexual roles. Although Miyazaki does similarly present many strong female protagonists in his films, through his nostalgia for past technological and mythological forms, he in effect incorporates such an "emancipated" woman into the larger controlling structure of the traditional patriarchal family.

Oshii does not indulge in a rose-tinted nostalgia for a very good reason: It would undermine the very thing he is trying to accomplish through his films. Nostalgia serves to reassure viewers, making them feel more comfortable. Nostalgia can restrict the further development of self; in the words of the Puppet Master: "Your desire to remain as you are is what ultimately limits you." Unlike Miyazaki, Oshii is trying to shake up the viewers, and by so doing makes the viewers begin thinking critically about why they are uncomfortable. Both filmmakers are actively engaged in questioning mainstream Japanese society, but because Miyazaki's films are essentially more reassuring than Oshii's, Miyazaki's films have fared better both commercially and critically.

THE FUTURE OF THE "STRAY DOG"

In his mid-fifties at the time of this writing, Oshii has become one of the elder statesmen of Japanese animation, while his pioneering use of computer graphics and digital animation has placed him at the forefront of twenty-first-century cinema. His use of such techniques, though, questions the ways in which we perceive the world and how we interact with the technology engulfing us every day. Oshii takes advantage of his position as director to deploy his own brand of social criticism, using his films as a springboard.

Oshii's two most recent directorial projects are a perfect example of the complementary contradictions showcased through much of his work. The first, which was released June 2003 in Japan, is a live-action short called ".50 Woman," part of a larger omnibus work called *Killers*. Oshii's fellow directors on *Killers* were

Kazuhiro Kiuchi (author of the manga *Be-Bop High School* and director of the film *Kyōhansha*), Shundō Ōkawa (director of the film *Double Deception*), Takanori Tsujimoto, and Shūji Kawata. When compared to Oshii's relatively expensive and labor-intensive animated works, the filming of *Killers* seems positively frugal. Each of the five segments took an average of 4.4 days to film, with Oshii's ".50 Woman" taking the least time, only 2 days.[19] Even though he worked with what he says was his smallest budget ever, he managed to incorporate an impressive-looking rifle costing one million yen (approximately US $8,500), which took up half of the budget.[20] The story in Oshii's segment is about a hit woman whose job is to assassinate a corrupt movie producer. As she waits patiently for her prey, she consumes a smorgasbord of food, documented and tallied onscreen for viewers. These scenes are executed in such a sensual way that according to film critic Mark Schilling, Oshii's ".50 Woman" segment "plays like an erotic daydream-cum-food commercial."[21] The film also can be read as a commentary about Oshii's relation to the film industry in Japan, as the role of the producer is played by Toshio Suzuki of Studio Ghibli, who is coproducing Oshii's newest animated film. As seen in the segment, Oshii positions himself outside of mainstream Japanese cinema, taking shots at the power of the industry. Not only is the segment about lethal women, guns, and food (recurring themes in Oshii's works), but it is a subversive wink at those who would try to control his films.

Oshii's next major project is the eagerly anticipated sequel to *Ghost in the Shell*. Titled *Innocence,* as of this writing the film is scheduled to be released in Japan in the spring of 2004. (It has also been announced that Go Fish, a division of Dreamworks SKG, will handle the U.S. version of the film, which is slated for a fall 2004 release.) As the film is still in the production stages, its creators and staff are reticent to say too much about it. *Innocence* promises to be more erotic than the first *Ghost in the Shell* film, although the precise meaning of the word is unclear. (Oshii's only comment on it has been that "[t]he usage of the word 'erotic' comes from my personal vocabulary."[22]) Based on preliminary footage, *Innocence* looks as if it will continue Oshii's questioning of what it means to be human in the modern world. Using the latest in computer animation technology, the film uses seemingly cel-drawn characters atop deep and complex computer-generated backgrounds, the juxtaposition serving to illustrate how perceptions of reality are increasingly mediated through technology.

Oshii also has a number of other projects that are either ongoing or will be produced in the near future. Recently he supervised a pair of short documentaries about the city of Tokyo, furthering the idea of the city as subject that he has explored in a number of previous fictional works. He is scheduled to supervise a two- to three-episode series called *Fūjin Monogatari,* written by the winner of the Anime Plan Grand Prix writing contest. It also has been announced that Oshii is developing a project for the 2005 World Expo to be held in Aichi, Japan. In keeping with the expo's theme of "Nature's Wisdom," Oshii will oversee the production of an exhibit consisting of a series of video screens designed to make passersby feel as if they are immersed in nature. The project promises to be a fascinating look at the intersection of technology and the natural world.

Mamoru Oshii's films have only just begun to garner critical and commercial attention outside of Japan. I hope that this book serves to focus a bit more consideration on his films and on Japanese animation in general. It is unlikely that Oshii's films, although celebrated both in Japan and abroad, will ever surpass the popular acclaim of the films of Hayao Miyazaki. Oshii is one of the great auteurs of Japanese anime, and his films are too questioning and cerebral to find general acceptance among the moviegoing masses. And although he certainly wants his films to be successful, Oshii is far too much of a stray dog to join the popular filmmaking pack for very long.

MAMORU OSHII FILMOGRAPHY

INFORMATION ABOUT THE PROJECTS in which Mamoru Oshii has been involved is given in the following order: English title; Japanese title (if different); release date (format); Oshii's role in the project.

One-Hit Kanta
Ippatsu Kanta-kun
series aired September 1977 to September 1978 (53 TV episodes)
storyboards (4 episodes); direction (2 episodes)

Time Bokan Series: Yattaman
Taimu Bokan Shirīzu: Yattāman
series aired January 1977 to January 1979 (108 TV episodes)
storyboards (2 episodes); general assistant director (second half of the
    series)

Science Ninja Team Gatchaman II
Kagaku Ninja-tai Gatchaman II
series aired October 1978 to September 1979 (52 TV episodes)
storyboards (3 episodes); direction (3 episodes)

Magical Girl Tickle
Majokko Chikkuru
series aired March 1978 to January 1979 (45 TV episodes)
storyboards (1 episode)

Time Bokan Series: Zendaman
Taimu Bokan Shirīzu: Zendaman
series aired February 1979 to January 1980 (52 TV episodes)
storyboards (10 episodes); direction (9 episodes); storyboard retouch (1
    episode)

Nils's Mysterious Journey
Nirusu no Fushigi-na Tabi
series aired January 1980 to March 1981 (52 TV eps.)
storyboards (11 episodes); direction (18 episodes)

Time Bokan Series: Time Patrol Team Otasukeman
Taimu Bokan Shirīzu: Taimu Patorōru-tai Otasukeman
series aired February 1980 to January 1981 (53 TV episodes)
storyboards (6 episodes)

Time Bokan Series: Yattodetaman
Taimu Bokan Shirīzu: Yattodetaman
series aired February 1981 to February 1982 (52 TV episodes)
storyboards (6 episodes)

World Masterpiece Stories
Sekai Meisaku Monogatari
series aired April 1981 to September 1981 (24 TV episodes)
opening storyboards; direction

Tear of the Dragon's Eye
Ryūno Me no Namida
June 1981 (film)
storyboards; direction

Sherlock Holmes
Shārokku Hōmuzu
1981 (pilot film)
storyboards

The Fullmoon Tradition: Indra
1981 (pilot film)
original story; planning; storyboards; direction

Nils's Mysterious Journey (film version)
Nirusu no Fushigi-na Tabi
1983 (film)
storyboards; direction

Belle and Sebastian
Meiken Jorī
April 1981 to June 1982 (52 TV episodes)
storyboards (2 episodes); direction (2 episodes); production assistant (2
    episodes)

G (Gold) Raitan
G (Gōrudo) Raidan
March 1981 to February 1982 (52 TV episodes)
storyboards (2 episodes)

Miss Machiko
Maicchangu Machiko-sensei
October 1981 to July 1983 (95 TV episodes)
storyboards (1 episode)

Urusei Yatsura
October 1981 to March 1986 (218 TV episodes)
chief director (episodes 1 to 106); storyboards (21 episodes); direction
    (24 episodes); screenplay (7 episodes); storyboard reorganization
    (1 episode)

Urusei Yatsura Spring Special
"Haruda Tobidase" *Urusei Yatsura* Special
April 1982 (two-part TV special shown between episodes 21 and 22 of
    the TV series)
storyboards and direction (first half)

Urusei Yatsura Kansai Electric TV Commercials
1982 (pair of public service announcements for Kansai Denryoku
    [Kansai Electric Company])
storyboards

Urusei Yatsura: Only You
Urusei Yatsura: Onrī Yū
February 1983 (film)
film adaptation; storyboards; director

Urusei Yatsura 2: Beautiful Dreamer
Urusei Yatsura: Byūtifuru Dorīmā
February 1984 (film)
screenplay; director

Dashing Kappei
Dasshu Kappei
October 1981 to December 1982 (65 TV episodes)
storyboards (1 episode)

Time Bokan Series: Ippatsuman Returns
Time Bokan Series: Gyakuten Ippatsuman

February 1982 to March 1983 (58 TV episodes)
storyboards (7 episodes)

Little Mrs. Pepperpot
Supūn Obasan
April 1983 to March 1984 (130 TV episodes)
screenplay (1 episode); storyboards (1 episode)

The Yearling
Koshika Monogatari
November 1983 to January 1985 (52 TV episodes)
storyboards (2 episodes)

Dallos
December 1983 to June 1984 (4 OVA episodes)
director; screenplay (3 episodes); storyboards (3 episodes); direction (3
    episodes)

Angel's Egg
Tenshi no Tamago
December 1985 (OVA)
original story (with Yoshitaka Amano); screenplay; director

The Red Spectacles
Akai Megane
February 1987 (film)
screenplay; director

Zillion
Akai Kōdan Jirion
April 1987 to December 1987 (31 TV episodes)
storyboards (2 episodes)

Twilight Q 2: Labyrinth Objects File 538
Towairaito Q 2: Meikyū Bukken File 538
August 1987 (OVA)
original story; screenplay; director

Mobile Police Patlabor
Kidō Keisatsu Patoreibā
April 1988 to December 1988 (6 OVA episodes)
director, storyboards

Mobile Police Patlabor
Kidō Keisatsu Patoreibā

July 1989 (film)
director

Glory to the Ancestors
Gosenzo-sama Banbanzai!
August 1989 to January 1990 (6 OVA episodes)
original story; screenplay; director; storyboards

Maroko
March 1990 (film)
original story; screenplay; director

Mobile Police Patlabor (Patlabor on Television)
Kidō Keisatsu Patoreibā (Patlabor on Television)
October 1989 to September 1990 (47 TV episodes)
script (5 episodes)

Mobile Police Patlabor (New Video Series)
Kidō Keisatsu Patoreibā (Shin Bideo Shirīzu)
November 1990 to April 1992 (16 OVA episodes)
script (4 episodes)

Stray Dog: Kerberos Panzer Cops
Stray Dog Keruberosu Jigoku no Banken
March 1991 (film)
original story; screenplay; director

Talking Head
October 1992 (film)
director; screenplay

Mobile Police Patlabor 2 the Movie
Kidō Keisatsu Patoreibā 2 the Movie
August 1993
director

Ghost in the Shell
Kōkaku Kidōtai
September 1995
director

Remnant 6
Uchū Kamotsusen Remunanto 6
August 1996
coordinating supervisor

Jin-Roh
February 2000
original story; screenplay

Blood the Last Vampire
November 2000
supervising producer

Avalon
November 2000
director

Mini Pato
Fall 2001 (3 episodes)
screenplay

Killers
(".50 Woman" segment only)
2002
screenplay; director

Innocence
planned for Spring 2004
screenplay; director

NOTES

CHAPTER I

1. Janet Pocorobba, "Freedom within Bounds: A Conversation with Donald Richie," *Kyoto Journal* 41 (Summer 1999): 19.
2. Alex Kerr, *Dogs and Demons: Tales from the Dark Side of Japan* (New York: Hill and Wang, 2001), 327.
3. Harry Knowles, "Mamoru Oshii's *Avalon* Review," *Ain't It Cool News,* May 7, 2001, http://www.aintitcool.com/display.cgi?id=8928.
4. "Chat with the Wachowski Brothers," *Official Matrix Website,* November 6, 1999, http://whatisthematrix.warnerbros.com/cmp/larryandychat.html.
5. "Multimedia Grand Prix '96," *Digital Content Association of Japan Homepage,* July 31, 2001, http://www.dcaj.or.jp/d-con/con/mmgp/96awards/souhyo_e/ji_so.htm.
6. Scott Frazier, interview with the author, Dallas, TX, August 31, 2002.
7. James Cameron, "Ghost in the Shell," *Manga Entertainment—Official Australian Website,* October 30, 2000, http://www.manga.com.au/gits4.html.
8. Scott Frazier, "Anime Production Panel," speech presented at AnimeFest 2002, Dallas, TX, August 31, 2002.
9. This and other elements of Oshii's early biography presented here are from "Gaburieru no Yūutsu: Oshii Mamoru Kōshiki Saito," ("Gabriel's Melancholy: Oshii Mamoru Official Site"), http://www.oshiimamoru.com.
10. Mamoru Oshii, "A Stray Dog Goes to Cannes," *Artists Liaison Ltd. Homepage,* February 11, 2002, http://www.artistsliaisonltd.com/flash/english/special/6th/oshii1–1.html.
11. Tony Rayns, "Game Master," *Sight & Sound* 12 (November 2002): 30.
12. Carl Gustav Horn, "Mamoru Oshii," in *Anime Interviews: The First Five Years of Animerica Anime & Manga Monthly (1992–1997),* ed. Trish Ledoux (San Francisco: Cadence Books, 1997): 134–135.
13. Lucien James and Oliver DeDoncker, "Just a Chat Before I Go: Kenji Kawai on the Run," *Akadot.com,* December 19, 2001, http://www.akadot.com/article/article-kawai1.html.

14. *FLCL,* vol. 1, DVD, directed by Kazuya Tsurumaki (Los Angeles: Synch-Point, 2002). Interestingly, this comment is only in the English dub and does not appear in the original Japanese dialogue.

15. Carl Gustav Horn, "At the Carpenter Center: The *PULP* Mamoru Oshii Interview," *PULP* 5 (September 2001): 15.

CHAPTER 2

1. Kenzaburo Oe, *Japan, the Ambiguous, and Myself: The Nobel Prize Speech and Other Lectures* (New York: Kodansha International, 1995).

2. Susan J. Napier, "Hybrid Identities—Oe, Japan, and the West," in *Return to Japan: From "Pilgrimage" to the West,* ed. Yoichi Nagashima (Oakville, CT: Aarhus University Press, 2001): 321.

3. "The World's Most Popular Female Comic Artist . . . Rumiko Takahashi," *Viz.com,* http://viz.com/products/series/takahashi/interview_02.html.

4. Seiji Horibuchi, "Rumiko Takahashi," in *Anime Interviews: The First Five Years of Animerica Anime & Manga Monthly (1992–1997),* ed. Trish Ledoux (San Francisco: Cadence Books, 1997): 20.

5. Harold David, "The Elegant Enigmas of Mamoru Oshii," *Anime-Fantastique* 1 (Spring 1999): 8.

6. Horibuchi, "Rumiko Takahashi," 19.

7. Mark Siegel, "Foreigner as Alien in Japanese Science Fantasy," *Science Fiction Studies* 12, no. 37 (November 1985): 257.

8. Jonathan Clements, "Sex with the Girl Next Door: The Roots of the Anime Erotic," in Helen McCarthy and Jonathan Clements, *The Erotic Anime Movie Guide* (Woodstock, NY: Overlook Press, 1999): 95.

9. Ibid., 105.

10. Another equally acceptable term is OAV, an acronym that transposes the last two words of the phrase.

11. Shigeru Watanabe, "Part 2: Dallos, the World's First OVA (Original Video Animation)," *Artists Liason Ltd. Homepage,* December 14, 2000, http://www.artistsliaisonltd.com/flash/english/special/4th/watanabe2–1.html.

12. Jonathan Clements and Helen McCarthy, *The Anime Encyclopedia: A Guide to Japanese Animation Since 1917* (Berkeley, CA: Stone Bridge Press, 2001): 79.

13. Ibid.

14. "Speculate about *Jin-Roh,*" *Jin-Roh: The Wolf Brigade,* special ed. DVD, directed by Hiroyuki Kitakubo (Cypress, CA: Bandai Entertainment, 2001).

15. Yūji Moriyama, commentary audio track, *Project A-ko,* DVD, directed by Katsuhiko Nishijima, New York: U.S. Manga Corps, 2002.

16. Takayuki Karahashi, "Leiji Matsumoto," in *Anime Interviews,* ed. Ledoux, 151.
17. Daisetz T. Suzuki, *Zen and Japanese Culture* (Princeton, NJ: Princeton University Press, 1959): 220.
18. Ibid., 435
19. Horn, "Mamoru Oshii," 139.
20. Mamoru Oshii, e-mail to the author, translated by Yoshiki Sakurai, March 15, 2003.
21. Toshifumi Yoshida, "Mamoru Oshii," translated by Andy Nakatani, *Animerica* 9 (June 2001): 40.
22. *Harai-gushi* literally means "purification skewer." It is a stick with strips of paper folded in a zigzag pattern attached to one end, used in Shinto for purification rituals.
23. Yoshida, "Mamoru Oshii," 40.
24. Susan J. Napier, *Anime from Akira to Princess Mononoke: Experiencing Contemporary Japanese Animation* (New York: Palgrave, 2000): 20.
25. Stephen Mansfield, "Tokyo, the Organic Labyrinth," *Japan Quarterly* (July-September 1998): 31–41.
26. Mary Douglas, *Purity and Danger: An Analysis of Concepts of Pollution and Taboo* (New York: Routledge, 2002).
27. Napier, *Anime from Akira to Princess Mononoke,* 12.
28. David, "The Elegant Enigmas of Mamoru Oshii," 8.

CHAPTER 3

1. Yūji Moriyama, commentary audio track, *Project A-ko.*
2. Ibid.
3. Clements and McCarthy, *The Anime Encyclopedia,* 427.
4. From Genkosha's *Animation Video Collectors Guide,* quoted in Horn, "Mamoru Oshii," 134.
5. "Yoshitaka Amano," *AnimeJump.com* (March 1999), http://www.animejump.com/cgi-bin/go.cgi?go=features/yoshitaka-amano/amano.
6. Charles McCarter, "Flights of Fantasy," *EX: The Online World of Anime & Manga* 4, no. 7 (1999), http://www.ex.org/4.7/04-feature_amano1.html.
7. Doug Ranney, "The Masters of Animation: An Unprecedented Opportunity," *Animation World Magazine,* September 1, 1997, http://mag.awn.com/index.php3?ltype=all&sort=date&article_no=702&page=3.
8. For more examples of religion in anime, see Antonia Levi, *Samurai from Outer Space: Understanding Japanese Animation* (Chicago: Open Court, 1996).

9. Owen Thomas, "Amusing Himself to Death: Kazuya Tsurumaki Speaks About the Logic and Illogic That Went into Creating *FLCL*," *Akadot.com,* October 17, 2001. http://www.akadot.com/article/article-tsurumaki1.html.

10. Scott Frazier, interview with the author, Dallas, TX, August 31, 2002.

11. Carl Gustav Horn, interview with the author, San Francisco, CA, March 1, 2003.

12. This translation is from Ellis S. Krauss, *Japanese Radicals Revisited* (Berkeley: University of California Press, 1974): 89.

13. Venetia Newall, *An Egg at Easter: A Folklore Study* (Bloomington: Indiana University Press, 1971): 30.

14. W. G. Aston (translator), *Nihongi* (London: George Allen & Unwin, 1956): 1–2.

15. Newall, *An Egg at Easter,* 175.

16. Ibid., 158.

17. Carl Gustav Horn, "Anime," in *Japan Edge: The Insider's Guide to Japanese Pop Subculture,* ed. Annette Roman (San Francisco: Cadence Books, 1999): 39.

18. Mamoru Oshii, e-mail to the author, March 15, 2003.

19. Susan J. Napier, "Liminal Worlds and Liminal Girls: Femininity and Fantasy in Japanese Animation," paper presented at Schoolgirls and Mobilesuits, Minneapolis College of Art and Design, September 28, 2002.

20. Charles McCarter, "Peering Into the Mists of Avalon: An Interview with Oshii Mamoru," *EX: The Online World of Anime & Manga,* June 16, 2001, http://www.ex.org/articles/2001/2001.6.16-exclusive-peering_into_the_mists_of_avalon-pg1.html

21. Oshii, e-mail to the author.

CHAPTER 4

1. "Gaburieru no Yūutsu: Oshii Mamoru Kōshiki Saito," http://www.oshiimamoru.com.

2. Lorraine Savage, "Anime Symposium Part 3: Anime Creation and Production: The Making of *Ghost in the Shell* (with Mamoru Oshii)," *The Rose,* no. 60 (October 1999), http://home.comcast.net/~hasshin/symp3.html.

3. "Kidō Keisatsu Patoreibā 2 wo Megutte: Jidai ni Keri wo Tsukeru Tameni," *Oshii Mamoru Zenshigoto: Urusei Yatsura Kara Avaron Made* (Tokyo: Kinema Junpo, 2001): 89. English translation from: "Around the Movie *Patlabor 2:* To Put an End to the Era," trans. Ryoko Toyama, *Nausicaa.net,* http://www.nausicaa.net/miyazaki/interviews/m_oshii_patlabor2.html.

4. Ibid.
5. Horn, "At the Carpenter Center," 15.Chapter 5

CHAPTER 5

1. "All About *Patlabor WXIII*," Supplemental disc, *Patlabor WXIII,* special ed. DVD, directed by Fumihiko Takayama (Des Moines, IA: Pioneer Entertainment, 2003).
2. Kerr, *Dogs and Demons,* 11.
3. Kenneth Lee, Edward Kwon, Charles McCarter, and the *EX* Staff, "Anime Expo 2000: Takada Akemi Guest of Honor Panel," *EX: The Online World of Anime & Manga* 5, no. 5 (2000), http://www.ex.org/5.5/16-feature_axp_takada.html.
4. Avery M. Tom, "Never Forget Your Protective Headgear!" *Animerica* 2, no. 6 (June 1994): 6.
5. Charles McCarter, "Record of an Illustrator: Interview with Izubuchi Yutaka," *EX: The Online World of Anime & Manga* 4, no. 6 (1999), http://www.ex.org/4.6/04-feature_izubuchi.html.
6. "Tatsunoko Wins 'Author's Right' to *Macross,*" *AnimeNewsNetwork.com,* January 20, 2003, http://www.animenewsnetwork.com/article.php?id=3072.
7. Takayuki Karahashi, "Masami Yuki," *Animerica* 5, no. 12 (December 1997): 9.
8. Amos Wong, "Inside Production I.G.," *Newtype USA* 2, no. 4 (April 2003): 30.
9. A seventh episode of this OVA series was produced, but it was produced after the original six and was not written or directed by Oshii.
10. Bruce Sterling, "Preface," in *Mirrorshades: The Cyberpunk Anthology,* ed. Bruce Sterling (New York: Ace Books, 1986): xiii.
11. Karl Marx, *Early Writings,* trans. Rodney Livingstone and Gregor Benton (New York: Penguin Books, 1992): 324.
12. Heather Hicks, "Striking Cyborgs: Reworking the 'Human' in Marge Piercy's *He She and It,*" in *reload: rethinking women + cyberculture,* eds. Mary Flanagan and Austin Booth (Cambridge, MA: The MIT Press. 2002): 95.
13. Krauss, *Japanese Radicals Revisited,* 5.
14. Patricia G. Steinhoff, "Student Conflict," in *Conflict in Japan,* eds. Ellis S. Krauss, Thomas P. Rohlen, and Patricia G. Steinhoff (Honolulu: University of Hawaii Press, 1984): 174.
15. "Meet the Director," *Patlabor The Mobile Police: The TV Series,* volume 1, DVD, directed by Naoyuki Yoshinaga (New York: U.S. Manga Corps, 2001).

16. Patrick Macias, *TokyoScope: The Japanese Cult Film Companion* (San Francisco: Cadence Books, 2001): 25.
17. Takashi Oshiguchi, "Yutaka Izubuchi, Toiler in the Vineyards of Anime," *Animerica* 2, no. 6 (June 1994): 5.
18. Yoshida, "Mamoru Oshii," 38.
19. For a fascinating look at the significance and meaning of numbers in Japanese popular culture, see Thomas Crump, *The Japanese Numbers Game: The Use and Understanding of Numbers in Modern Japan* (New York: Routledge, 1992).
20. Oshii, e-mail to the author, March 15, 2003.
21. Thanks to Assaf K. Dekel for e-mailing me about the significance of the number 26 (June 10, 2002).
22. Jean Baudrillard, *The System of Objects,* trans. James Benedict (New York: Verso, 1996): 121.
23. Yoshida, "Mamoru Oshii," 39.
24. Steinhoff, "Student Conflict," 182.
25. Rayns, "Game Master," 28–29.
26. Frazier, interview with the author.
27. Oshii, e-mail to the author.
28. Horn, "Mamoru Oshii," 139.
29. For an in-depth examination of mediated perception in *Patlabor 2,* see Christopher Bolton, "The Mecha's Blind Spot: *Patlabor 2* and the Phenomenology of Anime," *Science Fiction Studies* 29, no. 88 (November 2002): 453–474.
30. Michael Fisch, "Nation, War, and Japan's Future in the Science Fiction *Anime* Film *Patlabor II,*" *Science Fiction Studies* 27, no. 79 (March 2000): 61.
31. "All About *Patlabor WXIII,*" *Patlabor WXIII,* DVD.
32. "The Consolidated Design of the Creating Process for *MiniPato,*" *MiniPato* disc, *Patlabor WXIII,* special ed. DVD, directed by Fumihiko Takayama, Des Moines, IA: Pioneer Entertainment, 2003.

CHAPTER 6

1. Horn, "Mamoru Oshii," 138.
2. Ibid., 137.
3. Masamune Shirow, *Ghost in the Shell* (Milwaukie, OR: Dark Horse Comics, 1995): 307.
4. "Animation, Anime, and Spawn: Cartoons Just Grew Up," television program, HBO, May 19, 1998.
5. Hiroyuki Yamaga, commentary audio track, *Royal Space Force: The Wings of Honneamise,* DVD, directed by Hiroyuki Yamaga (Chicago: Manga Entertainment, 2000).

6. Mark Schilling. *Contemporary Japanese Film* (New York: Weather-hill, 1999): 237.
7. Sterling, "Preface," xiii
8. Takayuki Tatsumi, "The Japanese Reflection of Mirrorshades," in *Storming the Reality Studio: A Casebook of Cyberpunk and Post-modern Fiction,* ed. Larry McCaffery (Durham, NC: Duke University Press, 1991): 366–373.
9. Trish Ledoux, "Masamune Shirow," in *Anime Interviews: The First Five Years of Animerica Anime & Manga Monthly (1992–1997),* ed. Trish Ledoux (San Francisco: Cadence Books, 1997): 39.
10. Emru Townsend, "Marvin Gleicher," *The Critical Eye* (Summer 1996), http://purpleplanetmedia.com/eye/inte/mgleicher–2.shtml.
11. David Nerlich, "'Irresponsible Pictures': The Art of Anime," *IF Magazine* 27 (September 2000): 60.
12. William Gibson, "My Own Private Tokyo," *Wired* (September 2001): 117–119.
13. "Ichiban: Ten Reasons Why the Sun Still Rises in the East," *Wired* (September 2001): 120–125.
14. David Morley and Kevin Robins, "Techno-Orientalism: Futures, Foreigners and Phobias," *New Formations* 16 (Spring 1992): 154.
15. Toshiya Ueno, "Japanimation and Techno-Orientalism: Japan as the Sub-Empire of Signs," *Documentary Box* 9 (December 31, 1996): 3.
16. Toshiya Ueno, "Techno-Orientalism and Media-Tribalism: On Japanese Animation and Rave Culture," *Third Text* 47 (Summer 1999): 98.
17. "Japanese Government Policies in Education, Science, Sports and Culture," Year 2000 White Paper, *Ministry of Education Website,* http://wwwwp.mext.go.jp/eky2000/.
18. Ueno, "Japanimation and Techno-Orientalism," 3–4.
19. Frederik L. Schodt, *Inside the Robot Kingdom: Japan, Mechatronics, and the Coming Robotopia* (Tokyo: Kodansha International, 1988): 14.
20. "Ghost in the Shell Production Report," *Ghost in the Shell,* DVD, distributed by Manga Entertainment, 1998.
21. Carl Silvio, "Reconfiguring the Radical Cyborg in Mamoru Oshii's *Ghost in the Shell,*" *Science Fiction Studies* 26, no. 77 (March 1999): 56.
22. Ibid., 65.
23. Ibid., 66.
24. Anne Balsamo, *Technologies of the Gendered Body: Reading Cyborg Women* (Durham, NC: Duke University Press, 1996): 9.
25. Yuko Nakano, "Women and Buddhism—Blood Impurity and Motherhood," trans. Alison Watts, in *Women and Religion in Japan,* eds. Akiko Okuda and Haruko Okano (Weisbaden: Harrassowitz Verlag, 1998): 78.
26. Ichirō Hori, "Shamanism in Japan," *Japanese Journal of Religious Studies* 2, no. 4 (December 1975): 233.

27. Napier, *Anime: From Akira to Princess Mononoke,* 113.
28. Ibid., 108–111.
29. Bernard F. Batto, *Slaying the Dragon: Mythmaking in the Biblical Tradition* (Louisville, KY: Westminster/John Knox Press, 1992): 45–6.
30. Teigo Yoshida, "The Feminine in Japanese Folk Religion: Polluted or Divine?" in *Unwrapping Japan: Society and Culture in Anthropological Perspective,* ed. Eyal Ben-Ari, Brian Moeran, and James Valentine (Honolulu: University of Hawaii Press, 1990): 58–77.
31. Nakano, "Women and Buddhism—Blood Impurity and Motherhood," 65–85.
32. Margaret M. Lock, *East Asian Medicine in Urban Japan: Varieties of Medical Experience* (Berkeley: University of California Press, 1980): 182.
33. Nakano, "Women and Buddhism—Blood Impurity and Motherhood," 70.
34. Hicks, "Striking Cyborgs," 100.
35. Ibid., 101.
36. Donna Haraway, "A Cyborg Manifesto: Science, Technology and Socialist-Feminism in the Late Twentieth Century," in *Simians, Cyborgs and Women: The Reinvention of Nature* (London: Free Association Books, 1991): 181.
37. Livia Monnet, "Towards the Feminine Sublime, or the Story of 'A Twinkling Monad, Shape-Shifting Across Dimension': Intermediality, Fantasy and Special Effects in Cyberpunk Film and Animation," *Japan Forum* 14, no. 2 (September 2002): 231.
38. Napier, *Anime: From Akira to Princess Mononoke,* 272.
39. "Scrolls to Screen: The History and Culture of Anime," *The Animatrix,* DVD (Burbank, CA: Warner Brothers, 2003).
40. For an in-depth look at the various shots referenced in *The Matrix,* see Kukhee Choo, "The Influence of Japanese Animation on U.S. Visual Communication Media," Master's thesis, University of Texas at Austin, 2001.
41. Wong, "Inside Production I.G.," 32.
42. Taro Kanamoto, "Special Anniversary Interview: Oshii Mamoru," *Raijin Game & Anime* 1 (December 18, 2002): 7.

CHAPTER 7

1. "Interviewing Mamoru Oshii," Official Production I.G. website, http://www2.production-ig.co.jp/eng2/oshii1.htm.
2. Mamoru Oshii, *Hellhounds: Panzer Cops,* vol. 1 (Milwaukie, OR: Dark Horse Comics, 1994): 26.
3. "Interviewing Tetsuya Nishio," Official Production I.G. website, http://www2.production-ig.co.jp/eng2/nishio.htm.

4. Luis Reyes, "Chatting with Ishikawa: The 'I' of Production I.G. Spends a Few Minutes with *Akadot*," *Akadot.com*, August 15, 2001, http://www.akadot.com/article/article-ishikawa1.html.
5. "Speculate about *Jin-Roh*," *Jin-Roh* DVD, 2001.
6. Oshii, e-mail to the author, March 15, 2003.
7. Jack Zipes, *The Trials and Tribulations of Little Red Riding Hood: Versions of the Tale in Sociocultural Context* (South Hadley, MA: Bergin & Garvey Publishers, 1983): 17.
8. Ibid., 17–18.
9. Yoshida, "Mamoru Oshii," 37.
10. Ibid.
11. Takashi Oshiguchi, "From the Forest: On *Jin-Roh* and the Popularity of Anime Movies," *Animerica* 9, no. 5 (June 2001): 66.
12. A more accurate translation of "Oshii Juku" would be "Oshii Cram School," although "Team Oshii" has become the accepted translation. (Students in Japan often attend cram schools in the evenings after their regular school in order to score higher on high school and college entrance exams.) Much of the information of the inner workings of Team Oshii is from Frasier, interview with the author, August 31, 2002.
13. Oshii, e-mail to the author.
14. Frazier, interview with the author.
15. Clements and McCarthy, *The Anime Encyclopedia*, 71.
16. "SciFi.com Chat Transcript: Anime Director Hiroyuki Kitakubo," *SciFi.com*, August 1, 2000, http://www.scifi.com/transcripts/2000/kitakubo.html.
17. "Mamoru Oshii and Production I.G.," *AnimeJump.com* (March 1999), http://www.animejump.com/cgi-bin/go.cgi?go=features/mamoru-oshii/oshii.
18. Christopher MacDonald, "Interview: Production I.G.," *AnimeNews-Network.com*, August 1, 2000, http://www.animenewsnetwork.com/feature.php?id=24.
19. Frazier, interview with the author.
20. Reyes, "Chatting with Ishikawa."
21. Sharon Kinsella, "What's Behind the Fetishism of Japanese School Uniforms?" *Fashion Theory* 6, no. 2 (June 2002): 219.
22. Sara Ellis and Luis Reyes, "Kenji Kamiyama on Anime: *Blood* Script Writer Talks About His Career," *Akadot.com*, August 13, 2001, http://www.akadot.com/article/article-kamiyama1.html.
23. Frazier, interview with the author.
24. Reyes, "Chatting with Ishikawa."
25. Carl Gustav Horn, "Streaks of Red and White: The Short Long Time of the *Blood* Anime," forthcoming.
26. Wong, "Inside Production I.G.," 30.
27. Ellis and Reyes, "Kenji Kamiyama on Anime."
28. Horn, interview with the author, March 1, 2003.

CHAPTER 8

1. Oshii, e-mail to the author, March 15, 2003.
2. Shinishi Ishikawa, "Avalon," trans. Mayumi Kaneko, *Shift Japan* 51 (February 2001), http://www.shift.jp.org/051/avalon/.
3. Betting on online games: Scott Steinberg and Brian Lam, "Soldiers of Fortune," *Wired* 11, no. 7 (July 2003): 60. Selling game information: Justin Hall, "Galaxies Auctions—It Has Already Begun," *Game Girl Advance,* July 14, 2003, http://www.gamegirladvance.com/archives/2003/07/14/galaxies_auctions_it_has_already_begun.html.
4. Rayns, "Game Master," 30.
5. Taro Kanamoto, "The Creators' Chat Room: Oshii Mamoru," *Raijin Game & Anime* 3 (January 1, 2003): 9.
6. Rayns, "Game Master," 30.
7. Oshii, e-mail to the author.
8. For more examples of portrayals of Morgan in modern film, see Jacqueline de Weever, "Morgan and the Problem of Incest," in *Cinema Arthuriana: Essays on Arthurian Film,* ed. Kevin J. Harty (New York: Garland Publishing, 1991): 145–156, and Maureen Fries, "How to Handle a Woman, or Morgan at the Movies," in *King Arthur on Film: New Essays on Arthurian Cinema,* ed. Kevin J. Harty (Jefferson, NC: McFarland and Company, 1999): 67–80.
9. Raymond H. Thompson, *The Return from Avalon: A Study of the Arthurian Legend in Modern Fiction* (Westport, CT: Greenwood Press, 1985): 77–78.
10. Ibid., 85.
11. Eri Izawa, "The Romantic, Passionate Japanese in Anime: A Look at the Hidden Japanese Soul," in *Japan Pop!: Inside the World of Japanese Popular Culture,* ed. Timothy J. Craig (Armonk, NY: M. E. Sharpe, 2000): 140–141.
12. Daniel Mackay, *The Fantasy Role-Playing Game: A New Performing Art* (Jefferson, NC: McFarland & Company, 2001): 23.
13. Laurel Anderson Tryforos, "Questing by Computer: Arthurian Themes in Computer Games," *Avalon to Camelot* 2, no. 2 (1986): 15–16.
14. Yuji Oniki, "Tokyo Diary No. 5," in *Japan Edge: The Insider's Guide to Japanese Pop Subculture,* ed. Annette Roman (San Francisco: Cadence Books, 1999): 159.
15. Jean Baudrillard, *Simulacra and Simulation,* trans. Sheila Faria Glaser (Ann Arbor: University of Michigan Press, 1994): 1.
16. Robert Woodhead, e-mail to the author, April 1, 2003.
17. John Rhys, *Studies in the Arthurian Legend* (Oxford: Clarendon Press, 1891): 358.
18. Kanamoto, "The Creators' Chat Room," 8.
19. Laurence Reymond, "Entretien Avec Mamoru Oshii," *Fluctuat.net,* March 15, 2002, http://www.fluctuat.net/cinema/interview/oshii2.htm.

20. Oshii, e-mail to the author.
21. Rayns, "Game Master," 31.
22. Oshii, e-mail to the author.

CHAPTER 9

1. See Choo, "The Influence of Japanese Animation on U.S. Visual Communication Media," and J. P. Telotte, *Science Fiction Film* (Cambridge: Cambridge University Press, 2001): 112–116.
2. Horn, "Anime," 19.
3. Napier, *Anime from Akira to Princess Mononoke,* 12.
4. Melek Ortabasi, "Fictional Fantasy or Historical Fact? The Search for Japanese Identity in Miyazaki Hayao's *Mononokehime,*" in *A Century of Popular Culture in Japan,* ed. Douglas Slaymaker (Lewiston, NY: The Edwin Mellen Press, 2000): 218–219.
5. Susan J. Napier, "Confronting Master Narratives: History as Vision in Miyazaki Hayao's Cinema of De-assurance," *Positions: East Asia Cultures Critique* 9, no. 2 (2001): 471.
6. Marilyn Ivy, *Discourses of the Vanishing* (Chicago: University of Chicago Press, 1995): 105.
7. Brian Moeran, "Reading Japanese in Katei Gahō: The Art of Being an Upperclass Woman," in *Women, Media and Consumption in Japan,* ed. Lise Skov and Brian Moeran (Honolulu: University of Hawaii Press, 1995): 121.
8. Napier, *Anime from Akira to Princess Mononoke,* 25.
9. Yoshida, "Mamoru Oshii," 39.
10. Helen McCarthy, *Hayao Miyazaki: Master of Japanese Animation* (Berkeley, CA: Stone Bridge Press, 1999): 79–80.
11. Anne Cooper-Chen, *Mass Communication in Japan* (Ames: Iowa State University Press, 1997): 211–212.
12. See Silvio, "Reconfiguring the Radical Cyborg in Mamoru Oshii's *Ghost in the Shell,*" and Frederik L. Schodt, *Dreamland Japan: Writings on Modern Manga* (Berkeley, CA: Stone Bridge Press, 1996): 279–280.
13. See Jennifer Robertson, *Tazarazuka: Sexual Politics and Popular Culture in Modern Japan* (Berkeley: University of California Press, 1998).
14. Gerald Figal, *Civilization and Monsters: Spirits of Modernity in Meiji Japan* (Durham, NC: Duke University Press, 1999): 97
15. Ibid.
16. Ibid., 175.
17. Ibid., 177.
18. Ibid., 178.

19. "*Killers* Official Homepage," http://www.killers.jp/intro/intro.html.
20. Kanamoto, "The Creators' Chat Room," 11.
21. Mark Schilling, "Shoot 'Em Up, in Bits," *Japan Times,* June 25, 2003, http://www.japantimes.com/cgi-bin/getarticle.pl5?ff20030625a2.htm.
22. Oshii, e-mail to the author.

BIBLIOGRAPHY

Note: The preponderance of Internet sources in the bibliography is indicative of the highly wired nature of the anime fan community. Many articles and interviews that appeared online only.

"All About *Patlabor WXIII*." Supplemental disc. *Patlabor WXIII*, special ed. DVD. Directed by Fumihiko Takayama. Des Moines, IA: Pioneer Entertainment, 2003.

"Animation, Anime, and Spawn: Cartoons Just Grew Up." Television program. Home Box Office. May 19, 1998.

Aston, W. G. (translator). *Nihongi*. London: George Allen & Unwin, 1956.

Balsamo, Anne. *Technologies of the Gendered Body: Reading Cyborg Women*. Durham, NC: Duke University Press, 1996.

Batto, Bernard F. *Slaying the Dragon: Mythmaking in the Biblical Tradition*. Louisville, KY: Westminster/John Knox Press, 1992.

Baudrillard, Jean. *Simulacra and Simulation*. Translated by Sheila Faria Glaser. Ann Arbor: University of Michigan Press, 1994.

———. *The System of Objects*. Translated by James Benedict. New York: Verso, 1996.

Bolton, Christopher. "The Mecha's Blind Spot: *Patlabor 2* and the Phenomenology of Anime." *Science Fiction Studies* 29, no. 88 (November 2002): 453–474.

Cameron, James. "Ghost in the Shell." *Manga Entertainment—Official Australian Website,* October 30, 2000. http://www.manga.com.au/gits4.html (accessed June 26, 2003).

"Chat with the Wachowski Brothers." *Official Matrix Website.* November 6, 1999. http://whatisthematrix.warnerbros.com/cmp/larryandychat.html (accessed June 26, 2003).

Choo, Kukhee. "The Influence of Japanese Animation on U.S. Visual Communication Media." Master's thesis, University of Texas at Austin, 2001.

Clements, Jonathan, and Helen McCarthy. *The Anime Encyclopedia: A Guide to Japanese Animation Since 1917*. Berkeley, CA: Stone Bridge Press, 2001.

"The Consolidated Design of the Creating Process for *MiniPato*." *Mini-Pato* disc. *Patlabor WXIII*, special ed. DVD. Directed by Fumihiko Takayama. Des Moines, IA: Pioneer Entertainment, 2003.

Cooper-Chen, Anne. *Mass Communication in Japan*. Ames: Iowa State University Press, 1997.

Crump, Thomas. *The Japanese Numbers Game: The Use and Understanding of Numbers in Modern Japan*. New York: Routledge, 1992.

David, Harold. "The Elegant Enigmas of Mamoru Oshii." *AnimeFantastique* 1 (Spring 1999): 6–9.

de Weever, Jacqueline. "Morgan and the Problem of Incest." In *Cinema Arthuriana: Essays on Arthurian Film,* edited by Kevin J. Harty, 145–156. New York: Garland Publishing, 1991.

Douglas, Mary. *Purity and Danger: An Analysis of Concepts of Pollution and Taboo*. New York: Routledge, 2002.

Ellis, Sara, and Luis Reyes. "Kenji Kamiyama on Anime: *Blood* Script Writer Talks about His Career." *Akadot.com,* August 13, 2001. http://www.akadot.com/article/article-kamiyama1.html (accessed June 25, 2003).

Figal, Gerald. *Civilization and Monsters: Spirits of Modernity in Meiji Japan*. Durham, NC: Duke University Press, 1999.

Fisch, Michael. "Nation, War, and Japan's Future in the Science Fiction Anime Film *Patlabor II.*" *Science Fiction Studies* 27, no. 79 (March 2000): 49–68.

FLCL. Volume 1. DVD. Directed by Kazuya Tsurumaki. Los Angeles: Synch-Point, 2002.

Frazier, Scott. "Anime Production Panel." Speech presented at AnimeFest 2002. Dallas, TX, August 31, 2002.

Fries, Maureen. "How to Handle a Woman, or Morgan at the Movies." In *King Arthur on Film: New Essays on Arthurian Cinema,* edited by Kevin J. Harty, 67–80. Jefferson, NC: McFarland and Company, 1999.

"Gaburieru no Yūutsu: Oshii Mamoru Kōshiki Saito" ("Gabriel's Melancholy: Oshii Mamoru Official Site"). http://www.oshiimamoru.com (accessed August 31, 2002).

"Ghost in the Shell Production Report." *Ghost in the Shell*. DVD. Directed by Mamoru Oshii. Chicago: Manga Entertainment, 1998.

Gibson, William. "My Own Private Tokyo." *Wired* (September 2001): 117–119.

Hall, Justin. "Galaxies Auctions—It Has Already Begun." *Game Girl Advance,* July 14, 2003. http://www.gamegirladvance.com/archives/2003/07/14/galaxies_auctions_it_has_already_begun.html (accessed August 6, 2003).

Haraway, Donna. "A Cyborg Manifesto: Science, Technology and Socialist-Feminism in the Late Twentieth Century." In *Simians, Cyborgs and Women: The Reinvention of Nature,* 149–181. London: Free Association Books, 1991.

Hicks, Heather. "Striking Cyborgs: Reworking the 'Human' in Marge Piercy's *He She and It.*" In *reload: rethinking women + cyberculture,* edited by Mary Flanagan and Austin Booth, 85–106. Cambridge, MA: The MIT Press, 2002.

Hori, Ichirō. "Shamanism in Japan." *Japanese Journal of Religious Studies* 2, no. 4 (December 1975): 231–287.

Horibuchi, Seiji. "Rumiko Takahashi." In *Anime Interviews: The First Five Years of Animerica Anime & Manga Monthly (1992–1997),* edited by Trish Ledoux, 16–25. San Francisco: Cadence Books, 1997.

Horn, Carl Gustav. "Anime." In *Japan Edge: The Insider's Guide to Japanese Pop Subculture,* edited by Annette Roman, 13–41. San Francisco: Cadence Books, 1999.

———. "At the Carpenter Center: The *PULP* Mamoru Oshii Interview." *PULP* 5 (September 2001): 10–17.

———. "Mamoru Oshii." In *Anime Interviews: The First Five Years of Animerica Anime & Manga Monthly (1992–1997),* edited by Trish Ledoux, 134–41. San Francisco: Cadence Books, 1997.

———. "Streaks of Red and White: The Short Long Time of the *Blood* Anime." Forthcoming.

"Ichiban: Ten Reasons Why the Sun Still Rises in the East." *Wired* (September 2001): 120–125.

"Interviewing Mamoru Oshii." Official Production I.G. website, http://www2.production-ig.co.jp/eng2/oshii1.htm (accessed September 19, 2002; site now discontinued).

"Interviewing Tetsuya Nishio." Official Production I.G. website, http://www2.production-ig.co.jp/eng2/nishio.htm (accessed September 19, 2002; site now discontinued).

Ishikawa, Shinishi. "Avalon." Translated by Mayumi Kaneko. *Shift Japan* 51 (February 2001). http://www.shift.jp.org/051/avalon/ (accessed June 30, 2003).

Ivy, Marilyn. *Discourses of the Vanishing.* Chicago: University of Chicago Press, 1995.

Izawa, Eri. "The Romantic, Passionate Japanese in Anime: A Look at the Hidden Japanese Soul." In *Japan Pop!: Inside the World of Japanese Popular Culture,* edited by Timothy J. Craig, 138–153. Armonk, NY: M. E. Sharpe, 2000.

James, Lucien, and Oliver DeDoncker. "Just a Chat Before I Go: Kenji Kawai on the Run." *Akadot.com,* December 19, 2001. http://www.akadot.com/article/article-kawai1.html (accessed June 26 2003).

"Japanese Government Policies in Education, Science, Sports and Culture." Year 2000 White Paper. Japanese Ministry of Education Website, http://wwwwp.mext.go.jp/eky2000/ (accessed April 30, 2002).

Kanamoto, Taro. "The Creators' Chat Room: Oshii Mamoru." *Raijin Game & Anime* 3 (January 1, 2003): 8–11.

————. "Special Anniversary Interview: Oshii Mamoru." *Raijin Game & Anime* 1 (December 18, 2002): 6–7.

Karahashi, Takayuki. "Leiji Matsumoto." In *Anime Interviews: The First Five Years of Animerica Anime & Manga Monthly (1992–1997)*, edited by Trish Ledoux, 150–163. San Francisco: Cadence Books, 1997.

Karahashi, Takayuki. "Masami Yuki." *Animerica* 5, no. 12 (December 1997): 8–9, 26–29.

"Kidō Keisatsu Patoreibā 2 wo Megutte: Jidai ni Keri wo Tsukeru Tameni." *Oshii Mamoru Zenshigoto: Urusei Yatsura Kara Avaron Made.* Tokyo: Kinema Junpo, 2001. English translation from: "Around the Movie *Patlabor 2:* To Put an End to the Era," translated by Ryoko Toyama. *Nausicaa.net,* http://www.nausicaa.net/miyazaki/interviews/m_oshii_patlabor2.html (accessed June 26, 2003).

"*Killers* Official Homepage." http://www.killers.jp/intro/intro.html (accessed May 27, 2003).

Kinsella, Sharon. "What's Behind the Fetishism of Japanese School Uniforms?" *Fashion Theory* 6, no. 2 (June 2002): 215–238.

Kerr, Alex. *Dogs and Demons: Tales from the Dark Side of Japan.* New York: Hill and Wang, 2001.

Knowles, Harry. "Mamoru Oshii's *Avalon* Review." *Ain't It Cool News,* May 7, 2001. http://www.aintitcool.com/display.cgi?id=8928 (accessed June 26, 2003).

Krauss, Ellis S. *Japanese Radicals Revisited.* Berkeley: University of California Press, 1974.

Lee, Kenneth, Edward Kwon, Charles McCarter, and the *EX* Staff. "Anime Expo 2000: Takada Akemi Guest of Honor Panel." *EX: The Online World of Anime & Manga* 5, no. 5 (2000). http://www.ex.org/5.5/16-feature_axp_takada.html (accessed June 27, 2003).

Ledoux, Trish. "Masamune Shirow." In *Anime Interviews: The First Five Years of Animerica Anime & Manga Monthly (1992–1997)*, edited by Trish Ledoux, 38–45. San Francisco: Cadence Books, 1997.

Levi, Antonia. *Samurai from Outer Space: Understanding Japanese Animation.* Chicago: Open Court, 1996.

Lock, Margaret M. *East Asian Medicine in Urban Japan: Varieties of Medical Experience.* Berkeley: University of California Press, 1980.

MacDonald, Christopher. "Interview: Production I.G." *AnimeNewsNetwork.com,* August 1, 2000. http://www.animenewsnetwork.com/feature.php?id=24 (accessed April 28 2003).

Macias, Patrick. *TokyoScope: The Japanese Cult Film Companion.* San Francisco: Cadence Books, 2001.

Mackay, Daniel. *The Fantasy Role-Playing Game: A New Performing Art.* Jefferson, NC: McFarland & Company, 2001.

"Mamoru Oshii and Production I.G." *AnimeJump.com,* March 1999. http://www.animejump.com/cgi-bin/go.cgi?go=features/mamoru-oshii/oshii (accessed August 19, 2002).

Mansfield, Stephen. "Tokyo, the Organic Labyrinth." *Japan Quarterly* (July-September 1998): 31–41.

Marx, Karl. *Early Writings.* Translated by Rodney Livingstone and Gregor Benton. New York: Penguin Books, 1992.

McCarter, Charles. "Flights of Fantasy." *EX: The Online World of Anime & Manga* 4, no. 7 (1999). http://www.ex.org/4.7/04-feature_amano1.html (accessed June 26, 2003).

———. "Peering into the Mists of Avalon: An Interview with Oshii Mamoru." *EX: The Online World of Anime & Manga,* June 16, 2001. http://www.ex.org/articles/2001/2001.6.16-exclusive-peering_into_the_mists_of_avalon-pg1.html (accessed June 26, 2003).

———. "Record of an Illustrator: Interview with Izubuchi Yutaka." *EX: The Online World of Anime & Manga* 4, no. 6 (1999). http://www.ex.org/4.6/04-feature_izubuchi.html (accessed June 27, 2003).

McCarthy, Helen. *Hayao Miyazaki: Master of Japanese Animation.* Berkeley, CA: Stone Bridge Press, 1999.

McCarthy, Helen and Jonathan Clements. *The Erotic Anime Movie Guide.* Woodstock, NY: Overlook Press, 1999.

"Meet the Director." *Patlabor The Mobile Police: The TV Series.* Volume 1. DVD. Directed by Naoyuki Yoshinaga. New York: U.S. Manga Corps, 2001.

Moeran, Brian. "Reading Japanese in Katei Gahō: The Art of Being an Upperclass Woman." In *Women, Media and Consumption in Japan,* edited by Lise Skov and Brian Moeran, 111–142. Honolulu: University of Hawai'i Press, 1995.

Monnet, Livia. "Towards the Feminine Sublime, or the Story of 'A Twinkling Monad, Shape-Shifting Across Dimension': Intermediality, Fantasy and Special Effects in Cyberpunk Film and Animation." *Japan Forum* 14, no. 2 (September 2002): 225–268.

Moriyama, Yūji. Commentary audio track. *Project A-ko.* DVD. Directed by Katsuhiko Nishijima. New York: U.S. Manga Corps, 2002.

Morley, David, and Kevin Robins. "Techno-Orientalism: Futures, Foreigners and Phobias." *New Formations* 16 (Spring 1992): 136–156.

"Multimedia Grand Prix '96." *Digital Content Association of Japan Homepage,* July 31, 2001. http://www.dcaj.or.jp/d-con/con/mmgp/96awards/souhyo_e/ji_so.htm (accessed August 22, 2002; site now discontinued).

Nakano, Yuko. "Women and Buddhism—Blood Impurity and Motherhood." Translated by Alison Watts. In *Women and Religion in Japan,* edited by Akiko Okuda and Haruko Okano, 65–85. Weisbaden: Harrassowitz Verlag, 1998.

Napier, Susan J. *Anime from Akira to Princess Mononoke: Experiencing Contemporary Japanese Animation.* New York: Palgrave, 2000.

———. "Confronting Master Narratives: History as Vision in Miyazaki Hayao's Cinema of De-assurance." *Positions: East Asia Cultures Critique* 9, no. 2 (2001): 467–493.

————. "Hybrid Identities—Oe, Japan, and the West." In *Return to Japan: From "Pilgrimage" to the West,* edited by Yoichi Nagashima, 320–328. Oakville, CT: Aarhus University Press, 2001.

————. "Liminal Worlds and Liminal Girls: Femininity and Fantasy in Japanese Animation." Paper presented at Schoolgirls and Mobilesuits, Minneapolis College of Art and Design, Minneapolis, September 28, 2002.

Nerlich, David. "'Irresponsible Pictures':The Art of Anime." *IF Magazine* 27 (September 2000): 58–61.

Newall, Venetia. *An Egg at Easter: A Folklore Study.* Bloomington: Indiana University Press, 1971.

Oe, Kenzaburo. *Japan, the Ambiguous, and Myself: The Nobel Prize Speech and Other Lectures.* New York: Kodansha International, 1995.

Oniki, Yuji. "Tokyo Diary No. 5." In *Japan Edge: The Insider's Guide to Japanese Pop Subculture,* edited by Annette Roman, 158–159. San Francisco: Cadence Books, 1999.

Ortabasi, Melek. "Fictional Fantasy or Historical Fact? The Search for Japanese Identity in Miyazaki Hayao's *Mononokehime.*" In *A Century of Popular Culture in Japan,* edited by Douglas Slaymaker, 199–228. Lewiston, NY: Edwin Mellen Press, 2000.

Oshiguchi, Takashi. "From the Forest: On *Jin-Roh* and the Popularity of Anime Movies." *Animerica* 9, no. 5 (June 2001): 66.

————. "Yutaka Izubuchi, Toiler in the Vineyards of Anime." *Animerica* 2, no. 6 (June 1994): 4–9.

Oshii, Mamoru. *Hellhounds: Panzer Cops.* Vol. 1. Milwaukie, OR: Dark Horse Comics, 1994.

————. "A Stray Dog Goes to Cannes." *Artists Liason Ltd. Homepage,* February 11, 2002. http://www.artistsliaisonltd.com/flash/english/special/6th/oshii1–1.html (accessed August 22, 2002; site now discontinued).

Pocorobba, Janet. "Freedom within Bounds: A Conversation with Donald Richie." *Kyoto Journal* 41 (Summer 1999): 8–20.

Ranney, Doug. "The Masters of Animation: An Unprecedented Opportunity." *Animation World Magazine,* September 1, 1997. http://mag.awn.com/index.php3?ltype=all&sort=date&article_no=702&page=3 (accessed June 26, 2003).

Rayns, Tony. "Game Master." *Sight & Sound* 12 (November 2002): 28–31.

Reyes, Luis. "Chatting with Ishikawa: The 'I' of Production I.G. Spends a Few Minutes with *Akadot.*" *Akadot.com,* August 15, 2001. http://www.akadot.com/article/article-ishikawa1.html (accessed June 27, 2003).

Reymond, Laurence. "Entretien Avec Mamoru Oshii." *Fluctuat.net,* March 15, 2002. http://www.fluctuat.net/cinema/interview/oshii2.htm (accessed June 23, 2003).

Robertson, Jennifer. *Tazarazuka: Sexual Politics and Popular Culture in Modern Japan*. Berkeley: University of California Press, 1998.

Rhys, John. *Studies in the Arthurian Legend*. Oxford: Clarendon Press, 1891.

Savage, Lorraine. "Anime Symposium Part 3: Anime Creation and Production: The Making of *Ghost in the Shell* (with Mamoru Oshii)." *The Rose*, no. 60 (October 1999). http://home.comcast.net/~hasshin/symp3.html (accessed June 27, 2003).

Schilling, Mark. *Contemporary Japanese Film*. New York: Weatherhill, 1999.

———. "Shoot 'Em Up, in Bits." *Japan Times*, June 25, 2003. http://www.japantimes.com/cgi-bin/getarticle.pl5?ff20030625a2.htm (accessed June 25, 2003).

Schodt, Frederik L. *Dreamland Japan: Writings on Modern Manga*. Berkeley, CA: Stone Bridge Press, 1996.

———. *Inside the Robot Kingdom: Japan, Mechatronics, and the Coming Robotopia*. Tokyo: Kodansha International, 1988.

"SciFi.com Chat Transcript: Anime Director Hiroyuki Kitakubo." *SciFi.com*, August 1, 2000. http://www.scifi.com/transcripts/2000/kitakubo.html (accessed June 30, 2003).

"Scrolls to Screen: The History and Culture of Anime." *The Animatrix*. DVD. Burbank, CA: Warner Brothers, 2003.

Shirow, Masamune. *Ghost in the Shell*. Milwaukie, OR: Dark Horse Comics, 1995.

Siegel, Mark. "Foreigner as Alien in Japanese Science Fantasy." *Science Fiction Studies* 12, no. 37 (November 1985): 252–263.

Silvio, Carl. "Reconfiguring the Radical Cyborg in Mamoru Oshii's *Ghost in the Shell*." *Science Fiction Studies* 26, no. 77 (March 1999): 54–72.

"Speculate about *Jin-Roh*." *Jin-Roh: The Wolf Brigade*, special ed. DVD. Directed by Hiroyuki Kitakubo. Cypress, CA: Bandai Entertainment, 2001.

Steinberg, Scott, and Brian Lam. "Soldiers of Fortune." *Wired* 11, no. 7 (July 2003): 60.

Steinhoff, Patricia G. "Student Conflict." In *Conflict in Japan*, edited by Ellis S. Krauss, Thomas P. Rohlen, and Patricia G. Steinhoff, 174–213. Honolulu: University of Hawai'i Press, 1984.

Sterling, Bruce. "Preface." In *Mirrorshades: The Cyberpunk Anthology*, edited by Bruce Sterling, ix-xvi. New York: Ace Books. 1986.

Suzuki, Daisetz T. *Zen and Japanese Culture*. Princeton, NJ: Princeton University Press, 1959.

Tatsumi, Takayuki. "The Japanese Reflection of Mirrorshades." In *Storming the Reality Studio: A Casebook of Cyberpunk and Postmodern Fiction*, edited by Larry McCaffery, 366–373. Durham, NC: Duke University Press, 1991.

"Tatsunoko Wins 'Author's Right' to *Macross.*" *AnimeNewsNetwork.com,* January 20, 2003. http://www.animenewsnetwork.com/article.php? id=3072 (accessed January 20, 2003).

Telotte, J. P. *Science Fiction Film.* Cambridge: Cambridge University Press, 2001.

Thomas, Owen. "Amusing Himself to Death: Kazuya Tsurumaki Speaks about the Logic and Illogic That Went into Creating *FLCL.*" *Akadot.com,* October 17, 2001. http://www.akadot.com/article/article-tsurumaki1.html (accessed June 26, 2003).

Thompson, Raymond H. *The Return from Avalon: A Study of the Arthurian Legend in Modern Fiction.* Westport, CT: Greenwood Press, 1985.

Tom, Avery M. "Never Forget Your Protective Headgear!" *Animerica* 2, no. 6 (June 1994): 6.

Townsend, Emru. "Marvin Gleicher." *The Critical Eye* (Summer 1996). http://purpleplanetmedia.com/eye/inte/mgleicher–2.shtml (accessed June 12, 2003).

Tryforos, Laurel Anderson. "Questing by Computer: Arthurian Themes in Computer Games." *Avalon to Camelot* 2, no. 2 (1986): 15–16.

Ueno, Toshiya. "Japanimation and Techno-Orientalism: Japan as the Sub-Empire of Signs." *Documentary Box* 9 (December 31, 1996): 1–5.

———. "Techno-Orientalism and Media-Tribalism: On Japanese Animation and Rave Culture." *Third Text* 47 (Summer 1999): 95–106.

Watanabe, Shigeru. "Part 2: Dallos, the World's First OVA (Original Video Animation)." *Artists Liason Ltd. Homepage,* December 14, 2000. http://www.artistsliaisonltd.com/flash/english/special/4th/watanabe2–1.html (accessed August 22, 2002; site now discontinued).

Wong, Amos. "Inside Production I.G." *Newtype USA* 2, no. 4 (April 2003): 26–33.

"The World's Most Popular Female Comic Artist . . . Rumiko Takahashi." *Viz.com.* http://viz.com/products/series/takahashi/interview_02.html (accessed August 22, 2002; site now discontinued).

Yamaga, Hiroyuki. Commentary audio track. *Royal Space Force: The Wings of Honneamise.* DVD. Directed by Hiroyuki Yamaga. Chicago: Manga Entertainment, 2000.

Yoshida, Teigo. "The Feminine in Japanese Folk Religion: Polluted or Divine?" In *Unwrapping Japan: Society and Culture in Anthropological Perspective,* edited by Eyal Ben-Ari, Brian Moeran, and James Valentine, 58–77. Honolulu: University of Hawai'i Press, 1990.

Yoshida, Toshifumi. "Mamoru Oshii." Translated by Andy Nakatani. *Animerica* 9, no. 5 (June 2001): 13–15, 36–40.

"Yoshitaka Amano." *AnimeJump.com* (March 1999). http://www.animejump.com/cgi-bin/go.cgi?go=features/yoshitaka-amano/amano (accessed June 26, 2003).

Zipes, Jack. *The Trials and Tribulations of Little Red Riding Hood: Versions of the Tale in Sociocultural Context.* South Hadley, MA: Bergin & Garvey Publishers, 1983.

INDEX